Knowledge and Belief in Politics

Knowledge and Belief in Politics

The Problem of Ideology

Edited by
ROBERT BENEWICK
R. N. BERKI
BHIKHU PAREKH

LONDON · GEORGE ALLEN & UNWIN LTD
Ruskin House   Museum Street

First published in 1973

© George Allen & Unwin Ltd 1973

ISBN 0 04 320088 5

Printed in Great Britain
in 11 point Baskerville type
By T. and A. Constable Ltd
Hopetoun Street, Edinburgh

Preface

Few concepts in the modern age have created more controversy in the discussion of social, moral and political issues than that of ideology. Ever since Destutt de Tracy coined the term 'ideology' to refer to a scientific study of the origin of ideas, its meaning has predictably undergone a series of historical mutations. While some nineteenth-century thinkers equated ideology with idealism, Marx used it to describe distorted and false consciousness. Following Marx, Karl Mannheim used the term to characterize a body of ideas determined by the thinker's social background. Not very long ago Hannah Arendt employed it to refer to ways of looking at man and society which explain political and social life in terms of one idea. More recently its meaning has undergone further dilutions and now it refers to almost any organized body of beliefs.

Amidst these and other changes in the meaning of the term 'ideology', it is possible to detect a cluster of certain common preoccupations. At the most basic level the problem of ideology is a problem about the nature of truth and objectivity. Is human reason capable of knowing the truth, of comprehending reality 'as it is'? Or is its approach to reality necessarily influenced by the thinker's values, personal or class interests and personal or social prejudices? Is human reason, to go a step further, a culturally neutral instrument, or is it a socially acquired capacity that is deeply permeated by the categories of thought characteristic of a particular historical epoch or society or class or some other social grouping? At another level the problem of ideology is about the internal structure and rationale of specific ideologies. How are the various beliefs that compose an ideology held together? Do they form a logically coherent whole? Or are they a disparate bundle of beliefs, bound together by nothing more than their adherents' firm conviction that they do logically hang together? At the third level are questions about the role and function of ideology in human affairs. Why do particular ideologies have a strong appeal for particular societies and particular sections of them? How does an ideology command and hold the loyalty of its members? Do human societies need ideologies to hold them together? Do developing societies need them more than those already established? How does an ideology influence the way a nation formulates its foreign policy or its pattern of economic development or its social structure?

These and other problems constitute the principal concerns of the essays comprising this volume. As there is sufficient literature on the history of the concept of ideology we thought it best to concentrate on other equally important issues. The opening essays analyse some general philosophical problems encountered in the study of ideology, either independently or in relation to specific thinkers. Other contributions initially examine specific ideologies like pluralism, federalism, conservatism, socialism, apartheid and racialism. The role of ideology in holding societies together and in determining its domestic and foreign policies is examined in the remaining essays. We are only too aware that there are other topics which could have also been profitably discussed in the volume. We would have liked, for example, to include an essay dealing with the role of ideology in the natural sciences. However, we like to believe that the volume as it is covers most of the important issues connected with the question of ideology.

The volume grew out of a series of seminars organized by the Department of Political Studies, University of Hull, during the session 1971-2. We are grateful to Professor C. H. Dodd for his encouragement and support and to the University of Hull for the financial assistance which made the organization of the seminars possible. We are also indebted to our colleagues who participated in the seminars and to our contributors both for presenting the papers at the seminars and for revising them for this collection. In every way this has been a cooperative effort.

Robert Benewick
R. N. Berki
Bhikhu Parekh

Contents

CONTENTS

Contributors

ANTHONY ARBLASTER,
Lecturer, Department of Political Theory and Institutions,
University of Sheffield

ROBERT BENEWICK,
Reader in Politics,
University of Sussex

R. N. BERKI,
Lecturer, Department of Political Studies,
University of Hull

MALCOLM CROSS,
Lecturer in Sociology,
Civil Service College

ADRIAN CUNNINGHAM,
Lecturer, Department of Religious Studies,
University of Lancaster

C. H. DODD,
Professor of Political Studies,
University of Hull

ROBERT E. DOWSE,
Reader, Department of Politics,
University of Exeter

W. H. GREENLEAF,
Professor of Politics,
University College of Wales, Swansea

PRESTON KING,
Professor of Government,
University of Nairobi

STEPHEN KIRBY,
Lecturer, Department of Political Studies,
University of Hull

CONTRIBUTORS

BHIKHU PAREKH,
Lecturer, Department of Political Studies
University of Hull

W. G. RUNCIMAN,
Fellow of Trinity College, Cambridge

JOHN SAVILLE,
Professor of Social and Economic History,
University of Hull

HAROLD WOLPE,
Lecturer, Department of Sociology and Law,
Polytechnic of North London

Ideology and Social Science

W. G. RUNCIMAN

I start from the assumption, which I had better make explicit, that the problem posed by the title of this paper is peculiar to the social, as opposed to the physical and biological, sciences. There is a sense in which these can, if you wish, be said to have a problem of ideology too. If, in the manner of T. S. Kuhn or, before Kuhn, of N. R. Hanson,[1] we think of a scientific theory less as a set of connected laws and more as one way among others of looking at the world, then the choice between rival theories is perhaps a little more like a choice between social and political philosophies than used to be supposed by positivist philosophies of science. But apart from the detailed criticism to which views of this type have themselves been subjected,[2] I take it for granted in any case that there *is* a difference between a set of connected scientific laws and a *Weltanschauung*; that scientific theories, however haphazard the process by which they are arrived at and however provisional their status at any given time, stand or fall by being publicly tested against potentially disconfirming evidence; and that scientific progress can roughly be described as a cumulative demonstration that specified sets of operationally definable terms are co-extensive. The construction of wide-ranging and well-tested theories is, to be sure, the common goal of the social sciences too. But the question which this still leaves open is whether the social sciences are at the same time 'ideological' in some way which makes them incompletely 'scientific' in the conventional sense.

I take it also for granted that we are not concerned with either the motives of social scientists or the uses to which their findings may be put. Both questions are of moral as well as practical importance; but they are common to the sciences of man and of nature alike. The practice of a particular branch of academic inquiry may be morally undesirable not simply because the information made available as a result may be put to immoral use but because the mere execution of the research may already produce effects which it would be immoral not to prevent. Indeed, this may well arise more frequently in the social sciences than the natural, since according to the moral values held by most of its practitioners the scientific investigation of one person's behaviour by another can, under at least some circumstances, constitute a violation of the freedom and dignity of the person investigated. But despite this the validity of the research, if carried out, will be logically a separate matter—as separate as the morality of eugenics from the validity of molecular biology or of the Manhattan Project from the quality of the nuclear research which made the destruction of Hiroshima and Nagasaki possible.

It is of course true that the connection between a social scientist's moral and political views and his academic work is apt to be closer than a physical scientist's. Indeed, it is common to see economists, in particular, categorized as left-wing or right-wing not simply as private citizens but as economists, whereas there is not in the same way such a thing as left-wing or right-wing physics. But this does not demonstrate that economic science as such is in some way inherently infected with ideology; it demonstrates only that economists cannot answer the questions which private citizens are apt to be most concerned to put to them. A left-wing economist is so described because he inclines—as he is perfectly entitled to do—to hope that the answers to these questions will turn out to accord with his own political preferences. He hopes and believes that, for example, the conjunction of rapid inflation and slow growth is not the result of the trade unions' success in pursuit of their wage claims to the degree that economists of rival political persuasion would have him believe. But if it were one day empirically demonstrated that they are, he would have to accept it, whether or not he would still be disposed to argue that the unions were morally and politically justified in behaving as they had. There is some-times the additional complication that a social scientist may help to make his hopes and beliefs come true by the very vehemence with which he proclaims that they will—the so-called 'bandwagon effect' or 'self-fulfilling prophecy'. But this still does not bridge the gap between what he hopes is true and will make come true if he can and the relations of cause and effect which, even if yet undiscovered, must actually be opera-ting to produce the result which he and his colleagues observe. Both natural and social scientists may have a strong emotional commitment to one rather than another possible solution of controversial problems in their field. But the correctness of the one or the other is no more a logical function of the researcher's prejudices in the case of twentieth-century arguments over wage drift and cost push than in the case of sixteenth-century arguments over the number of Jupiter's moons.

I propose also to take for granted that two traditional argu-ments sometimes advanced in favour of the inherently ideo-logical character of social science can be dismissed, although I recognize that they are not by any means negligible arguments and that their influence is still widely felt. The first is what can be called the sociology of knowledge argument—the argument, that is, that social theory even of the most ostensibly scientific kind is always the ideology of a class, meaning by this not merely that it is so framed as to serve the political interests of the class from which it springs but also that that class imposes its own criterion of validation for it. No doubt, there are as a matter of historical fact social theories of which this holds true; indeed, I shall later on in this paper refer to one of them. Nor am I saying that there is nothing to be learnt from the writings on this topic of such authors as Mannheim, Lukacs or Gold-mann. But if taken as a general philosophical claim about the validity of social theory it is, as has been pointed out time and again, self-defeating. If social theory can *never* be objective and scientific, then how much less so can the sociology of knowledge itself? To talk of validity is necessarily to talk of validity in-dependent of origin; and as soon as we concede, as in practice everyone does, that at least some parts of at least some social theories are as much matters of fact as the findings of physical or biological science, then we are no longer dealing with a branch of academic study inherently and totally class-bound but only with a succession of theories which may or may not be distorted in the particular case by the social circumstances under which they are conceived and propagated.

The second form of argument I propose to dismiss is that deriving from Max Weber's distinction between 'value-relevance', so-called, and 'value-freedom', since it too, if construed as an argument for relativism, leads only to a further dilemma. Weber appears to have held that although the sociologist can and must practise his discipline with the same lack of bias and the same attention to empirical testability as the engineer, his *Kulturwertideen* are bound to enter into the formulation of his concepts and the hypotheses employing them in a way that the engineer's don't enter into the formulation of his. Now it is true, as I have remarked already, that our values are 'relevant' to what social scientists study in the sense that we all hold moral and political views about human behaviour in a way that we don't about the behaviour of the things that are studied by engineers. But as a claim about the *validity* of social-scientific theories, Weber's argument rests on the tacit elision of theoretical presuppositions with value judgements. Weber is perfectly right in saying, for example, that 'every historical comparison assumes that a choice has been made by reference to cultural significance which, by excluding an infinite number of given facts, both general and particular, determines the purpose and direction of the imputation of causes'.[3] But in the first place, nothing follows from this that makes social-scientific theory less scientific, or less objective, or less testable in principle than natural-scientific theory; and in the second, the theories of natural science rest just as much as those of social science on presuppositions not themselves derivable from the observations they seek to explain. If, as a matter of ascertainable fact, a particular social scientist's moral and political values influence the construction of his would-be theories more than the natural scientist's do his, this is a matter of psychology, not of logic. The success of the theory is to be judged on other grounds. Weber's distinction leads only to one or other of two alternatives. Either values *are* peculiarly 'relevant' to social science, but in a sense which makes no difference to the scientific standing of the theory in question, or else the term 'value' is being so used as to build them by definition into natural-scientific just as much as social-scientific theories.[4]

This may seem to invite the suggestion that there is really no problem about ideology in social science after all. But there is; and to anyone disposed to deny it the simplest rejoinder is to proffer some examples. Admittedly, there is an enormous number of propositions advanced in the literature of social science which are as 'scientific', on any definition, as any in the literature of the natural. But it is just as easy to find examples which are radically and unmistakably different in both form and style from anything ever to be found in a natural-scientific text. Here are five examples which I have chosen from fairly disparate sources as all being, in their various ways, typical of the kind of academic argument which has no counterpart in physical or biological science, and which invites unavoidable disputes about 'ideological' content:

(1) 'Focusing on the problem of stability, we might emphasize the following facts about the American political system:

1. There are very few citizens who have no means by which to express their wishes effectively enough to influence the government. The right to vote is virtually universal, and almost everywhere there are competing parties or factions trying to garner votes. Even such groups as the Negroes in the South, whose legal right to vote is often denied in practice, have pressure groups, such as the National Association for the Advancement of Coloured Peoples, that have demonstrated their not inconsiderable political effectiveness. Moreover, there is no large segment of the population that is everywhere deprived of the vote. The votes of Northern Negroes can and do benefit Southern Negroes to some extent.' (Harry M. Johnson, *Sociology: A Systematic Introduction.*)

(2) 'The happy system of policy on which European states have succeeded in preserving this balance; the degree of moderation which has, in adjusting their treaties, become habitual even to victorious and powerful monarchies, does honour to mankind, and may give hopes of a lasting felicity to be derived from a pre-possession, never, perhaps, equally strong in any former period, or among any number of nations,

that the first conquering people will ruin themselves, as well as their rivals.' (Adam Ferguson, *An Essay on Civil Society.*)

(3) 'When the Greeks exposed unwanted children at birth, they showed how seriously they interpreted the exacting conditions of their existence, and followed the example of nature, which exerts its own selection and control by allowing only the strongest to survive.' (Maurice Bowra, *The Greek Experience.*)

(4) 'The example is taken from the Calvinistic Independents: but it will also serve excellently to describe the stance of Methodism before temporal authority. This surrender was implicit in Methodism's origin—in the Toryism of its founder and in his ambivalent attitude to the Established Church. From the outset the Wesleyans fell ambiguously between Dissent and the Establishment, and did their utmost to make the worst of both worlds, serving as apologists for an authority in whose eyes they were an object of ridicule or condescension, but never of trust.' (E. P. Thompson, *The Making of the English Working Class.*)

(5) 'Only the give and take of a free society's internal struggles offers some guarantee that the products of the society will not accumulate in the hands of a few power-holders, and that men may develop and bring up their children without fear of persecution. And, as we have seen, democracy requires institutions which support conflict and disagreement as well as those which sustain legitimacy and consensus.' (S. M. Lipset, *Political Man.*)

The obvious comment which these examples invite is that in all of them facts are being somehow blurred with values: Johnson is looking at the political disabilities of twentieth-century American Negroes through suspiciously rosy lenses; Ferguson is at the same time affirming approbation of a particular state of international relations in the mid-eighteenth century and predicting a relative durability for it; Bowra is hinting, by a quasi-descriptive use of the dangerous term 'nature', at an apologia for the practice of infanticide among the ancient Greeks; Thompson is implicitly endorsing ridicule of the Wesleyans on the ground of what he sees as the reason for which they incurred it; Lipset is recommending liberal democracy on the American model through the tacit invocation of an ostensibly empirical generalization about 'freedom from persecution' which might well on closer inspection turn out to be circular. The question which they raise is thus not merely whether social scientists do advance ideological presuppositions under the guise of academic objectivity so much as whether they can help doing otherwise.

To give an adequate answer, however, it is not enough just to examine whether the factual content in the passages quoted can be sifted out in such examples as these from the evaluative. It may be that the links between ostensibly factual propositions of doubtful testability and ostensibly evaluative propositions with implicit descriptive claims can be dissolved by a wave of the magic wand of the is/ought distinction. But this will still leave open the question whether the 'ideological' content of the passage taken as a whole will have been exhausted in the process. The difficulty is not that the complexity of the relation between facts and values calls the distinction itself into question, but that there underlies the relation in each particular case of this kind a whole further complex of implicit presuppositions in which facts and values are intermingled once again in their turn. To get to grips with the problem, therefore, requires not simply a logical dissection of one or more selected passages, but the analysis of the whole context within which a selected passage occurs.

Of the five works from which my examples were taken, the one which can, I think, be most instructively analysed along these lines is Thompson's. I have chosen it for three reasons: first, because it is widely known and admired and I would expect most readers of this paper to have at least some acquaintance with the sort of issues with which it deals; second, because Thompson himself quite explicitly raises the question of ideology and social science; and third, because it deals with the people and events of a period in which I have no vested interest. This carries the disadvantage that I shall be dealing with arguments whose validity, to the degree that they rest on the interpretation of historical evidence, I am not competent to assess. But I hope it will be outweighed by the benefit that I am as open to persuasion by one school of nineteenth-century historians as by another.

Thompson's book is a long one and covers a number of complex questions, sometimes in close detail. Its general theme, however, is the extent and nature of working-class radicalism in England in the first third of the nineteenth century, and its principal purpose is, in Thompson's own words, to quarrel with the orthodoxies which 'tend to obscure the agency of working people, the degree to which they contributed, by conscious efforts, to the making of history' and to 'rescue the poor stockinger, the Luddite cropper, the "obsolete" hand-loom weaver, the "utopian" artisan, and even the deluded follower of Joanna Southcott, from the enormous condescension of posterity.'[5] The arguments directed to this purpose are supported by a substantial body of empirical evidence drawn from primary sources. But they are at the same time couched and presented in terms of a complex of related assumptions which go beyond such factual conclusions as the evidence (if trustworthy) requires. Different readers would no doubt be disposed to summarize these assumptions in different ways according to their own ideological presuppositions. But it seems to me that there are four principal assumptions of the kind with which I am concerned here.

The first assumption is about the nature and assessment of economic well-being. It is true that in the postscript to the Pelican edition of his book Thompson has qualified his chapter on 'Standards and Experiences' by conceding more merit to the work of historical demographers and statisticians than he had originally been willing to do. Indeed, he says that he has let the chapter stand unaltered 'only as a polemic'. But he does not retract his view that the Industrial Revolution was experienced as immiseration by the overwhelming majority of industrial workers and that their relation to their employers grew progressively more 'exploitive' during the period. This view is evidently not to be refuted by statistics for increasing *per capita* consumption of tea and sugar or calculation of the nutritional value of the potato. Nor is it to be refuted by evidence, even if convincing, that pre-industrial, pre-urban England was not the golden age of later romantic idealization or that exploitation was as intense in the relations between working people and small landlords, artisans or publicans as between working people and the owners of great estates, factories or mills. They were immiserated and exploited because they felt themselves to be so, and that is what economic well-being is, or should be, acknowledged to be about.

The second assumption is about the ideological character of contemporary political economy itself. The Poor Law Amendment Act of 1834 and its administration constituted, in Thompson's words, 'perhaps the most sustained attempt to impose an ideological dogma, in defiance of the evidence of human need, in English history'.[6] It is not simply that the model of a so-called 'natural' economy was mistaken because, as it turned out, technological progress would enable productivity to increase yet faster than population. Men like Chadwick and Kay were not just well-intentioned physicians to the body politic whose ignorance of later scientific discovery caused them to practise remedies which, after a century of academic progress, we know to have been unsoundly based. There was built into their creed something more than a belief about the determinants of wage rates and the relation of un- or under-employment to production and prices. They also believed that the lot of the poor—of the losers, that is, in the struggle with either the machines or the other unwilling recruits to the army of surplus labour who were depriving them of a livelihood—could only be improved by encouraging motives of frugality and prudence and discouraging motives of improvidence and idleness. From this, it was but a step to blaming the poor for their own misfortunes and imposing upon them an alien and odious discipline whose effects, so far from persuading the economists that their policies were mistaken, served only to confirm the prejudices with which they had undertaken them.

The third assumption is about the relation of religious dogma to social conduct. In the passage which I have already quoted Thompson links the attitude of Methodism to the established church to what he calls its 'surrender' to the temporal order. In the same chapter he goes on to consider the relation of Methodist theology to industrial rather than political discipline in terms which require no further comment:

It is difficult to conceive of a more essential disorganization of human life, a pollution of the sources of spontaneity bound to reflect itself in every aspect of personality. Since joy was associated with sin and guilt, and pain (Christ's wounds) with goodness and love, so every impulse became twisted into the reverse, and it became natural to suppose that man or child only found grace in God's eyes when performing painful, laborious or self-denying tasks. To labour and to sorrow was to find pleasure, and masochism was 'Love'. It is inconceivable that men could actually *live* like this; but many Methodists did their best.[7]

The fourth assumption is about the essentially repressive nature of the political control exercised by the English governing class during and after the Napoleonic wars. There seems no doubt that this policy is partly, at least, to be explained by the events that followed 1789 in France, and the resulting identification of domestic democratic agitation with radical Jacobin revolutionism. But the result, as it affected the political organization of working people, was to ally the aristocratic and manufacturing interest against them in a deliberately 'counter-revolutionary war'. In this war, so far from being seen as the aggressors they should be seen as resisting a simultaneous intensification of economic exploitation and political oppression each of which reinforced the other. Luddism, in its political aspect, is on Thompson's view not an attack on the principle of private property so much as a demand for a restoration of constitutional rights by journeymen and artisans justifiably resentful of their exclusion from the franchise; and the policy of the war-time Ministry is not a defence against French agents and conspiracies of assassination so much as 'sheer counter-revolutionary opportunism'.

These very short summaries are of course a simplication of Thompson's arguments. But they do, I hope, fairly represent the principal themes which he seeks to present over and above a recital of demonstrable facts and a suggested explanation of their causes. To me, as a reader with no first-hand knowledge of any of the sources for the period, this presentation is very persuasive. Indeed, I find it hard to see how any reader, whatever his own political persuasion and however substantial his disagreement with Thompson's attributions of causes and effects, could fail to be moved by the conditions which Thompson describes and to sympathize with the poor stockingers, 'obsolete' hand-loom weavers and the rest who are the avowed heroes and heroines of his story. Moral indignation, as Thompson recognizes, is a dangerous impulse in the historian; but it is a perfectly proper response in his readers, and there are many passages in Thompson's book where it is mine. But where ideological assumptions are being argued, whether explicitly or not, there is always another side; if there weren't, Thompson would not himself be arguing. We aren't *bound* by his evidence, even if it is entirely well-founded, to accept his views of the Industrial Revolution, Political Economy, Methodism, and the Government and Parliament of Sidmouth or Pitt. And speaking, as I must emphasize again, without any claim to specialist knowledge, I find that three possible counter-arguments occur to me which, while leaving Thompson's evidence unquestioned, might lead one to wish to qualify those views.

First, there is the question of the relation of population to resources. No doubt the assumptions on which the political economy of Malthus (or for that matter Ricardo) rested should not have been held to be axiomatic in the way that they were. But equally, there can be little doubt that the political economy of England during Thompson's period *was*, like that of many industrializing nations during our own period, in a Malthusian state—that is to say, an expanding economy was under pressure from a swiftly expanding population at the same time as there was pressure for the use of the investible surplus generated by the economy for both capital investment and military expenditure rather than increment of *per capita* purchasing power. The real benefits of the Industrial Revolution, in terms of income *per capita*, were postponed.[8] Historians are, apparently, uncertain about the precise causes of the spectacular population increase. But whether it was due to a rising birth-rate, a falling death-rate, a net inflow of Irish immigrants, or all three, the economy was supporting double the number of mouths within fifty years.[9] Disraeli, who was no friend to political economy, gives a vivid contemporary picture of the impact of these numbers in the famous dialogue about 'two nations' in *Sybil*. In Ireland, of course, there was widespread starvation. But in England there was not; and in this sense there was an increase in economic well-being, not because there was a rise in income and resources *per capita* but because the economy was supporting more *capita*. Or to look at it the other way round: it was the *capita* as well as the economy keeping the average of well-being down during Thompson's period.

Now it doesn't necessarily follow from this that for members of the governing class to preach birth control to the workers was either sensible or humane. There can be two views about this, then as now. To J. S. Mill in 1859: 'The fact itself, of causing the existence of a human being, is one of the most responsible actions in the range of human life. To undertake this responsibility—to bestow a life which may be either a curse or a blessing—unless the being on whom it is to be bestowed will have at least the ordinary chances of a desirable existence, is a crime against that being. And in a country either over-peopled, or threatened with being so, to produce children, beyond a very small number, with the effect of reducing the reward of labour by their competition, is a serious offence against all who live by the remuneration of their labour.'[10] But then contrast with this Dr Han Suyin in 1971: 'The exploited in the world are very conscious of the genocidal policies of racism. That is why in Africa many of the populations are hostile to family planning. They know that the population explosion theory is a racist invented myth. They know that they are under- not over-populated and that their poverty is not because of too many people, but that to be a minority is to be weak.'[11] I have no intention of trying to arbitrate between these two opposite views, whether for developing Britain in the 1850s or developing Afro-Asia in the 1970s. But whichever way one's particular moral and political values may incline one, it is salutary to recognize that beyond a certain point no developing country can have it both ways. It may be better at any given state of development to support more people with consequently lower average resources; it may be better to improve more substantially the well-being of fewer people. But England in the Napoleonic wars was not in a position, whatever its governing class had tried to do, to break through at a single stroke into the virtuous spiral of rapidly rising population and still more rapidly rising average living standards for them all.

The second, and related, question on which alternative views remain possible is the central one of exploitation. I don't mean by this that Thompson is wrong on matters where Sir John Clapham, or Professor T. S. Ashton, are right. I mean only that whether he is or not I remain uncertain what exactly is the sense in which it is appropriate to say that the English working class of Thompson's period was being exploited in some way or to some degree other than the working class of whatever times or places are being implicitly contrasted with it. Is it that a small elite of greedy or fortunate employers and landowners were enabled to amass vastly more personal wealth than the rest of the population could ever dream of? This certainly roused the indignation of many of the workers whom Thompson describes, as indeed it does his own. But this wealth, precisely because concentrated in so very few hands,[12] would have made proportionately little difference to everyone else even if compulsorily redistributed among them. Suppose, for the sake of argument, that the government of the time had actually done this: would the workers then have ceased altogether to be 'exploited'? I would not think so. Perhaps then the exploitation lies in the amount of the surplus product extracted from the labour force. But by this measure the Chinese villager (according to an authority accepted by Barrington Moore in his *Social Origins of Dictatorship and Democracy*)[13] was more exploited after the Communist Revolution than before—which suggests that exploitation is more a matter of what a society does with its surplus product than of how extortionately it extracts it. Then is exploitation a matter of good government and bad? Well: it's hard not to believe that the miseries of the Industrial Revolution *could* have been alleviated to some degree by swifter and more efficacious legislation. But aside from the doubtfulness of the wisdom of hindsight, exploitation is surely an economic rather than a political relationship, and even if an enlightened administration had done more to limit child labour, emancipate the trade unions and organize better provision than the workhouse for the old and unemployed, the working class would still have been selling their labour to employers who would not have paid for it with more than a proportion of the net surplus after overheads, interest charges, depreciation and reinvestment on research and development which it had helped to generate. Is exploitation then measured simply by the level of well-being of the industrial work force under one economic system rather than another? But in that case, we are back with the arguments over both the notional welfare of the unborn and the lack of a measure which would enable us to say that although below a certain point exploitation was present, above a certain point it was not. Once again, I am not seeking to argue for an answer of my own.[14] But I do want to make the point that exploitation is a concept easy to apply but hard to define; and to the extent that Thompson's argument rests on it, his interpretation is bound, even with full agreement on the evidence deployed, to be disputable.

Third and last, there is the question of what Thompson himself called the 'condescension of posterity'. This consists, I take it, in describing the poor stockinger and the Luddite cropper in terms irreconcilable with those in which they themselves experienced their economic and social relations. But then to be less condescending to some is perhaps to be more condescending to others. Let us agree that Clapham and Ashton have condescended to the croppers and stockingers. May not Thompson be condescending to Chadwick and Kay? The latter is, after all, the same person of whom G. M. Young felt moved to say (albeit with a later stage of his career in mind) that 'if history judged men less by the noise than by the difference they make, it is hard to think of any name in the Victorian age which deserves to stand above or even beside Kay-Shuttleworth's';[15] and if the test is people's own experience in the context of their own class and time, I dare say G. M. Young is in this case no more guilty of the optical illusions of hindsight than Thompson is. The English Establishment of the early nineteenth century was undoubtedly callous by twentieth-century English standards. But by these anachronistic standards it was altogether a callous, and even a brutal, age. Duelling, public executions and bare-knuckle prizefights continued for a generation after Thompson's period ends, and Christian English gentlemen to whom it was perfectly acceptable that naval ratings could be flogged to death with the cat-o'-nine-tails for striking a superior officer were unlikely to be lenient to civil disobedience in time of war, or threatened revolution, or both. Their morality, like their religion (or lack of it) may to a later generation be both puzzling and distasteful. But presented more understandingly in their own context, as Thompson so convincingly presents the Luddites and the Friendly Societies, I suspect that the Benthamites and even the Wesleyans might be less puzzling and distasteful than his account makes them appear.[16]

How, then, since these issues are so evidently debatable, should Thompson's book be used to unravel the relation of ideology and social science? Where exactly does its debatability lie? It follows from what I said earlier that the first move to be made is to see whether it is possible to sift out an unmistakably evaluative content, with which even those who agree with Thompson's account of the facts are not thereby bound to concur, from an unmistakably factual content which even those whose moral and political preferences are entirely incompatible with Thompson's are bound to accept unless they can dispute the empirical evidence from which it derives. From this standpoint it is at once clear that there is indeed a connection between Thompson's ideology and his account of the events he describes which manifests itself in two different ways. In the first sort of case Thompson is arguing in the manner of the hypothetical 'left-wing' economist whom I cited earlier; that is to say, he is presenting matters of fact about which no definitive conclusions can be established in such a way as to accord with the hopes, or even expectations, that spring from his 'ideological' presuppositions. In the second he is quite explicitly deploying the evidence he has collected in the service of an evaluation of the Industrial Revolution as such.

An example of the first kind which is even clearer than Thompson's view of the economic policies which might best have alleviated the industrial workers' sufferings is his view of Francis Place, whose 'great political sagacity', attributed to him by the Webbs in their *History of Trade Unionism*, Thompson flatly denies. This supposed sagacity rests on his as it were Fabian moderation relative to men like Gravener Henson or Peter Moore, the Radical MP for Coventry. Thompson's opinion is that they were right where Place was wrong, and that Place, influenced both by a conventional belief in the efficacy of the laws of supply and demand and by his own experience in the atypical industry of small tailoring, was 'grossly self-deluded as to the probable consequences of repeal'[17] of the Combination Acts and unjustified in the grounds on which he pushed Henson's rival Bill aside. Now the consequences of repeal are of course an observable matter of fact; but the consequences which

27

would have followed from the pursuit of an alternative strategy to Place's are, although also a matter of fact, an unverifiable one, since the alternative was not pursued. The argument over Place's 'sagacity' accordingly rests on whether the aim which to Thompson, as to the Webbs, is the desirable one—that is, the maximum amelioration of the political and economic disabilities of the working class—could have been better achieved by the Radicals, who may have been weaker on tactics but were in Thompson's view sounder on doctrine, than by Place, who even if he was doing the right thing was doing it in part, at least, for a mistaken reason. In this argument, there is a fairly intricate interplay between judgements of fact and of value, and a verdict on Place's sagacity will incorporate both. But it is perfectly possible to see where and how they relate to each other and what, therefore, would be meant by saying that it is possible to take a more or less 'left-wing' view either of the effects of Place's actions or of the degree to which those actions and the calculations which inspired them are to be admired, as the Webbs did, or not.

An example of the second kind, which effectively embraces all those I have cited already, is Thompson's avowed claim that the historical sociologist is and must be 'concerned with making some judgements of value upon the whole process entailed in the Industrial Revolution, of which we ourselves are an end-product'.[18] The sense in which he 'must' is not, of course, that of a logical compulsion: it would be better to say that historians and/or sociologists do all as a matter of fact have moral and political values, although very different ones, and that they cannot help applying them to any such narrative of events once they are satisfied as to the validity of the evidence on which it rests. But nobody can question that we all do this, though we may recognize that our different and often irreconcilable values neither entail nor are entailed by any facts which the historical sociologist may discover. Thompson leaves the reader in no doubt that by his moral standards, at least, the employers, political economists, Wesleyans and government ministers whose conduct he narrates are to be strongly disapproved. It is not, clearly, so simple a matter as just deciding in the light of one's own individual values whether the Industrial Revolution taken as a whole was or was not a 'Good Thing'. Whatever the moral and political criteria different observers may be disposed to apply, serious evaluation of so complex a historical process and the participants involved in it is an intricate and subtle affair, and in actual argument many value-judgements of what can be called a 'non-basic' kind[19] are effectively dependent on factual assumptions. But it is always possible, however intricate and subtle the argument may have become, to separate disagreement about the evidence for what the participants thought, said and did from disagreement about the criteria according to which those thoughts, words and deeds are to be commended or deplored.

Yet after all this has been said, we have still to settle the question whether any proffered conclusions about living standards, exploitation, repression or Methodism are not still discretionary in a way that the natural scientist's are not, aside from either disagreement over hypothetical might-have-beens on the one hand or differences in explicitly moral or political principles on the other. Consider for example Thompson's remark in his concluding chapter that 'There is a sense in which we may describe popular Radicalism in these years as an intellectual culture.'[20] I cannot see that this can be construed as a value-judgement in the way that Thompson's remarks about the Wesleyans or political economists can. It does not depend on Thompson's notions of which of the members of that culture behaved well or badly or of what in general is or is not a desirable social state of affairs. No doubt in accordance with Thompson's values to say that popular Radicalism was an intellectual culture is to praise it. But even someone according to whose values that was a thoroughly bad thing might still agree that it should indeed be described in those terms. To do so, moreover, is not simply to adopt an arbitrary convention of the form of 'if it's more than 4 feet high we shall call it a tree and if it's less we shall call it a bush'—what philosophers sometimes call a 'characterizing' as opposed to an 'appraising' value-judgement.[21] It is to represent, or if you like to depict, the culture in question in a term which Thompson regards as appropriate to the meaning which the experiences he describes had to the participants themselves—the labourers, artisans, shopkeepers, schoolmasters and clerks who in Thompson's words 'formed a picture of the organization of society, out of their own experience and with the help of their hard-won and erratic education, which was above all a political picture'.[22] This characterization is, naturally, directly based on the empirical evidence which Thompson presents. But it is not a matter simply of reportage either. Any characterization of this kind, even if based on evidence about which rival observers are not in dispute, can (and in practice will) be presented by rival observers in different terms which are not equivalent in meaning. Let us suppose that we go over Thompson's arguments again and that we discount, wherever we detect them, all his distaste for the Methodists, his disapproval of the moderates, his admiration for the leaders of the working class and his hatred of the governments and employers of his period. We would still not be left with an account which no other observer as familiar as Thompson with all the evidence Thompson used could presume to dispute; and the dispute which would still be possible would not be a dispute either about facts or about values.

Now to propose that a full resolution of the problem of ideology in social science involves elucidating an intermediate category between facts and values is to risk becoming embroiled in a long succession of unsettled philosophical controversies. All I can do in this paper is to draw briefly on some ideas which I have sought to develop somewhat more fully elsewhere.[23] I am, however, convinced that discussion of these topics has suffered from a too exclusive preoccupation with the logic of sociological explanation on the one hand and of moral or political value-judgements on the other. To see where the irreducible difference does *not* lie between the sciences of man and of nature, it is enough to list the standard procedures of academic inquiry common to both: observation (whether direct or indirect); classification (which is necessarily in terms of some sort of theoretical presupposition); narration (answering the question what happened that calls to be explained); and explanation (which at a minimum will show how the explanandum came to be possible and at best will link the explanandum to the values of one or more independent variables, possibly but not necessarily by reference to an articulated set of general laws). No doubt there is the obvious difference between most of the natural and most of the social sciences that we are much better able to ground our suggested explanations in a presumptive theory in the first than the second; but this is not a difference of principle and has nothing to do with the problem of ideology. If there is after all a difference of kind between social and natural science it lies not in the fact that either explanation or evaluation are different in one or the other case but in the fact that there is an *additional* problem which arises where human action is the object of study, and that the additional problem is a problem not of classification, narration or explanation but of description.

Let me go back to my last example from Thompson— describing the popular radicalism of a given period as 'an intellectual culture'. This, if you like, is a matter of classification. But it is classification for a different purpose from the classification which is a preliminary to scientific explanation. It is a matter of telling the reader not what something *is*, but what it is *like*; and it does not arise in the study of natural events as opposed to human actions because in the study of natural events there is no problem of meaning apart from that which is decided by the modification and development of scientific theory. It is only in the study of human institutions and behaviour that even where an explanation has (whether rightly or wrongly) been accepted as correct by rival observers there can still be a difference of view between them as to the terms in which the experience of the people observed should be framed. Now this opposition between meanings and causes has a long history in the philosophy of social science. But those who have most insisted on the contrast, like Dilthey or Jaspers or Colling-wood, have always tended to exaggerate the conclusion to be drawn from it. They have used it to argue that explanation must therefore be different in some more than trivial sense where human action is the object of study. But why should this follow? To explain human institutions and behaviour, if it can be done, involves the same sort of reasoning and requires the same sort of justification as explaining anything else, and although *forms* of explanation will differ widely according to the type of explanandum involved, this is a difference within the sciences of man and nature just as much as between them. The problem of meaning arises because even if there is nothing left to explain the observer has to choose in what terms to charac-terize the assumptions which informed his subjects' motives and purposes and the significance which their roles and actions had to themselves. Thus two observers who had all the same evidence before them and who were entirely agreed on the assignation of causes and effects could still differ over whether the popular radicalism of Thompson's period could appropriately be called an 'intellectual culture'; and the difference would not necessarily be bound up (even though in practice it might) with conflicting impulses towards praise or blame any more than with conflicting explanatory hypotheses.

This ineluctable discretion which the social scientist has in framing and applying the concepts he thinks apposite to the states of mind of the people whose experience he describes means that there can never be a single authoritative account of the Industrial Revolution (or the French Revolution, or the Decline and Fall of the Roman Empire, or indeed any 'historical individual', in Rickert's and Max Weber's phrase). This holds quite apart from either the trivial question of what happens to interest you or the less trivial but logically equally separate question of which side may have enlisted your sympathies. It is not just a matter of selection. Obviously, no description is ever 'complete', and different observers will choose different aspects or features of a 'historical individual' from each other to present as essentially constitutive of it. But the incompleteness of any description applies as much to natural as to social science: a geologist's account of the Ice Age no more tells everything about it than either Thompson's or Clapham's account of the Industrial Revolution. The difference is that where human behaviour is involved, no conceptual framework can be descriptively neutral as between different possible characterizations, since the conceptualization called for is of, among other things, the conceptualizations of those whose behaviour is to be described. The slightly odd-sounding question 'What was the Ice Age like?' would no doubt be answered differently by one geologist from another; but nothing of any significance would hinge on the difference—the facts listed could in principle be added to indefinitely on request, but that would be all. The question 'What was early nineteenth-century Methodism like?', on the other hand, is altogether different. We may reject Thompson's account as tendentious and controversial. But what would be a wholly non-tendentious and uncontroversial substitute? *Whatever* terms are used to denote and characterize the beliefs, values and attitudes of the Methodists in question may be rejected as inapposite by a second observer, whether or not he agrees with either the implicit value-judgements or the proffered explanations of the first.

The diagnosis of any account of human behaviour which, like Thompson's, goes beyond simple reportage is accordingly a much more subtle affair than the acceptance or rejection of a charge of political bias. Not only must the account in question be considered as a whole and all of its latent presuppositions made explicit, but any allegedly 'ideological' presuppositions must be so analysed as to recognize the difference between first, untestable suppositions of fact which would, if vindicated, accord with the moral or political predilections of the author, second, imputations by the author of praise or blame arising out of his recital of testable facts and suggested causes, and third, exercise of unavoidable discretion by the author in the choice of the terms which, in his view, best characterize the conditions and events which he describes as experienced by the actual persons concerned. In Thompson's discussions of the assessment of well-being, the nature and extent of exploitation, the character of early nineteenth-century religious and political dogma and the motives and purposes of those in control of the coercive apparatus of the state, all three are present throughout. They are difficult to disentangle not only from the recital of documented facts with which they are interwoven but from each other, and the reader who feels moved to dispute Thompson's conclusions may be reacting against any or all of them. I offer no verdict on how far such a reaction would or would not be justified. But I do claim that Thompson's book shows in what way and to what degree the possibility is bound to arise.

The problem of ideology in social science thus dissolves into three, once we have excluded the altogether separate questions of the morality of the motives which may inspire it and of the uses to which it may be put. The first two of the three are, although in different ways, questions of 'values'. But the third is not, and it is for that very reason more intractable. The disentanglement of the values, whether Left or Right, from the social science, whether right or wrong, is often difficult enough. But to say that the content of a social-scientific text is influenced by its author's values entails that their presence can be detected;

B

and if they can be detected, they can in principle be discounted by someone who does not share them. We need only ask whether the conclusion offered can be accepted by someone whose values are not, as it happens, the same. What cannot be discounted in the same way are the presuppositions which underlie the vocabulary of intentions and motives, meanings and roles, in terms of which the thoughts and actions of the social scientist's subjects are described. Whether these too should be called 'ideological' is then a matter of verbal convention: etymologically, at least, it seems as proper to use it here as in the other two cases. But the difficulties they pose for the practising sociologist are not the same, and it is important not to confuse them. The fundamental difference of kind between the natural and the social sciences is neither that explanation is different in the one case from the other nor that evaluation is somehow intrinsic to the latter: it is that there is an area of discretion in the framing and application of concepts in the sciences of self-conscious human behaviour from which the natural sciences are spared. If that is what is meant by saying that the social but not the natural sciences are 'inherently' ideological, then the claim is true; but if what is meant is that they and not the natural sciences are logically inseparable from value-judgements, then it is false.

NOTES AND REFERENCES

1. T. S. Kuhn, *The Structure of Scientific Revolutions* (University of Chicago Press, 1962); N. R. Hanson, *Patterns of Discovery* (Cambridge University Press, 1970).

2. Cf. I. Lakatos (ed.), *Criticism and the Growth of Knowledge* (Cambridge University Press, 1970).

3. Max Weber, *The Methodology of Social Sciences* (Glencoe, Ill., 1949).

4. This argument is developed further in W. G. Runciman, *A Critique of Max Weber's Philosophy of Social Science* (Cambridge University Press, 1972), sec. III.

5. E. P. Thompson, *The Making of the English Working Class* (London, Gollancz, 1964), p. 12.

6. Ibid., p. 267.

7. Ibid., p. 372.

8. The gross national income of Great Britain is estimated to have risen from £340m. in 1831 to £523m. by the year of the Great Exhibition—which, for example, the redoubtable Gravener Henson of the framework knitters, who had been jailed for complicity in Luddism in 1817-18, only just lived to see; and it was not until the following decades that there was an incontrovertible increase in real wages.

9. Scotland and Ireland lie outside Thompson's argument except as sources of net migration into England and Wales, where the census figures show an increase in total from 10·164m. in 1811 to 20·066m. in 1861.

10. J. S. Mill, *On Liberty* (Oxford University Press, 1912), Ch. 5.

11. 'Race Relations and the Third World', *Race*, XIII (1971), p. 9.

12. Even for 1841, J. F. C. Harrison, *The Early Victorians* (London, Weidenfeld, 1971), p. 21, speaks of 'the overwhelming size of the labouring population and the numerical tininess of all other sections of the community'.

13. Barrington Moore, Jr., *Social Origins of Dictatorship and Democracy* (Boston, 1966; Penguin, 1969), p. 227: 'The Communist regime forged a new link between the village and the national government. It became evident to every peasant that his daily life depended on a national political power. Through this new link the Communists pumped out of the village, C. K. Yang estimates, even more than the landlord rentier and the Kuomintang had taken before.' The term 'exploitation' seems less apt, however, because first, 'the new and larger burden was more equally distributed' and second, 'to extract more resources from the peasants could only be preliminary to solving the basic problem of increasing economic output all around'.

14. Even if 'exploitation' is explicitly defined by reference to well-being, argument will continue far beyond such relatively straightforward matters as the measurement of real incomes; contrast, for example, the view of W. R. Greg in 1851 that working-class expenditure on beer, spirits and tobacco, being greater than the 'total annual revenue of the Kingdom', was 'sufficient evidence of their material advance' (cited by John Burnett, *Plenty and Want: A Social History of Diet in England from 1815 to the Present Day* (London, Penguin, 1968), p. 140) with the remark of Geoffrey Best, *Mid-Victorian Britain, 1851-75* (London, Weidenfeld, 1971), p. 93, that 'A London artisan with demonstrably rising real wages and shortening hours of work may still have been having to pay so much more of his income for so persistently inadequate a home, and consequently losing so unnecessarily high a proportion of his infant children, that one would be hard put to it to say whether he was "better off" or not'. In fact, I suspect that the emotive charge that 'exploitation' carries derives precisely from the indignation aroused among those of egalitarian sympathies by the spectacle of some people wallowing in luxury while others are dying of neglect: in the uncompromising dictum of Babeuf, when anyone is starving it is a crime to have more than enough. But by this criterion, all readers of this paper are exploiters of the people of Bangladesh, and although it may be that we are all, to varying degrees, to be reprehended morally on that account, 'exploitation' has then become less, not more, useful as a sociological term.

15. G. M. Young, *Victorian England: Portrait of an Age* (Oxford University Press, 1953), 2nd ed., p. 89.

16. Cf. Chapter 1 ('The Distorting Mirror') of W. L. Burn, *The Age of Equipoise* (London, Unwin, 1964) on the pitfalls of 'selective Victorianism'.

17. Thompson, op. cit., p. 520.

18. Ibid., p. 444.

19. Cf. A. K. Sen, *Collective Choice and Social Welfare* (Edinburgh, Oliver & Boyd, 1970), sec. 5.4.

20. Op. cit., p. 711.

21. See Ernest Nagel, *The Structure of Science* (London, Routledge, 1966), p. 492.

22. Op. cit., p. 712.

23. See W. G. Runciman, 'Describing', *Mind*, LXXXI (1972), pp. 372-388 and cf. *A Critique of Max Weber's Philosophy of Social Science*, sec. VI.

35

Reflections on Projections:
The Range of Ideology

ADRIAN CUNNINGHAM

Arising from some problems in relating ideology and religion, this paper re-examines the origins of the concept of ideology by asking what is presupposed by such a theory or theories—looking again at origins to see if it will help sort out some of the contemporary confusions of the term. If I am right, these origins are closely connected with questions of language, rationality, relationship and historicity *as a complex* within a deistic view of the world in the late eighteenth century and especially characteristic of Herder. The dropping of the deistic view enables a specific and strong sense of ideology to emerge, but at the same time leads to fragmentation and narrowness. I am not suggesting that the coherence can be restored by restoring the deism. Rather I am suggesting that the narrowness of and lacunae in most uses of the term 'ideology' are linked with the neglect of the religious context of its roots, a neglect compounded in the problems of a representative figure like Marx over the differences between projection and reflection, and between myth, religion and ideology. The difficulties here have not only had severe consequences in the Marxist tradition where most of the work has been done—it shows up especially in the treatment of aesthetics—but also outside it.

The fairly recent revival of interest in the problem and analysis of ideology is an immensely important one. The question has been so long off the Anglo-Saxon agenda (if it was ever on) that there was bound to be a period of initial confusion. There being no readily acceptable categories available, each contributor has often had to define the term for his own use. This is understandable, but the debate as a whole seems to stay within an unnecessarily narrow framework. A problem that cuts across existing disciplines of knowledge is already parcelled out among them so that the depths of the problem are trivialized and certain fundamental critiques of the existing system of knowledge evaded.

There seem to me two major components in the present revival: an increasing attention to the significance of 'superstructural' problems in the self-evaluation of the Marxist tradition, and a set of problems in the social sciences over the relation between fact and value, the relation between apparently discontinuous language games, etc. Both of these concerns, separately and in combination, have provided some important specific analyses and a good deal of methodological clarification —though it often seems that in the social and political sciences there is more clarification than application.

My own problem, as someone interested in cultural analysis (for want of a better term), especially with regard to religion and to art, is that very little of this work is actually of a great deal of use for approaching the problems thrown up in the course of such study. In the Marxist tradition, for example, despite some work of classic status, there remain key confusions and lacunae in the study of art, and with regard to religion there is almost nothing of any value. With regard to the second component, the now customary declaration of personal position that prefaces work touching on ideological themes often seems to indicate an evasion of central problems of method by an individual modesty which is more than just a recognition of the lack of consensus in many areas. It tends to imply a vague individualistic and perhaps positivist framework *against* which the original critique of ideology as part of a search for common meanings was directed. Such a framework may be workable in questions where ideas and beliefs can be studied as political theories, or in the manner of the history of ideas. But if the concept is as deeply connected with romantic and Hegelian thinking as I shall argue, then it cannot be simply detached from that context and, as it were, screwed on to common-sense Anglo-Saxon social science

37

as an exciting new attachment: the ingenuity involved is often intriguing but the enterprise remains unconvincing. The student of religion, moreover, is necessarily faced with questions of embodied beliefs, common meanings, feelings, traditions, liturgical and ecclesiastical practices, which only temporarily allow of that kind of useful abstraction. And these common meanings and feelings run continuously from the relatively systematized theoretical level of theology, where the self-identification of the tradition is continually re-examined and re-established, to levels of everyday consciousness and practice, where the self-identification of the person is established, and back again. This very simultaneity of elements has often been the reason for dismissing religion and/or its scientific study; on the contrary, it would seem to me to offer, in a more than usually coherent form, just those *ranges* of relations between ideas and practices, individuals and collectives, which are or should be a central part of the enterprise of social science.

The scientific study of ideas and beliefs ranges across the history of ideas, literary criticism, art history, the study of religion, the social sciences, in its project (as I take it) of locating its particular object within the structural grammar of ideas and feelings of a period, tradition or movement; in some cases, establishing continuities over very different periods and diverse cultures. Since its concern is with meanings—their continuities and discontinuities, their range and variety of levels, their social and individual determinations—such study necessarily involves epistemological considerations as well as the more obvious question of the possible truth or falsity of the ideas studied.

Part of the importance of the present opportunity in this field is that we may be able to avoid the series of historic splits in the history of this study, or rather reconstitute the wholeness of the inquiry precisely in order to make specific studies more scientific. Seen from the religious studies angle, this means that whilst the strong and most specific sense of ideology is able to emerge with the work of Marx this is at the expense of those areas of meaning that cannot be readily accommodated to it (especially questions of art, religion, ethics). The attention of an over-compensatory move in later work to just these areas is characterized by a further separation of the study of religion from the study of cultural history (Weber, Durkheim). And the study of religion in its turn again splits into sociology, history of religions, phenomenology, and branches of theology.

The exceptions of a major kind to this fragmentation are some of the studies generated by the examination of the Protestantism-capitalism hypothesis (recently those of Swanson and in particular Walzer),[1] and the area of anthropology of religion, which has produced important material for recent methodological discussions (e.g. Winch, Horton, Gellner).[2] The very foreignness of the primary religions demands an ongoing hermeneutic enterprise, so that questions of meaning and communication are immediately present in a way that they may not be for the sociologist, even the sociologist of contemporary religion. In their very different ways the work of Lévi-Strauss, Ricoeur, and Eliade illustrates this, as do recent writings of Spiro and Geertz.[3] Studies of this kind do, however, need supplementation by the tools that the student of ideologies deploys to avoid the danger that understanding everything ends in justifying everything. Just as Marx saw the social Darwinists reading bourgeois society back into the animal kingdom, and Lévi-Strauss suggests that the religion-as-fantasy account of totemism was itself a fantasy of middle-class anthropologists, we might suspect that quite a part of, for example, Eliade's work, is shaped by a traditionalist and conservative ideological position.

The recent breaks with the tacit agreement to keep sociological and theological inquiry carefully separate were long overdue,[4] and whilst 'socio-theology'[5] is an off-putting term, the problems confronted are, at least, substantial ones (e.g. Berger, Bellah).[6] These resistances to fragmentation have, however, yet to get confidently beyond either the use of material from primary religions merely as a source for methodological clarification, or, rather general accounts of the historical and social nature of human meanings and projections.[7] And this is especially so with regard to the modern Christian traditions which both need investigation in their own right and because their study would practically and theoretically lead to a refinement and consolidation of existing approaches.[8]

If I may summarily, and with reference mainly to the Catholic tradition, give some examples, these would include the following. The study of political movements with religious connections (the Sillon, Christian Democracy, the Action Française, Catholic Action, etc.) is generally lacking in both structural and phenomenological accounts of the religious milieux and specific inheritances of doctrinal and experiential traditions. Similarly, the investigation of the idea of the family in the Catholic tradition would certainly throw further light on conservatism, corporatism and some versions of syndicalism, but only if it included, on at least an equal level of seriousness with other *data*, the theological, scriptural and milieux determinations of this theme. Or again, the current debate over contraception has many of the features of an ideology except that the power situation it maintains has no *obvious* link with general social-economic forces. Whatever may be the case elsewhere, in religion, even over so practical a matter as this, the 'relative autonomy of the superstructure' seems peculiarly marked, and the area as a whole thus a key one for testing the sophistication of theories of ideology.

At a further level the nature of the church as a trans-historical, trans-national and trans-class institution (with many of the features of Gramsci's 'egemonia') has rarely been investigated beyond the elaboration of church-denomination-sect typologies wholly internal to the specialized sociology of religion. Yet this must raise important issues for social class analysis, as well as for the relative weighting and inter-action of weak and strong senses of ideology. At the most theoretical level, if questions of ideology are closely related to problems arising from the historicity of human beings, the apparent relativity of knowledge and the attendant problems of interpretation, then the first area in which they were consistently pursued was theology. A lot of the labour currently expended in theoretical clarification of these topics often arrives, in a different style, at hypotheses and conclusions parallel to those available, especially in German theology, more than fifty years ago. The problem of the accurate dating of scripture, the historicity of the Gospels, the quest for the 'historical Jesus', the relation between inspiration, myth and history, the different models offered for the development of doctrine and tradition—these and other matters generated a vast literature which provides important theoretical tools and examples of general use outside the original context.

In drawing attention to what might be gained for the study

of ideology from the religious area, and vice versa, I am not suggesting that in every particular discussion the critic must master half a dozen 'disciplines' before his work can have value. Rather, that his work will be restricted and limited if it does not operate with at least an implicit understanding of the parallels and interconnections with other areas of inquiry, and of the *range of connected implications and presuppositions that make ideology and its study possible*. Among these implications and presuppositions I would, summarily, emphasize the following:

1. Ideology is part of a range of terms like 'Weltanschauung' and 'spirit of the age' which arise from the discovery, concomitant with romanticism, that we inhabit, as Wordsworth said 'a world we both see and half create'—that we invest the world with meanings rather than read them off from it, that collectively and individually we construct our reality.
2. That this construction is inseparable from our being social, linguistic creatures.
3. Given the social nature of language we should expect not only connections between it and the world we construct, but if this constructive activity and language define us as human, then we should expect links between language and rationality of a constitutive, and not merely secondary or subsequent kind.
4. The co-inherence of language, rationality, world construction and sociality is inseparable from the fact that we are historical beings.
5. The dynamic and dialectical nature of construction and the plasticity within it means that we are self-transcendent beings.[9] The *post festum* nature of most sorts of inquiry is only possible because we continually transcend particular situations. That is, historicity is simultaneously the specific situatedness of human beings and their overcoming of, change of, or active confirmation of, it.
6. Language, meanings, symbols have their own reality, they are primary parts of our experience and not merely ideas 'about' it.
7. Consciously and/or unconsciously, collectively and/or individually, our actions have an intentionality or attitude towards the future, a certain expectation of it, without which they are

unintelligible. (Whether this intentionality derives from fundamental and pretty fixed needs of our nature, i.e. is expressive of
an essence, or is to be conceived quite differently, is an important
issue in the handling of this presupposition.)

8. More specifically, false consciousness remains consciousness,
a systematic mode of pre-selecting what reflexion will deal with,
where the absence of a factor may be as, or more important
than, the presence of another. It is not a simple error of fact that
might be quickly remedied. Nor is it a disability like short-
sightedness. It has necessarily to do with modes and styles of
life, with wants, desires and their shaping influence on present
conduct, with what seem to be the obvious and natural directions in which the world either is or ought to be running.
Difficulties here may be clarified but certainly not resolved by a
fact/report or fact/value distinction. Just as there are no reports
that are not related to facts so there are no facts that are not
reported, and analogously, with values.

9. Just as the fact/report, fact/value distinctions may have
limited use in this area, so may the fears of the 'genetic fallacy'
often be misplaced. For we are, typically, dealing with embodied beliefs, styles of life, historical and material possibilities
as much as correct concepts. Concepts may be valid apart from
their origins, but in the contexts where ideological analysis is
most useful this kind of validity may be only abstract, partial,
shadowy, incomplete.

10. In this view absolute, fixed, conceptions of truth, of any
consequence, are no longer possible. In some cases it might be
said, *not yet* possible. For if no significant ideas, beliefs, etc. have
been wholly separate from interests, it may be less a question of
how social interests distort 'truth' as what social interests allow
the possibility of 'more truth' to emerge—truth here understood as the most comprehensive, profound, open, undominating
ideas and values.

What defines *ideology* in this complex is the association of
general interests with the merely partial interests of a specific
group; the ideas, beliefs, 'structures of feeling'[10] involved being
characterized by insufficient comprehensiveness and historical
awareness.[11] In the *strong*, Marxist, sense these partial interests
are those of the bourgeois class seen in the light of a wholly
different future that can be envisaged from *within* bourgeois

society.[12] In a weaker and qualified sense, ideology can be used with regard to classes prior to the bourgeoisie, or groups other than classes, Catholics for example. And, in an accepted but scientifically useless sense ideology describes beliefs, typically religious ones, that are not particularly related to any group or period and which, for a variety of reasons, are thought to be false.

If I am right in drawing attention to these presuppositions or concealed implications of the range within which ideology is located, then we should re-examine the origins of the term and its development to see why, especially in Anglo-Saxon discussions this has not been faced up to. In sum, these implications have almost nothing to do with Destutt de Tracy and the '*idéologues*',[13] and a lot to do with Herder and the Romantics. Only by understanding the Herderian roots of the questions can the subsequent developments be understood and, in particular, it is to the connections between language and rationality, meanings and historicity in Herder that we should attend.

In Herder's work, there is an examination of the connection between language and rationality which tends towards the conclusion that rationality *is* the use of language. His guiding premise is a refusal to completely separate out the various functions and powers of the human person;[14] and a dissatisfaction with theories in which language might be a steady transition from animal exclamation.[15] As Herder will later argue, the difference between freedom and natural aptitude hinges upon language, for language is our substitute for instinct. The issues of rationality, freedom, and language are thus directly connected. But if man has always been rational, then Herder will argue, so has he always been linguistic. The problem with *both* the divine gift and the humanly discovered conception of the origins of language is that they conceive human beings as rational before they invent or are given language. It is their both being wrong that allows Herder a way out; he rejects both views as they stand, but finally leaves open the question of God as ultimate source of rationality, meaning and language.

Language is not traceable or possibly reducible to a cause and effect relation starting from sensation, emotion, or reflection: rather, there is the whole person articulated by language, language is the central fact of this underivable complex.

Language is not so much the channel by which already acquired knowledge reaches us, it is rather the instrument and means of knowing. And this is as true of self-knowledge as of any other kind: for language provides a medium in which we can examine ourselves and it is in this examination that we come to be as persons. Herder is well aware of the point that language is always specific in its utterance yet universal in its content (that purely private languages are, in the literal sense, impossible): the relation between individual and species is like that between my use of language and the fact of language as such—my use is wholly my own, yet contained, controlled and continually sustained by the independence of language, regardless of my usage. Further and crucially, it is not just that the language question is a fine example of how individuals and groups are to be related: it is from language or with language that the two are differentiated as much as they are connected. A word which identifies a part of reality for me is simultaneously and necessarily a communication to and from other people.

It is remarkable how this self-created inner sense of the spirit constitutes in its very origin also a means of communication. Man cannot conceive the first thought, cannot form the first reflexive judgment, without experiencing a kind of dialogue within his own mind, or without feeling impelled towards engaging in a dialogue with other minds. Essentially, therefore, the first human thought prepares communication with other beings; whatever I grasp directly assumes the form of both an identifying symbol for myself and a communicating symbol for others.[16]

Language for Herder, then, exists as that in which man finds himself already indissolubly and constitutively connected with other men and other times. It is an integral part of the process of the emergence of the self in the emergent presence of other selves—that range of the relations between I and Thou which will occupy figures as diverse as Humboldt, Schleiermacher, Feuerbach and Buber.[17]

It is a mystery in which reality, self, creativity and meaning are focused to reveal the unending striving towards the totally human. But all this is seen as a symphony whose totality is known only to God.

For Herder responds in a brilliant way to the general enlightenment problem of reconciling the universality of reason with a steadily growing recognition of the diversity of cultures and historical epochs, the new awareness that there may be as many forms of rationality as there are languages. The diversity of cultures and historical periods is not to be organized in a hierarchy of development towards true rationality. We do 'live in a world we ourselves create', and it may be true that 'humanity (*Humanität*) is the end of human nature; and with this end God has put their own fate into the hands of mankind.'[18] But this end is not teleological in a historical sense. 'Humanity' does not come as a future perfect society.

The question of moral diversity was not, of course, new. Locke, for example, is partly prompted to a rational, demonstrable system of ethics by just such considerations. The difference is that diversity has now encroached upon the criteria of rationality as well as practice, custom or passion; for if the mind is active and not passive then a whole dimension of constraints upon diversity has gone,[19] and more basic levels of human unity have to be found. Thus historicism in its reaction to rationalism revives or preserves elements of pre-rationalist, religious modes and yet is even more precarious. For if the deist underpinnings, or the Herderian developmental powers (*Kräfte*), with their finally religious implications, were to go—as they did for the more radical thinkers—then either a new collective subject of history (e.g. the proletariat) would have to be found, or the dizzy miasma of complete diversity faced—and somehow lived through. In Herder historicity is controlled by an underlying conception which in part draws on ancient concepts of fullness and diversity in creation and partly on the deistic 'best of all possible worlds'. The conception is that of history as a drama without a *dénouement*, a cosmic symphony in which every part is significant in itself. Later movements are not superior to early ones, or closer to any ultimate goal—it is God alone who hears the whole, the total sense of all the movements, the infinite complexity of the continuing development of *Humanität* in all its varied forms. In a real sense, the *Humanität* which is the end of human nature exists only for God.

The Herderian response to the challenge of change and universality, of a becoming without terminus, is, in fact, that of an historicized form of the traditional concept of *being*. Behind all variety and historical progression we find a simultaneity; an ultimate identity is manifest in the remotest details of all forms of creativity. Herder's formulation of the problem of historicity within a dynamic deistic pluralism directly affects the question of 'progress'. For within the dominant forms of European rationality, to challenge progress is to challenge the lynchpin of rationality itself. The denial of perfection drives a wedge into that connection of truth, beauty and goodness that has sustained it. For this connection only has validating conviction if perfection is possible: if it is not, then the edifice tends to collapse and we seem left with either sheer banal diversity or sheer nothingness—a consideration which keeps Herder a Christian, for God is the only guarantor of meaningfulness.

In the universal striving for development wholes are events rather than substances and are thus inconceivable unless 'existence' means continual activity. At every point diversity transforms itself towards unity, but this is at no point a unilinear process: traditions may internally correct themselves or transform themselves but there is no clear way of judging between them, their final coherence exists only for God. Thus rationality *is* universal, but *not* for man—though he can derive comfort and coherence of life from the fact that there is in the end a universal rationality to the total system.

I have underscored the controlling nature of the deism in Herder for it leads directly into that expressivity of spirit in history and culture in Hegel which provides the basic paradigm for all subsequent studies of *Weltanschauungen*. Any attempt to study the style of a movement or period in relation, say, both to architecture and philosophy in this tradition raises problems of what the 'subject' expressed here is and the position from which the wholeness of the expressions can be seen: 'God', *Kräfte*, spirit, totality, the human essence, 'culture' can all act as variants of this holism.[20]

Of course we should not wish to approach the question in the way Herder did, but if the influential nature of this paradigm is correct and if the presuppositions of ideology are as I suggest, then short of wholly abandoning the greater part of the methods available to us, the issues involved here will require very careful examination if a more unified study of beliefs and ideas is to be negotiable.

It should require no emphasis that in Hegel's radical systematization and transformation of some of Herder's insights the deistic emphasis and the notion of *Kräfte* are replaced by Spirit, that an end to the self-expression of Spirit is posited, and that this process of self-expression is characterized as self-estrangement and final reconciliation. And the general relation between this and Marx's further radicalization has been investigated in various directions. But there are certain specific problems in Marx's development in this connection which need comment, for whilst they provide a scientifically useful strong concept of ideology, they leave undeveloped and to one side the complex of questions of the relations of language and rationality, meaning and historicity, opened up by Herder as elements of a potentially unified theory, and they have an important influence not only on the Marxist tradition, but also indirectly on its critics—current concepts of ideology deriving from this interaction.

Lichtheim's observation, in one of the best concise accounts available, is largely quite correct: 'The Marxian concept of ideology thus fuses two different principles: Hegel's insight into the transitory character of successive manifestations of spirit, and Feuerbach's materialist inversion of Hegel, with its stress on the this-worldly of natural existence . . . An explosive mixture.'[21] But I shall want to add to it a complication in the light of the previous discussion. For the examination of religion in the mature Hegel and its critique by Feuerbach, and Marx's distinctive critique of both, play a central role in his general development and especially on the question of ideology. Many of the problems that arise may, I think, be traced back to his one-sided adaptation of Feuerbach. If I am right the Marxian view of ideology is, at important points, confused because, besides overlooking a third principle (that of the specific level of language and rationality suggested by Herder) it is *not* a fusion of Lichtheim's two different principles.

It is not a fusion for at least one reason, namely, Feuerbach's view is not in itself unified. It is rather a shifting alliance between a simple reflective view of human beings deriving from Enlightenment materialism and a view in which human beings

create the world they perceive, associated with romantic philosophy. An ambiguity that becomes evident as soon as one asks
if the 'world' is a world of objects, or a world which constitutively contains human projects, meanings and interactions.
That is, Feuerbach's central category of the 'projection' of
human realities into a religious world has ambivalent characteristics.[22]

1. Religion is a misperceiving of what is in fact there, in the
way in which an object may be misperceived; as if religion were
a pair of distorting spectacles, or a veil lying over something—
without religion, reality will be seen as it is, and that 'as it is' is
object-like. The question here is of a correct, exact or incorrect,
distorted *reflection* of what-is-there-to-be-reflected. One already
notes the undialectical nature of this, and possibly any, optical
metaphor; between an object and a mirror there can be no
dialectic and no history—at most a history of various distortions,
various distorting spectacles, not a history of *history-making*.
The unveiling or unmasking of distortion, the removal of
garb or disguise is important, but the aim is to reveal the
object for correct reflection. The limitations of such an emphasis
should be clear, but it has a conveniently positive aspect: there
can be no doubt about the objectivity of the object and hence
what the criteria for true reflection are: for *reflection excludes active
perception*. It is to this simple position that Feuerbach will drop
back whenever troubled by the problem raised about criteria
on his second view.

2. On the second view, 'projection' is more properly used,
that is, in a way different from and finally irreconcilable with
reflection. As Hegel uses self-alienation or projection of spirit
in creation, so Feuerbach uses self-alienation or projection of
man in religion. In both cases the emphasis lies upon (*a*) the
wholeness of what is projected, (*b*) the process, the active
process, of projection and (*c*) following these—the most important break with reflection—the fact that whilst a correct
reflection can only contain passively a mirror image (light being
given as constant presence), projection allows and enforces
many further complex problems: *what* projects; *upon what* does it
project; *through what medium* does it project? Or, since *difference* is
constitutive of projection as it is not of reflection, what is a
correct or incorrect projection? Does the question have any

sense? A reflection is always less real than its object, a projection may well not be—it would be strange to think of a map as less real than the terrain. What might be 'false' for example about Mercator's, or any other, cartographic projection? It is a rendering rather than a distortion of the object, enabling us to correctly, that is, appropriately and usefully for purposes of a neutrally human kind, come to terms with what we experience and what we want to do. The example might seem a little tendentious but is, I think, allowable; it brings out the world-constructing activity of human beings, which raises important questions about the criteria according to which our projections are validated or invalidated. All too often it seems assumed that projections are *ipso facto* false, and attention moves, evasively, to the true/false reflection model.

Besides the notion of an enlarged (and not necessarily, on that account, distorted) image, projection also carries further and other connotations: mapping, setting out, distancing in order to see more clearly and become familiar with; a design, pattern or forecast; a task, an attempt, a possible intention. These differences of implication in projection and reflection carry through in their application to directly human capacities. Reflexion, as a turning back on the self and its development, is obviously a crucial part of our experience and central to any historical or philosophical analysis. But it is Marx, if anyone, who has taught us that what we reflect upon is men in pursuit of their needs and aims, in their indefinite and constitutive self-transcendence as beings defined by having a future. To adapt his own phrase, reflexion is *post-festum*, history-making is a matter of creative projection—a Promethean rather than Columban matter.

With reflection one is comparing things, as it were, out there with things in here—the crudity of the conception is also an offer of simple verification—but this is not the case with projection, or at least not so evidently. With projection one at least raises the possibility that one is comparing one projection with another. While there can be only one correct reflection, what happens (to put it not wholly seriously) when Feuerbach's projection theory is submitted to analysis in terms of a Freudian projection theory? In so far as Feuerbach resolves the discrepancy of the two terms, it is by a simple collapse of the tension between them, ending finally in a very banal materialism.

49

This is to consider the two terms in their most extensive range, but this is something that it seems to me needs doing, for the dangers of simple and loosely deployed optical metaphors are still considerable. If many of Marx's successors have been led astray by the reflection metaphor, a fair number of his philosophical critics seem, rather quaintly, to think that perception has something basically to do with eye-balls.[23]

In taking up and criticizing Feuerbach's position, Marx also takes up the ambiguity and does not resolve it in a satisfactory manner.[24] In both his references to religion and to ideology the ambiguity remains; between images of unmasking, unveiling, stripping off, 'de-disguising', revealing what is really there to be seen and what, but for the veil, *could* (and therefore should) have been seen; and images of a more complex kind in which distortion enters as an active structuring of the ways in which the world is constructed and perceived, and which, given certain historical conditions, *could not* have been seen otherwise. The difficulty this poses for the theory of ideology is increased by his non-revision of the early assumption that religion *is* ideology.

If religion is seen not only as a false projection but as *the* distorting factor in human self-knowledge then a Feuerbachian argument need not, though it may, canvass the possibility of multiple and constitutive human projections. Whereas if a theory of ideology, in fact of ideologies in the very varied forms of law, politics, art, 'everyday consciousness' is to be set out, then it *presupposes* not only divisions of mental from material labour but connections between consciousness and historicity, rationality and situation, that is, of multiple projections and projection as a human fact.[25]

Thus, Marx's revision of Feuerbach raises questions of general projection and the relativity of knowledge which Feuerbach did not need to consider. Paradoxically perhaps, Marx's radicalization of Feuerbach's analysis of religion by implicitly bringing general projection to the fore and thus making comparisons not between projection and fact, but between projection and projection, may reopen certain possibilities for the discussion of religion and related forms of belief that Feuerbach seemed finally to have closed.

It is possible that the non-pursuit of such questions and problems by Marx is connected with his general lack of interest in religion and his assumption that, in this area at least, Feuerbach's account would stand. It does seem that for religion he retains a Feuerbachian analysis which he does not employ elsewhere.

Two examples from *A Contribution to the Critique of Political Economy* (1859) will confirm this. One concerns aesthetics, the other the connection between myth and religion. In his discussion of the disproportion between artistic and material production Marx raises a fundamental problem: 'But the difficulty is not in grasping the idea that Greek art and *epos* are bound up with certain forms of social development. It rather lies in understanding why they still constitute with us a source of aesthetic enjoyment and in certain respects prevail as the standard and model beyond attainment.'[26] And we know that he probably read Aeschylus in the Greek text 'at least once a year' considering him, along with Shakespeare, the greatest dramatic genius the world had known.[27] His response to the difficulty is, therefore, quite staggeringly naive and psychologistic. Since we all love the 'artless ways of the child' and cannot become children again without becoming childish, 'Why should the social childhood of mankind, where it had obtained its most beautiful development, not exert an eternal charm as an age that will never return?'[28] The oddity lies not just in Marx's regression to psychologism in an area central to his own experience, it is that just what needs to be explained, and is evaded, far from being the simplicity and beauty of childhood, is the *contemporaneity* of Aeschylus with levels of our own experience: this raises questions about meanings of a trans-historical kind.

This part of *The Critique of Political Economy* also suggests a distinction between myth and ideology such that mythology is only negatively conditioned by economic forces; archaic society's undeveloped stage of production is connected with an uncomprehended external nature: 'All mythology overcomes and masters, and shapes, the forces of nature in and through the imagination: it disappears when real mastery over those forces begins.'[29] Ideology, on the other hand, is a reflection of alienated human relations. Whilst, for Marx, only in capitalism does society start to detach itself from natural determinations, and whilst there is an obvious general truth in the affinity between the rise of capitalist ideology and the humanization of

51

Christianity in Protestantism, Marx's distinction is a tricky one if, as he seems at times to want, religion is generally associated with primitive errors of perception. The development of Protestantism may mark a break with a nature-sacramental element of religion, but the whole complex argument over 'secularization' shows that this is in no way a simple or even yet complete break. Apart from the, in Marx's view, undifferentiated relations of things human and things natural in religion, it has almost always contained beliefs about human interactions which cannot be simply reduced to such primitive confusions or related to ideological reflections. Quite apart from its obvious ideological possibilities, the cosmogenic Adam myth, for example, is still very relevant to vast numbers of people. If we are to see the origin of capitalism as the origin of freedom from natural and mythic ties, then 'remnants' and 'traces' have a 400-year duration and depth that one would hardly expect from Marx's references. On the other hand, to describe them as 'anticipations' in religious or utopian disguise is to raise as many questions as it solves, for such 'anticipations' presuppose the trans-historical account of human beings which is just one of the points at issue.

The difficulties implied here can, I think, be made more precise by looking at Lefebvre's concise and accurate account of this topic. '. . . some representations are illusory, for they arise prior to the conditions under which concepts can be formed.'[30] An amazing statement if concepts is taken in its usual sense, but as Lefebvre's example of 'representations concerning the succession of events' before 'the concept of historical time had arisen' shows, what he means is adequate theoretical concepts in our sense. That is, in this minor example, he has blurred conceptual thinking and specifically contemporary theoretical adequacy. I draw attention to this slip for it may suggest a possible confusion in Marx's sparse comments on language between linguistic sociality as such and particular societal uses of language.

Related to these representations are the early cosmogenies/theogonies concerned with relations between life/death, female/male, elements of nature, subordination, superordination. Were these myths ideologies? Yes, in the sense that they supported the 'nascent inequalities' of men, but basically No because they antedate class divisions, and—to be noted—because these 'constructions of the human mind are works of art—more like monuments than abstract systems. They belong to the same category as styles in art history, compendia of moral wisdom, "cultures".'[31] That is, myths, styles, moral wisdom and 'cultures' seem about to vanish out of the Marxist frame of reference! Cosmogenies and myths are turned into ideologies 'only when they become ingredients in religion, especially in the great religions that lay claim to universality'. Now the 'abstract universality' of the great religions (if it is such)[32] could possibly be made plausible in the light of the possible connections of modern Protestantism and abstract universality; but whilst this might be a point of departure for a retrospective analysis, it is not an identity as is here assumed. Moreover, the division between theogonies and religion makes no substantial sense at all.

Because of his key role in the development of the theory of ideology I have emphasized the problem in Marx.[33] Whilst we can retain without change the strong sense of ideology he provides, its honest deployment requires, if my argument holds, that it and any other theory of ideology cannot be taken except in context with the wider if—at that stage—less scientific possibilities attendant on its birth. That is, that the questions of meaning, basic to the study of religion and the study of art, are not secondary features of a theory of ideology but historically, theoretically and practically *basic* elements in it. A proper reconstitution of the range of concepts within which ideology is located will be a difficult task. It requires an adequate Marxist account of language and epistemology, and an elucidation of basic human needs and interests, which alone, I think, make possible evaluations of consciousness as true/false.[34] In these areas, the study of religion provides an astringent test-case, and also, perhaps, some specific resources for attempts at a solution.

NOTES AND REFERENCES

1. Guy Swanson, *Religion and Regime* (Ann Arbor, University of Michigan Press, 1967); Michael Walzer, *The Revolution of the Saints* (New York, Atheneum, 1966).

2. Peter Winch, 'Understanding a Primitive Society', *American Philosophical Quarterly*, I (1964); Robin Horton, 'A Definition of Religion and its Uses', *Journal of the Royal Anthropological Institute*, 90 (1960); 'African Tradition and Western Science' in Bryan R. Wilson (ed.), *Rationality* (Oxford, Blackwell, 1970); 'Neo-Tylorianism: Sound Sense or Sinister Prejudice?', *Man* n.s. 3 (4 Dec. 1968); Ernest Gellner, 'Concepts and Society' in Dorothy Emmet and Alasdair MacIntyre (eds), *Sociological Theory and Philosophical Analysis* (London, Macmillan, 1970).

3. Claude Lévi-Strauss, *Totemism* (Harmondsworth, Penguin, 1969); Paul Ricoeur, *The Symbolism of Evil* (Boston, Beacon Press, 1969); Mircea Eliade, *Patterns in Comparative Religion* (London, Sheed and Ward, 1958); Melford E. Spiro, 'Religion: Problems of Definition and Explanation; Clifford Geertz, 'Religion as a Cultural System', both in Michael Banton (ed.), *Anthropological Approaches to the Study of Religion* (London, Tavistock, 1966).

4. Cf. especially Thomas Luckmann, *The Invisible Religion* (New York, Collier-Macmillan, 1967), Ch. I.

5. Roland Robertson's coinage in his important article 'The Sociology of Religion: Problems and Desiderata', *Religion* I (ii) (autumn 1971).

6. Peter Berger, *The Social Reality of Religion* (London, Faber, 1969) and *A Rumour of Angels* (London, Allen Lane, 1970); Robert Bellah, *Beyond Belief* (New York, Harper & Row, 1970); 'Symbolic Realism', *Journal for the Scientific Study of Religion* (spring 1971).

7. An important exception here might be the recent work of Mary Douglas, *Natural Symbols, Explorations in Cosmology* (London, Barrie & Jenkins, 1970).

8. With regard to the combination of approaches required in the study of beliefs, I wholly agree with Runciman, though I do not find his objections to the attempt to define religion satisfactory. W. G. Runciman: 'The Sociological Explanation of "Religious" Beliefs', *Sociology in its Place and Other Essays* (Cambridge University Press, 1970). In the short term, the general ignorance of the religious area indicates that care is necessary with regard to immediately incorporating religion into the general study of beliefs. More importantly, because religion contains highly specific features (worship, for example) specialized study—within a general study of beliefs—remains; and with it, the problem of definition.

9. Luckmann's discussion of this (op. cit.) as 'the anthropological *a priori*' is as illuminating as his decision to call all such self-transcendence 'religion' is confusing.

10. Cf. Raymond Williams, *The Long Revolution* (London, Chatto & Windus, 1961), pp. 48-71.

11. Cf. Istvan Meszaros, *Marx's Concept of Alienation* (London, Merlin Press, 1970) where he argues that genuine historical awareness presupposes social equality (p. 36f).

12. Cf. Jurgen Habermas, *Towards a Rational Society* (London, Heinemann Educational, 1971), p. 99; Alfred Schmidt, *The Concept of Nature in Marx* (London, New Left Books, 1971), p. 117f on the problems of 'ideologies' prior to bourgeois society.

13. Cf. F. Picavet, *Les Idéologues, essai sur l'histoire des idées et des théories scientifiques, philosophiques, religieuses en France depuis* 1789 (Paris, 1891), Chs 5-6; H. B. Acton, 'The Philosophy of Language in Revolutionary France', *Proceedings of the British Academy*, XLV (1959), pp. 199-219.

14. 'It matters not what one may call the entire disposition of his powers: reason, intellect, consciousness, etc. as long as these names are not to denote disconnected powers or merely a higher degree of animal powers. It is the totality of the organisation of all human powers, the entire economy of man's perceptive, cognitive and volitional nature, or rather it is the sole positive power of thinking

which, combined with a certain organisation of the body, is called mind in man, just as it becomes natural aptitude in animals; in man it gives rise to freedom, in animals it constitutes instinct. The difference however is not one of degree or of a "more or less" of given faculties or powers, but rather that of wholly dissimilar direction and development of all powers.' J. G. Herder, 'Treatise on the Origins of Language' in J. G. von Herder, F. M. Barnard (ed.). *On Social and Political Culture* (Cambridge University Press, 1969), p. 131.

15. Herder's view of language obviously owes something to Condillac (as in a more positive way it does to Monboddo), but the differences are crucial. Especially in context with his form of historicism, it indicates the complex range of possibilities for later theories of ideology—as the positivistic theories of language and perception of the *idéologues*, following Condillac, do not. The difficulty of fusing the views of de Tracy and Herder is exactly parallel to the ambiguity of 'reflection' and 'projection' vocabulary in Feuerbach and Marx, to be discussed later.

16. Op. cit., p. 141.

17. The I-Thou terminology is conventionally traced to Feuerbach. As Buber himself points out in *Between Man and Man* (London, 1948; Fontana, 1961), p. 17, it derives from the philological studies of Herder's friend, von Humboldt. It also plays an important role in Schleiermacher's work.

18. J. G. Herder, *Reflections on the Philosophy of the History of Mankind*, edited by F. E. Manuel (University of Chicago Press, 1968), p. 82.

19. The complex of problems about truth and the relativity of human beings is normally and usefully centred upon Kant, but Berlin is right in claiming Herder as the first articulate exponent of the indissolubility of fact and value. See Isaiah Berlin, 'Herder and the Enlightenment' in E. R. Wasserman (ed.), *Aspects of the Eighteenth Century* (Baltimore, Johns Hopkins, 1965), p. 95. Cf. John Macmurray, *The Self as Agent* (London, Faber, 1957), pp. 39-61.

20. The holistic emphasis in much historicism is obvious. Its presence in Huizinga and even in its apparent opponent Burckhardt (argued convincingly by E. H. Gombrich, *In Search of Cultural History* (Oxford, 1969), is less so. That it occurs in Jung's archetypes and Eliade's patterns is no surprise; that it occurs in parts of Lévi-Strauss would be so to many of his readers. I stress it not only because it is a major paradigm of the cultural sciences, but because it would so often seem to be thought that those, like the historicists, who formally confronted its basic problems are self-evidently wrong, or sadly *passé*. The debate over expressive totalities in French structuralism (cf. Maurice Godelier, 'System, Structure and Contradiction in Marx's Capital', in R. Miliband and J. Saville (eds.), *Socialist Register* (London, 1967)) is particularly important here; part of the fascination of certain forms of structuralism lies in their being the first major attempt to keep the paradigm whilst dissolving the 'subject'.

21. George Lichtheim, *The Concept of Ideology and Other Essays* (New York, Vintage, Random House, 1967), p. 16.

22. This is not the place for a detailed exegesis of Feuerbach; I am thinking primarily of *The Essence of Christianity*, tr. George Eliot (New York, Harper & Row, 1957), and *Principles of the Philosophy of the Future*, tr. M. H. Vogel (New York, Bobbs-Merrill, 1966); the later *Essence of Faith According to Luther*, tr. R. Mannheim (London, Harper & Row, 1967) is also interesting in this connection.

23. As Althusser's brilliant analysis of whether Marx 'stood Hegel on his head' or 'extracted the rational kernel' from his philosophy shows, Marx's metaphors need careful study—they are often very misleading (Louis Althusser, 'Contradiction and Overdetermination', *For Marx* (London, Allen Lane, 1969). With regard to the reflection metaphor one should note that its use in the *Critique of Hegel's Philosophy of Right*, tr. John O'Malley (Cambridge University Press, 1970), p. 25, is

based on a passage of Hegel where 'reflection' suggests mutual reflection or co-inherence—a possibility absent from the use of this metaphor in the Marxist tradition and not evident, I think, apart from this instance, in Marx himself.

24. In an important passage of *The German Ideology* (Moscow, 1964; London, Lawrence & Wishart, 1965), p. 37, we find in thirty lines: ideas as 'interwoven with material activity', 'direct efflux of material conditions', 'determined by a definite development of . . . productive forces', 'upside down as in a camera obscura', 'ideological reflexes', 'ideological echoes', 'nebulous images in the brain', and 'sublimates of material life processes'.

25. 'Objectification' suggests something far more definite and scientific than projection; but objectifications involve projections, and different types of objectification require classifying.

26. *A Contribution to the Critique of Political Economy*, tr. N. I. Stone (Chicago, 1904; London, Lawrence & Wishart, 1971), pp. 309-12.

27. Franz Mehring, *Karl Marx, the Story of his Life* (London, Allen & Unwin, 1936), p. 503.

28. Loc. cit.

29. Op. cit.

30. Henri Lefebvre, *The Sociology of Marx* (London, Allen Lane, 1968), p. 77.

31. Ibid., p. 78.

32. Ibid., p. 79.

33. John Mepham's stimulating interpretation, 'Ideology in *Capital*', *Radical Philosophy*, 2, 1972, appeared after this paper was completed.

34. Cf. my 'Objectivity and Human Needs in Marxism', *New Blackfriars*, May/June 1973.

Social and Political Thought and the Problem of Ideology

BHIKHU PAREKH

The most influential conception of rationality in Western thought, a conception that is *prima facie* highly plausible and has a good deal of attraction for intellectuals, goes back to the pre-Socratics and finds its noblest expression in the philosophy of Plato and Aristotle. On this, what for convenience I shall call the traditional view of rationality, thinking was essentially a contemplative activity in which the human mind soared above the contingencies of human existence and comprehended its subject matter without being influenced by any extra-rational factors issuing from the thinker's psychological or social background. Thinking, in other words, was regarded as a direct and unmediated encounter between the thinking mind and its objects of thought. The traditional view of rationality also drew a fairly neat distinction between theory and practice. Unlike the world of practice which arose from human wants and desires and thus from a lack of human self-sufficiency, theorizing was regarded as an unconstrained, free, and indeed useless activity in which the human mind was guided by nothing other than the disinterested desire to seek the truth. Aristotle expressed the distinction well when he described practice as an essentially human, and theory as an essentially divine, activity. As God is self-sufficient, he could not want or desire anything and could only be defined as self-thinking thought. Man therefore was believed to be most god-like when he was engaged in theorizing. Aristotle carried the argument to its logical conclusion when he suggested that the theoretical reason, *nous*, could not be inherent in the human organism but came from 'outside'[1] and was immortal. It was simple and changeless, and since it dealt with pure forms and did not depend on physical sensations and images to provide it with its subject matter, it was self-sufficient. As the theoretical reason was thus detachable from the human body, it was believed to be totally uninfluenced by its physical and social environment.

Man, on the traditional view of rationality, was essentially a theoretical being whose primary concern was to discover and contemplate the truth. In his pursuit of truth he was guided by nothing other than the disinterested concern to reach the truth. As practical interests distorted and corrupted thought, man, it was believed, could pursue the truth only if he had no interest in the practical outcome of his pursuit. The more the human reason was dissociated from passions and desires, the more it was considered capable of attaining the truth. It is worth noting that for Plato, Aristotle, Descartes and even Spinoza, desires and passions were not original properties of the human soul but the 'disturbances' it suffered as a result of its union with the body and which it could and should constantly endeavour to transcend. Not only was the human reason not influenced by human passion, it was not influenced by the surrounding society or the social position of the thinker either. That the thinker existed in a particular society was considered a historical contingency that in no way affected the operations of his reason. When the socially transcendent human reason discovered truths, they were naturally believed to be eternally valid.

While some of the beliefs of the traditional view of rationality were questioned by many Christian theologians, the first full-scale challenge to it was not mounted until the dawn of the modern era. The challenge came from two related but essentially different directions.[2]

The first attack was based on a psychological theory of human action that was initiated by Hobbes, refined by Locke, and perfected by the thinkers of the French Enlightenment. Man, it was argued, was essentially a practical being whose main concern in life was to pursue his happiness, to make the world a habitable place. Reason, it was argued further, was set in motion by human desires;[3] indeed, it was created by desires, so that the more a man desired, the greater the stimulus he had to think and therefore the greater his reason. As Voltaire, in his *Treatise of Metaphysics*, remarked, 'the passions are the wheels which make all these machines go'. Vauvenargues reflected the same attitude in his *Introduction to the Knowledge of the Human Mind* when he concluded that the true nature of man did not lie in reason but in the passions. Helvetius observed in his *Treatise on Man* that reason in itself was inert and was set in motion only by desires. As reason thus arose and operated within the overall context of practical interests and desires, its essential task was considered to be to serve passions, to find the best means of gratifying them. It was argued, further, that of all human passions the concern for personal interest was the 'most powerful, most important, most uniform, most lasting and most general' (Bentham). It was believed to be natural to man to 'prefer himself to mankind'; indeed, it was argued that this desire comes with us 'from the womb' and 'never leaves until we go into the grave' (Adam Smith). Now if a man was a creature compelled by his very nature to pursue his own interest, and if reason was only a means to satisfying human desires, it was very difficult to see how human thought could be other than self-interested. Not only in all his conscious activities but even in his unconscious desires and motivations man could not but be guided by considerations of self-interest. And this applied not merely to his practical activity but also to his intellectual activities.

The second major attack on the traditional theory of rationality came from the historicist school of which Hegel was the greatest philosopher. Kant had already paved the way for this line of attack by denying the objective and ontological unity of the world on which the traditional theory was based. He took the view that the world in itself had no order, no internal principles of unity, and that it was the perceiving subject who imposed order on his experiences and created a coherent perceptual universe out of the chaos of experience. However, as Kant had assumed that the human mind had an inherent structure, and that the principles it imposed were universally common, his view did not lead to epistemological subjectivism. But it did raise some acute problems. He had assumed that the human mind had fixed categories of understanding, without explaining how they came to be there in the first instance. He had further treated the human mind as if it somehow stood outside society and was not a product or even an integral part of society. He had also not asked if the human mind and its categories always remained the same or if they were subject to historical evolution.

Trying to meet the difficulties that Kant's epistemology had raised, Hegel argued that man was essentially a social creature, and society essentially a historical product. He thought that each society had a unique modality of consciousness, a *Volkgeist* that permeated and unified all its parts and gave it an internal unity and distinctive identity. The *Volkgeist*, further, was a manifestation of the world spirit, representing a particular stage in its successive historical manifestations. Hegel's philosophy implied that human thought was culturally and historically conditioned and could not transcend the categories and assumptions of its time. It implied further that human thinking was not an individual but a social activity, that man thought not as an individual but as a member of his society, and that the relationship between the human mind and its object was necessarily culturally mediated.

Both the psychological and the historicist attacks on the traditional theory of rationality were coordinated by Marx, which is why he is such a central figure in the discussion of ideology. Marx married liberal psychology to Hegel's historicism. Like Hegel he too divided history into several epochs, but unlike him his principle of division was not cultural but economic. Human thought for him was determined by interests as the liberals had argued; but he defined interest not in individual but in socio-historical terms. Each individual thought, he believed, in terms of the categories characteristic of his class, and what made him a representative of his class was the fact that he continued to wrestle with the same problems at the theoretical level that preoccupied other members of his class in actual life. He remained unable, Marx thought, to transcend the categories and assumptions of his class because ultimately, to put it somewhat crudely, it was not in his interest or in the interest of his class that he should do so. Such limited and distorted thought Marx called ideology.

The psychological and the historicist attacks on the traditional theory of rationality created a serious intellectual crisis and generated 'the problem of ideology'. They managed to cast serious doubts on the traditional theory, and yet what they proposed to put in its place destroyed human rationality and capacity ever to reach the truth. If self-interest was the ultimate spring of human conduct it was difficult to see how it did not permeate and distort thought, how a man could accept truths that went against his interest. One could of course argue that truth and interest always harmonized, or that it was in man's interest to pursue truth. But this was, to say the least, a highly questionable assumption and it in no way relieved the tension between liberal psychology and liberal epistemology. Similarly if all thought was historically conditioned as Hegel had argued, the idea of the Absolute could not make any sense, and even if it did, it was difficult to see how the historically limited mind of Hegel could claim to grasp the ways of the Absolute in their totality. Similarly, Marx too could not argue that while all thought was class determined he had somehow transcended the categories of his class or that interest had not distorted his thought. And therefore if they were to be consistent both he and Hegel had to argue that truth was relative to historical epoch or class, that man could never attain objective and universally valid truths, that there were as many different types of ration-ality as there were societies and classes, and that therefore mankind did not constitute a rational community capable of mutual comprehension.

The essence of the problem of ideology then was, and is, whether the historically, sociologically and psychologically naive traditional theory of rationality could be revised without destroying rationality altogether. In other words, can one bring down human reason from its seat in high heavens (as Greeks had imagined it) to the earth and locate it firmly and securely in the human world without losing it in the process? Or can the dignity and power of reason be secured only by pretending that it is a divine and transcendent faculty? In short, can reason be human (or humanized) without ceasing to be reason?

Of a number of attempts made to deal with this crisis of rationality, Mannheim's was one of the most significant. He saw the problem that Weber did not. And he did not feel committed to defending Marx and Hegel in a way that Lukács did. While he did not resolve the problem, he did face up to it and opened up an interesting line of inquiry. It will therefore be rewarding to consider in some detail his analysis and proposed resolution of the problem. In the next two sections I shall outline his position and criticize what appears to be a fundamental weakness in an otherwise stimulating analysis. In the final section I shall sketch very briefly the outlines of a theory of rationality that incorporates many of Mannheim's basic insights and avoids his mistakes.

I

Following Marx, Mannheim argues that human thought arises and operates in a definite social milieu. The process of knowing in his view is 'decisively' influenced at 'critical' points by 'extra-theoretical' or 'existential' factors. To every social situation, he argues, there pertains a definite point of view: a definite perspective on the world, a definite conceptual framework, a definite set of beliefs about man and society, a definite set of 'basic categories of thought', a definite standard for evaluating and validating knowledge. As he puts it, 'mental structures are inevitably differently formed in different social and historical settings' (238).[4] It is the social context that determines the way an individual defines and uses concepts, the way he contrasts them with other concepts, the sorts of concepts that are absent from his thought, the dominant models of his thought, the level of his abstraction and his theory of reality. Mannheim explains in some detail how this is so.

It is because their different social backgrounds give rise to different perspectives that two different persons, both reasoning accurately, judge the same object and define the same word very differently. Thus to a nineteenth-century German conservative, freedom meant the right of each estate to live according to its own privileges, while to a contemporary liberal, it meant precisely the absence of these privileges. That each side saw only one aspect of the concept is 'clearly and demonstrably connected with their respective positions in the social and political structure' (245). Similarly, conservatives generally use morphological categories of thought that enable them to grasp the totality of experience as a whole, whereas left-wing groups, concerned to change things, generally atomize a situation into its component elements in order that they can reassemble them anew (246). Take again, the differences in the thought-models of different individuals and groups. While the success of the natural sciences created a general desire to study social phenomena in mechanistic-atomistic terms, it is significant, thinks Mannheim, that not all the groups in society accepted their dominance. The landed nobility, the displaced classes and the peasantry were generally disinterested in and even resentful of any attempt to study society in scientific terms. This was so because the world view that the natural sciences represented 'belonged to a mode of life other than their own', was alien to their 'life-situation' (247). Mannheim offers a similar explanation of the difference in the level of intellectual abstraction of different individuals and groups. Why is it, he asks, that Marxism, which is so keen to trace the ideological origins of its opponents' thought, did not develop a general theory on this basis? And replies that this was because of the Marxists' subconscious reluctance to think out the implications of their insight to a point where they would have a 'disquieting effect' on their own position (249). In other words Marx did not develop a general theory of ideology because it would have shown that his own ideas were as ideological as those of his opponents.

The recognition of the 'infiltration of the social position of the investigator into the results of his study', Mannheim argues, entails a rejection of nearly all the basic assumptions of the traditional theory of rationality. Its biggest mistake was to detach human thinking from its social and activist context. It had naively assumed that thinking was a solitary and uniquely individual activity. In Mannheim's view, on the other hand, men are members of various groups and confront the world both practically and intellectually as members of these groups. As they think *with* some groups and *against* some others, thinking is basically a social, a collective, activity. 'Strictly speaking it is incorrect to say that the single individual thinks. Rather it is more correct to say that he participates in thinking further what men have thought before him' (3). Thinking, further, is not a contemplative but a practical activity and is integrally connected with the human need to respond to the world (15). Its problems, concepts, forms of thought are not *sui generis* or excogitated out of the human mind but arise in the course of transforming and grappling with the world. Thinking and acting, theory and practice, are not separate activities but two somewhat different dimensions of a single composite activity. Theory arises out of and reacts on practice, just as practical concerns generate and transform, and are in turn transformed by, theory.

As the traditional theory of rationality is based on false assumptions concerning the nature of thought, Mannheim goes on, its notions of truth and objectivity need to be radically revised. If all thought is practical, the idea of a disinterested pursuit of truth does not make any sense. And if all thought is socially determined the idea of absolute and universally valid truth does not make any sense either. To suggest that some forms of thought and criteria of validity are universally true is naive in the extreme. 'Such simple and unsophisticated ideas in their purity and naivety are reminiscent of some intellectual Eden that knows nothing of the upheaval of knowledge after the fall' (94). The discovery that thought is immersed in the life of society, that it has 'social and activist roots' (5), has already been made, and it is no longer possible to go back to the cosy and comforting but essentially invalid rationalism of the traditional theory of rationality. One can, of course, keep pointing to a few basic propositions of logic and mathematics and even of some of the natural sciences as examples of universally valid truth and continue chanting slogans about the dignity and purity of human thought. But that is no answer to a man who, deeply perplexed and bewildered by the sheer multiplicity and chaos of social and political thought, asks how 'the partisanship, the fragmentariness of our vision' can be transcended and how we can deal with the 'undoubted' fact that human ideas are profoundly conditioned by deep psychological and social forces (38). It is no use talking to him about the formal consistency or inconsistency of a theory, since his query is about the diversity of substantive interpretations of facts. And it is no use either to refer him to the verificationist criteria for evaluating different theories, since the social and political facts to which an appeal is being made can themselves be interpreted and described in so many different and conflicting ways. To put the point differently, the recognition of the 'inherently ideological character of all thought' (48), of the fact that the 'thought of all parties in all epochs is of an ideological character', has destroyed 'man's confidence in human thought in general' (37). And the fundamental problem that any well-considered theory of rationality must answer is as to how one can deal with this crisis in human self-confidence, without taking recourse to the already discredited Platonic, Cartesian and other forms of abstract rationalism, or to self-destructive scepticism and irrationalism, or to an 'ill-considered and sterile form of relativism . . . increasingly prevalent today' (237).

Mannheim's own answer to the crisis created by the knowledge of the existential determination of truth is along the following lines. Just as in personal life one acquires mastery over blind and unconscious impulses by first becoming aware of them, and then consciously controlling them, so too in his pursuit of knowledge man can acquire objectivity, not by ignoring or holding 'in abeyance' his interests and evaluations but only by recognizing and accepting them. And just as a patient needs a psycho-analyst to make him aware of his unconscious impulses and to help him to come to terms with and even conquer them, a society needs a sociologist of knowledge. The task of the sociologist of knowledge is threefold. First, he is to interpret and organize people's complex and chaotic ideas into coherent and intelligible perspectives. Second, he is to interpret and analyse these perspectives and classify them into a few basic styles of thinking. Having done this he is to take the third and final step of going 'behind' these basic styles of thinking, relating them to their relevant social backgrounds and showing how each perspective is existentially determined. This three-stage inquiry Mannheim calls sociology of knowledge. And its method of operation he calls 'relationism', that is, relating isolated ideas to a perspective, a perspective to a thought style, and relating the latter in turn to a life-situation. Relationism then is Mannheim's answer to relativism, and sociology of knowledge is his answer to ideology.

By analysing the life-experiences within which a perspective arises and from which it derives its meaning, the sociologist of knowledge, in Mannheim's view, is able to comprehend its inner significance and rationality. He is also able to show to its

c

adherents why they think the way they do, why they emphasize certain experiences and not others, why they value certain things and not others, why they use words and concepts one way rather than another. By thus demonstrating to them how their perspective reflects and articulates a *Weltanschauung* appropriate to their particular social position, he is able both to show them the one-sidedness of their perspective and to make them receptive to the insights of other perspectives. In seeing how various perspectives differ and why, the sociologist of knowledge, further, is able to go beyond them all and is in a position to create a higher level of abstraction that offers a 'common denominator', a common vocabulary and a common body of standards for translating the insights and results of one perspective in terms of another (270). He is able, in other words, to develop 'a more comprehensive basis of vision' (271), a dynamic and synthetic viewpoint that encompasses, explains and integrates conflicting perspectives.

Sociology of knowledge, Mannheim maintains, does no more than provide a common framework within which different perspectives can engage in a dialogue. Since a mere empirical demonstration of the origin of an idea tells us nothing about its validity, sociology of knowledge is not equipped to assess the validity of ideas, which, as the traditional theory of rationality had insisted, remains the preserve of epistemology (4). However, sociology of knowledge is not entirely irrelevant to epistemology. The knowledge of the origin of an idea clarifies its meaning and indicates how it is intended to be taken. It informs us, further, about the scope of the statement, the area of experience it is intended to cover; by thus indicating how its truth or falsity is to be ascertained, it guides us in deciding *how* it is to be validated and *within what limits* it is to be considered valid. In other words sociology of knowledge 'particularizes' the 'scope and the extent' of the validity of an idea or a theory (225). In Mannheim's cryptic and vague phrase, the value of the findings of the sociology of knowledge 'lies somewhere . . . between irrelevance to the establishment of truth on the one hand, and entire adequacy for determining the truth on the other'.

Since Mannheim is convinced that there is a 'close' relationship between the origin of an idea and its validity, between sociology of knowledge and epistemology, he argues that the 'fundamental presuppositions' of the traditional conception of epistemology should be radically revised (257). The 'self-sufficiency of epistemology', accepted as a self-evident truth by the traditional theory of rationality, is a myth. The traditional conception of epistemology is derived from the natural sciences; and since the historical-social perspective of the investigator is irrelevant to the validity of the knowledge acquired in these sciences, traditional epistemology has remained unhistorical and abstract. When therefore it is applied to the social sciences where the social position of the investigator is of utmost importance it leads to distortion. What we need to do therefore is to evolve a historically orientated epistemology that takes full account of the concrete interplay between existence and knowledge. Once the traditional epistemology is revised, says Mannheim, its notions of truth and objectivity have to be revised as well. Different perspectives have different insights into social reality and all we can hope for is to encourage a debate among them and arrive at a broader and richer insight, an insight that is more comprehensive and richer than any of them but not one that can pretend to represent 'truth as such'. A true social or political theory is not one that no one can deny but one that most men can accept. The idea of 'absolute truth' or 'truth in itself' is therefore inapplicable to the study of man. Besides, as a richer and more satisfactory conception of social reality can only be attained by integrating partial and narrower conceptions of reality, an 'indirect approach through social history' is in the end far more fruitful than 'a direct logical attack'. Truth, that is to say, is reached not by falsifying and knocking down theories but by understanding their social context, appreciating their partial insights, and incorporating them in a wider perspective.

II

Mannheim spoils a good thesis by exaggerating it. He says much that is interesting and valid and with which, as will become apparent in the next section, I agree. As we shall see later he is right to emphasize the social and activist context of social and political thought and to draw attention to some of the problems created by the remarkably different ways in which people see the same reality. He is right to criticize the traditional theory of rationality for its historical and sociological *naïveté*; and he is no less right to criticize Hegel and Marx for emphasizing the historicity of all thought but claiming inconsistently that their own theories somehow represented absolute truth. He is also right to see the narrowness of Marx's economism, and to want to define the category of social factors much more widely. Mannheim's own proposal for a sympathetic analysis and systematic synthesis of conflicting social and political theories does suggest a way out of the pluralist impasse and opens up an interesting line of inquiry. His basic mistake, however, was twofold. First, while he was right to see that human thought, especially social and political thought, cannot be dissociated from human interests, values, anxieties, cultural biases, etc., he went wrong in arguing that it was determined by any or all of them. In other words, he confused the fact that man is culturally conditioned with the dubious view that man is socially determined, and rejected only the economistic version of the determinist thesis, but not the thesis itself. Mannheim's second basic mistake was to confuse pluralism with relativism, the undoubted fact that different people see reality differently with the dubious view that they see different realities and that truth and reality are relative. These mistakes led his otherwise stimulating analysis into blind alleys.

Although Mannheim's entire analysis hinges on his basic thesis that knowledge is determined by social background, he never clearly defines any of the key terms involved. He does not explain what he means by knowledge. It is not clear, for example, if he means the total body of information that an individual has or only the systematic body of theoretical knowledge. That your name is John and that Paris is the capital of France can in one sense be called knowledge, but Mannheim clearly does not want to say that this type of knowledge is relative to different perspectives. By knowledge therefore he must be taken to mean systematic and organized knowledge. Even here, however, he qualifies his thesis by saying that not all but 'most of the domains of knowledge' are existentially determined. How the distinction between different types of knowledge is made and why only some of them are considered socially

SOCIAL AND POLITICAL THOUGHT

determined is nowhere explained. He is not even certain what domains of knowledge are existentially determined. He is clear that 'historical, political and social sciences' and 'ordinary thought' are determined and 'exact sciences' are not. But his attitude to logic is ambiguous. At times he suggests that its 'laws' are immune from social determination; but at other times he argues that even formal logic is acceptable and appears plausible only to certain types of society or to certain sections of it (22, 23).

Not only does he not give a coherent account of what type of knowledge is determined and why, he also does not explain what precisely he means by determinism. Sometimes knowledge is said to be 'casually' determined (54, 239); sometimes it is said to be 'conditioned' by existential factors; sometimes it is said to be 'closely connected' with or 'in harmony' with or 'in accord' with them (76, 148, 199); sometimes it 'corresponds' to them (33, 144); while at other times, as is more often the case, he is content to remark that it is 'no accident' that ideas and social background correspond (127, 223, 248, 249). Mannheim could, of course, argue, as in fact he does, that these and other expressions do not reflect any ambiguity in his thought but only represent different *types* and *levels* of correlation that can exist between thought-process and life-situation. Thus in some cases ideas are determined by social factors; in other cases, they are only conditioned by them; and in some other cases they only correspond to them. This would be a plausible thesis to maintain, but then it would mean that Mannheim is not justified in talking about existential *determination* of knowledge, since determination refers to but one particular type of relationship and an extremely strong one at that. What is more, in those cases where ideas are said to accord with or correspond to existential factors, he would not really be establishing any meaningful correlation between them, since merely to show that certain ideas happen to be vaguely associated with certain social backgrounds is not to say anything of real significance. Mannheim needs to show that this association is not a mere coincidence but due to the influence of social factors.

Mannheim, again, does not show what existential factors determine ideas, why they and not others should be singled out, and why they have this kind of influence. Unlike Montesquieu he does not assign any influence to climatic, geographical and other natural factors without showing why. One would have thought that they too are 'existential' factors. He is also not clear whether or not psychological factors 'determine' thought and to what degree. At times he assigns key role to 'collective-unconscious, volitional impulses' (104 ff) and argues that thought requires an 'emotional-unconscious undercurrent to assure the continuous orientation for knowledge in group life'. In his view it is 'impulsive, irrational factors' that furnish 'the real basis' for the development of society and of ideas. Knowing, he maintains, 'presupposes a community of knowing which grows primarily out of a community of experiencing prepared for in the sub-conscious' (28). Since the collective unconscious of a group has such a powerful influence on its ideas he devotes nearly eighteen pages to the discussion of how to control it (30-48). For the most part, however, Mannheim is not happy with such psycho-logical accounts; and while stressing their importance, he seems to want to explain them in sociological terms, generally taking the view that unconscious psychological influences are them-selves the result of social forces (223).

But when it comes to specifying social factors he is, again, ambivalent. Sometimes he takes every possible type of social grouping to be a determinant of ideas, and emphasizes the role of family, childhood experiences, occupational groups, etc. At other times, he follows Marx in regarding the class as all-important. At yet other times he stresses 'political interests' (148) as existentially very important. Sometimes he moves away from groups altogether and resorts to that capacious umbrella of social forces, social structure as a whole, and even the entire historical epoch as the existential determinants of ideas. Thus he says at various places that the rationalistic manner of thinking arose in the modern society because it was 'in accord with the needs of an *industrial society*', that the post-Romantic generation adopted a revolutionary view of society because it was 'in accord with the needs of *the time*', that psychic energies and forms of thought are transformed by 'social forces' (223). To say that social factors determine ideas is not really to say anything meaningful, unless one shows how the social factors are them-selves interrelated. Now either Mannheim should pick up one of them as all-important, or he should establish a pattern of interaction among them. He does neither. He is tempted to take the familiar Marxist line, but fights shy of its reductionism and naive economism. The result is that he keeps emphasizing different factors as they suit his argument, leaving his theory of social determinism incredibly chaotic.

Mannheim's basic thesis then is muddled. He does not clarify what types of ideas are determined by what types of existential factors; and he is not clear either on whether they are determined or conditioned or stimulated by them or whether they simply happen to correspond to them. What is worse his concern to establish his thesis leads him to make highly dubious assertions. Explaining why Marx did not develop a sociology of knowledge, he argues that it was because he did not want, albeit unconsciously, to jeopardize his own claim to represent an absolutely true theory of society (249). But how does Mannheim know that this was Marx's unconscious reason? Why cannot one admit that Marx did genuinely believe, however wrongly, that while the ideas of some classes were determined by interests, his own were not? Perhaps he was inconsistent, but what evidence does Mannheim have to jump to the conclusion that this inconsistency sprang from Marx's unconscious desire to distort the truth to bolster his scientific claims? Mannheim asserts, again, that much of modern sociology shies away from dealing historically and concretely with the problems of society and remains abstract and formalistic because it is afraid that otherwise its own internal contradictions, and those of capitalism itself, might become visible to others (249/50). The bourgeois discussion of freedom, Mannheim again insists, has always concentrated on political but never on social and economic freedom, because the bourgeoisie are fearful that this might pose a threat to their interests. In no case does he offer any evidence that this was or is really the intention of the parties concerned. He does not show, for example, that formalistic sociology is really committed to the defence of capitalism, or that the adoption of an historical approach will necessarily lead it to criticize it. The reasoning in each case is deductive and speculative and one could just as plausibly offer a totally different account of the phenomenon concerned.

Even if Mannheim's thesis could be correctly formulated, it would have to be rejected on a number of grounds. If all

No

thought is existentially determined, so is the thought that all thought is existentially determined, and therefore has no general validity. Again, a society is a system of roles and reciprocal relationships which cannot be sustained if its members do not have similar ideas on their position in society and the rights and duties it entails. In other words the existence of an organized society becomes impossible to explain if its members have different ideas corresponding to their different social backgrounds. Again, Mannheim's view rests on a naive conception of the nature of ideas. It assumes that as social conditions change ideas change automatically; but this is to treat ideas like a baggage that one can pick up and put down at will. It also implies that men cannot change their ideas unless they change their social group, and this not only denies all intellectual value to education, discussion, criticism, introspection and disturbing personal experiences, but also makes it impossible to explain the familiar fact that people do change their ideas without changing their social position.

Even though Mannheim's account of ideology and rationality is untenable, what he says about sociology of knowledge makes some very interesting points. His view that the knowledge of the life-situation of a person is useful in understanding his social and political ideas is valid and his belief that it is possible to work out a realm of debate where competing viewpoints can carry on a dialogue and come better to appreciate their partialities opens up an interesting line of inquiry. Even though he does not establish any clear relationship between the origin and the validity of an idea, he does manage to suggest that the two are related, although not in quite the way he proposes. His plea for both an historically orientated epistemology in social and political thought, and for a revision of the notions of objectivity and truth as they apply to the study of man, is backed up by some very powerful arguments.

The point, however, is that his sociology of knowledge is impossible if his theory of ideology is correct. In other words, paradoxically, his cure is only effective if his diagnosis is wrong. It is not at all clear how it is possible for holders of different perspectives ever to argue if their categories of thought and forms of consciousness are determined existentially. As each perspective is a self-enclosed world and no one can get out of it,

No Again trying to say the rejection of a criterion must be justifiable by that criterion Obviously cant be !

the possibility of a dialogue is foreclosed. This applies to the sociologist of knowledge as well who, despite Mannheim's rather naive theory of 'socially unattached intellectuals',[5] is as much a prisoner of his existentially determined perspective as anyone else, and therefore cannot have the ability to reconstruct other perspectives faithfully or to relate them to their adherents' life situation or provide a 'common denominator' between them. Further if different perspectives are to criticize each other, they must have *some* common standards to which they can appeal and whose general validity they must accept. This means that objective standards that Mannheim had earlier rejected and that indeed generated the problem of ideology in the first instance have now to be brought back through the backdoor, as he actually does in his reference to 'the direct examination of facts'. But once they are brought back, it becomes possible for different perspectives to communicate and criticize each other directly; and therefore sociology of knowledge is no longer necessary to provide a common vocabulary or a common realm of discourse. In other words, if all social and political thought is ideological, sociology of knowledge is impossible; if, on the other hand, it is not ideological, sociology of knowledge is not necessary to play the redemptive role that Mannheim assigns it.

III

Mannheim then has failed to provide a satisfactory theory of social and political rationality. As he mistakenly took a determinist and relativist view of social and political thought he remained unable to explain how social thought could be improved, how men could debate and discuss, how the partial insights of conflicting social and political theories could be synthesized. The problem for any well-considered theory of rationality, therefore, is how it can come to terms with the plurality of social and political thought without getting misled into determinist and relativist blind alleys. Below is sketched very briefly and tentatively the outline of one possible way of conceiving rationality.

We can take it as true that a human being does not exist in a vacuum but is a member of a society by whose cultural milieu he is necessarily conditioned. He grows up with its values, prejudices and categories of thought that are often too deep even for consciousness. His language too directs his perceptions and thoughts along definite channels. He occupies a definite position in society that delimits his range of experiences, and therefore influences the view he will be inclined to take of his fellow-men, the beliefs he will find plausible, the weight he will attach to an argument or to an account of human behaviour. The cultural ethos of his society moulds and shapes his mind; it disposes him to look at the world in a certain way and gives his consciousness a quality, a tone, a content, a rhythm, a structure. His reason, which is only the way his consciousness operates, is thus firmly and securely located in the culture of his community and is not a natural or transcendent faculty but a cultural capacity. Human mind, further, is a complex totality in which reason, passion, desire are all closely intertwined. It cannot therefore be broken up into separate parts each of which operates in isolation from the rest. Just as human feelings and emotions are not primeval raw forces but are already permeated by reason, so also human reason is immersed in the individual's values, interests, anxieties and aspirations. To abstract it from them is to distort it, to miss its inspiring and guiding principles. Thinking, in short, is not a cerebral or a mental process but a total human response, and it is not the human reason, nor the human mind, but the total human being who thinks and reasons. Further, man faces the world not in his sovereign loneliness but as a cultural being, as a being with a complex of values and attitudes. This is indeed what is involved in being human. *Contra* Mannheim he can, of course, change or modify some or most or even all of his values and attitudes but it is impossible to imagine a human being who has no definite way of looking at man and society, who is not orientated to the world in some definite way.

Intellectual inquiries differ in the way they involve the total human person. In the inquiries like logic and mathematics that are purely formal, one proposition follows from another with deductive rigour, leaving no room for preference or interpretation, and therefore human values and prejudices do not enter. In the natural sciences where there is room for interpretation and discretion, they do enter, but to a limited degree and not in a way that affects the substance of the theories developed. Thus whether or not the universe is a deterministic system and allows 'free will', whether or not it leaves room for God, whether its ultimate constituents are isolated and singular atoms or whether they constitute a 'community' are issues that do affect the scientist's personal values, emotions, world view, and therefore influence the way he describes his conception of the universe or what theories he finds persuasive and appealing. One has only to consider, for example, the way some scientists refuse to accept a deterministic conception of the universe, or the way they talk about the 'community' of atoms, or define the notions of absolute space and time. Again, not every scientific hypo- thesis can be completely verified, and a scientist has to decide if evidence for it is *sufficiently* strong and probability sufficiently high. And here one of the factors influencing his judgement is his view of the seriousness of the consequences issuing from making a mistake in accepting the hypothesis. Thus, for example, if the hypothesis under consideration was that a toxic ingredient was present in a drug in lethal quantity, the scientist would want a relatively high degree of confirmation before accepting it.[6]

The study of man is of a very different kind. Being a study of men like himself whose actions provoke attitudes of approval or disapproval, praise or condemnation, it *activates* the theorist's cul- tural values in a way that the study of nature or number does not. Human actions have a meaning that is not obvious and straightforward and has to be teased out. And this can only be done on the basis of what one expects men to be like, what one's experiences of men are like. What one says is capable of influenc- ing others, and therefore involves one's interests and values. One likes to see a certain type of world, a certain pattern of inter- personal relationship, and since theory is one mode of action one's theories and interpretations are unavoidably coloured by one's anxieties and aspirations as the testimonies of Plato, Augustine, Hobbes, Rousseau and Marx make so abundantly clear. A theorist, further, has a certain way of looking at the world. He is either a pessimist or an optimist; he either loathes conflict or welcomes it. And these attitudes influence his selection of facts, the importance he assigns them and the way he feels inclined to relate them. Again, his language is already charged with the ethos of his community and directs his thought, and therefore his choice and manner of relating facts, in a certain definite way. A language that offers no means of describing or referring to men separately from their caste or other social groupings would make it most difficult to develop a theory, e.g. of methodological or ontological individualism and would incline its users to look for only those aspects of human conduct in which individuals cooperate and act in a concerted manner.

Apart from this general fact that human prejudices, values, interests, attitudes, are activated by the study of man in a way they are not by other types of study, there are also several other reasons why the study of man is culturally conditioned. Unlike natural events human beings are historical creatures. They have a past that endures in the present; they are subject to historical change; and they can and do organize their personal and social life in so very different ways. Our moral life, for example, is a precipitate of several moralities: the Greco-Roman, Judaic, Christian, feudal and the contemporary bourgeois and socialist moralities. All these strands have given rise to a highly complex pattern of moral conduct that is by no means a coherent structure. What is more they are combined differently in different sections of society or by different individuals and generate unique patterns of moral conduct. A moral philosopher is no exception and therefore he will tend to offer an account of moral life that is faithful to his own moral experiences. But his moral experiences are not others' moral experiences; and therefore an account that strikes him as natural, accurate, obvious, true, strikes another as one-sided and even false. Kantian moral theory, for example, offers a perfectly valid account of the moral experiences of men who live a life of duty for duty's sake and generally take a legalistic attitude to life. But it cannot but strike as odd to those who take life less rigorously, who would bend a rule at the first available opportunity to make others happy. This does not mean that the Kantian moral theory is valid for some and not for others, but rather that it is able to account for certain types of moral experiences much better than others, and that therefore those to whom the former types of experience come naturally will be persuaded of its truth in a way that others would not be. *Contra* Mannheim it does not mean either that a moral philosopher cannot imagine what different types of moral experiences are like and take account of them in constructing his moral theory. However, imagination, like reason, is not some abstract faculty but is culturally conditioned and therefore there are limits to what a man can imagine. When a moral or social theorist tries to comprehend another society or an unfamiliar experience, he does not approach it with a blank mind but with a mind already accustomed to looking at man and society in a specific way. He can certainly stretch his imagination and revise his preconceptions, but there are limits to how far he can go. And even when he can imagine unfamiliar experiences, he needs to interpret and make sense of them, and here his own cultural assumptions and categories inescapably enter.

In social and political thought there is also the further question of theoretical discretion in conceptualizing experience. A concept can best be understood on the analogy of a beam of light; it has an unmistakable centre but a nebulous and hazy circumference and therefore covers a wide range at either end of which it merges into other concepts. An analysis of a concept therefore involves determining both its centre (its paradigmatic usage) and its range (that is, its permissible usages). Take, for example, the concept of man. We know how to use this concept and have generally no difficulty recognizing human beings. But suppose walking through the jungles of Africa I come across a tiny insect who greets me and strikes off an extremely pleasant conversation about the beauty of the jungle and its wild life, the misery and poverty of Africans, etc. How am I to describe this creature? It behaves like a man, and therefore I could call it a man. But it looks like an insect, and therefore I could refuse to call it a man. There is no reason why I could not take either view, and in each case I would be no more or no less objective or right than the person taking the opposite view. The same sort of problem comes up in less bizarre cases. Is the so-called psychic 'violence' violence or not? Is exploitation violence as the New Left insists? Or should the term violence be reserved only for the use of physical force? Is Aristotle's proportional equality to be called equality? Is the Greek city-'state' a state? Or is the term to be reserved only for the modern post-Renaissance state? Is university politics politics? Or is the term to be reserved only for the conduct of the affairs of the state? There are good and bad reasons for each side of the controversy, and therefore a theorist

77

has a discretion. Depending on how he uses each of the countless concepts that go to compose his theory, he will describe, interpret and relate the relevant phenomena differently.

Theories about man and society then are culturally conditioned and reflect the cultural orientation of their originators. Hence they appear plausible to those sharing their underlying cultural values and attitudes; to those who take a different view of man and society, they appear less convincing and persuasive. Not that they are true for one group and false for another, but rather that they appear true, self-evident, to one group but not to another. That all theories about man and society are permeated by their creators' cultural biases and values, and that they appear more plausible and persuasive to some but not to others, can be established not only on the basis of a philosophical analysis of the nature of thinking but also by showing empirically how there is hardly any social or moral or political theory that does not, as it were, give away its originator's identity.

Max Weber is one of the clearest examples of a thinker who believed that a social scientist could and should offer, and that he himself did offer, 'an unconditionally valid type of knowledge' that, in his favourite phrase, 'must be acknowledged as correct even by a Chinese'. Ignoring the vulgar Nazi criticism of his writings as essentially 'Jewish',[7] the crude Communist attack on him as a man concerned to make out a case for charismatic leadership and thereby for the Führer,[8] and ignoring also the rather crude neo-liberal attack on him as a man whose writings were inspired by a Machiavellian worship of power and German imperialism,[9] it is still possible to show that underlying Weber's sociological writings is a definite cultural bias, a definite *Weltanschauung*, a clearly identifiable body of moral values. He is an old-fashioned liberal who prizes individual liberty, above all the freedom of conscience, the freedom to make one's moral choices oneself. One of the important reasons why he separated fact and value was not that this might corrupt the objectivity of science but rather that it might create moral experts and give the scientist a power to prescribe moral values that might detract from the individual's unique moral status and dignity.[10] It is also this that explains his interest in and intense concern about the consequences of bureaucratization. Consider, for example, his following description of it:

... each man becomes a little cog in the machine and, aware of this, his one preoccupation is whether he can become a bigger cog ... it is horrible to think that the world could one day be filled with those little cogs, little men clinging to little jobs and striving towards bigger ones ... this passion for bureaucracy is enough to drive one to despair. It is as if we were deliberately to become men who need order and nothing but order, who become nervous and cowardly if for one moment this order wavers, and helpless if they are torn away from their total incorporation in it. That the world should know men but these; it is in such an evolution that we are already caught up, and the great question is therefore not how we can promote and hasten it, but what we can oppose to this machinery in order to keep a portion of mankind free from this parcelling-out of the soul, from this supreme mastery of the bureaucratic way of life.[11]

This is not a value-free statement but the remark of a man firmly committed to individual liberty. His liberalism comes out in a variety of other ways as well. As a secular rationalist he denies that the world is intrinsically rational; and as a good pluralist, he sees different religions as so many equally valid attempts to make some sense of it. Similarly he regards different moral systems as more or less equally valid ways of organizing moral life. Again, as a good liberal he takes the individual as the ultimate social reality, an unanalysable 'atom' of sociology, and issues the methodological prescription that any property involving reference to a collectivity must ultimately be resolved into concepts referring to actions of identifiable individuals. Again, he subscribes to the liberal view of man as an essentially rational being in whom irrationality is a deviation, an aberration, and deduces the methodological prescription, embodied in his theory of ideal type, that all 'irrational, affectually determined, elements of behaviour' should be treated 'as factors of deviation from a conceptually pure type of action'. Even without consulting a 'Chinese', someone who takes a different view of man and society, a Marx or a Tawney or a Samuelson,[12] for example, would quarrel with many of Weber's interpretations and explanations and offer a different account of the nature and rise of bureaucracy or capitalism or Protestantism or Calvinism.

Not only that Weber, the champion of 'unconditionally valid knowledge', himself does not produce a body of knowledge that 'even a Chinese' must accept; no other political or social scientist has so far done so either. Don Martindale[13] has shown in detail how many of the allegedly value-neutral socio-logical theorists rest on unmistakable normative foundations. Henry Murray and David McClelland have shown how theories of personality[14] project their authors' personal and cultural orientations. Charles Taylor has analysed Lipset's *Political Man* in considerable detail and shown how underlying his analysis is an unmistakable liberal preference for a society in which conflict is not suppressed but brought out into the open and integrated into the social framework, in which economic inequality is reduced, in which there is a large middle class and whose members are prepared to settle their differences by compromise and bargain.[15] After a careful survey of the researches on the Negro problem in America, Myrdal concluded that 'there is no piece of research on the Negro problem which does not contain valuation, explicit or implicit'. J. W. Bennett has shown in a most interesting article how researches into the Pueblo culture describe and account for the same basic facts so very differently.[16] Thompson, Benedict and others describe Hopi life as harmonious, organic, spontaneous, and involving minimum physical force; Goldfrank and Eggam, on the other hand, emphasize its deep social conditioning, its harshness, its coerciveness, and the emotional price it exacts from its members. These and other differences, as Bennett has shown, arise not from any carelessness in empirical research on the part of either group of writers, but essentially from the basic differences in their values, their attitudes to life, their cultural background, their prejudices, that lead them to select different facts, or to order the same facts differently, or to interpret and elucidate their meanings differently. Bertrand Russell was not entirely wrong when, commenting on the studies of the behaviour of rats by American and British psychologists, he remarked how American and British rats seemed to him to behave almost exactly as the Americans and Britishers did in their ordinary life. It is not difficult either to show how the study of the Third World by developmental experts says more about them than about the countries they study.[17]

Since social and political theories are unavoidably selective, partial and culturally conditioned, the only way to improve them is to force them to explain themselves, to articulate and justify their assumptions and choice of concepts, to defend their interpretations of facts and show why other interpretations are mistaken. By criticizing a theory we can show how it rests on dubious assumptions, or how its concepts are muddled, or how it does not account for certain types of experience and how it becomes incoherent and muddled when it tries to give a plausible account of them, or how it draws illegitimate inferences or is internally inconsistent. In other words the institutionalization of criticism, as Popper has rightly emphasized, is the basic precondition of improving social and political theories.[18]

If our earlier account of social and political theory is correct, Popper's theory of criticism, however, needs to be modified in several important respects. Popper argues that a theory can be falsified if it does not conform to facts. This does not take account of the twofold fact that facts can be interpreted differently and that facts themselves can be so very different. As we saw earlier, Kant's moral theory gives a satisfactory account of certain types of moral experience but not others. It would be wrong to say that the latter falsify his theory; rather they demonstrate how it is partial and limited, how its explanatory power and truth-content are limited. Similarly to a Bentham taking an egoistic view of man Jesus's martyrdom is as much an act of self-love or self-interest as Shylock's demand for a portion of flesh or Hitler's slaughter of Jews. This certainly goes against our ordinary evaluations of Christ's motives, but it would not do to use this as a 'fact' that falsifies Bentham's moral psychology, no more than our ordinary feeling that the earth is flat could be invoked to reject the scientific theory that the earth is round. Our ordinary evaluations can be wrong, or while admitting them at one level Bentham might rightly want to deny them at another.

The only way we can criticize Bentham's account of Christ's behaviour is by examining if and how he can show why self-love takes so very different forms in the cases of Shylock and Jesus, what secret pleasure Christ is pursuing in his martyrdom, why Bentham takes the view that man is necessarily an egocentric creature, how he would knock down other interpretations of

human conduct, etc. In other words, facts do not falsify a social
and political theory in a way that the discovery that there is no
cat in my room falsifies the assertion that there is. Rather they
impugn the validity of a theory by showing how in the course of
explaining them it is forced to become more and more muddled,
incoherent, ambiguous, bizarre. Facts destroy a social or political
theory not so much by falsifying it as by undermining its
integrity and credibility, by making it incoherent. In some
sense this is like the way a lawyer proves a hostile witness a liar.
He presents him with an inconvenient fact and asks him to
explain it. The latter might be able to explain it away, in which
case the lawyer presents him with another awkward fact. He
might be able to explain away this fact as well, and then the
lawyer presents him with yet another disturbing fact. And so on
until the man is cornered, exposed, rendered incoherent. Hobbes
or Bentham or Weber or Hegel, too, cannot be refuted, but
cornered by being patiently presented with inconvenient facts at
each stage of the argument. The more general methodological
point of this example is that coherence correspondence dicho-
tomy needs to be revised in discussing social and political
thought, since the most effective way to criticize a social theory
is not merely to expose its formal inconsistencies or to show that
it does not correspond to facts but rather to use *facts* to
demonstrate its incoherence, to use *empirical* evidence to demonstrate its *logical* weakness.

The second important respect in which Popper's theory of
criticism needs to be modified is directly related to the peculiar
character of social and political thought. As social and political
facts can be interpreted differently and given different meanings
and significance, our concern here, as Mannheim has argued, is
to understand each other, to benefit from each others' insights,
and ideally to acquire as comprehensive and rich a vision of
social life as possible, a vision to which each theory makes a
contribution and which unites all contestants at a deeper level
of understanding. What one needs, therefore, is not a boxing
match between different theories where each gets a point for
every punch it lands and the victory goes to the one who deals a
knock-out blow, as Popper's rather aggressive metaphors suggest,
but a sympathetic and imaginative dialogue in which each
contestant tries to learn from the rest. In this process of helping

each theory to understand what makes others tick, what they really mean, and why they have an appeal for their adherents, something like Mannheim's sociology of knowledge has a useful role. Even the sociology of knowledge, however, is a somewhat crude tool and needs to be supplemented by literature, art and philosophy that can present the insights of each theory in an imaginative way and increase their mutual comprehension. As social and political knowledge grows not merely by criticism but also by sympathy and imagination, as one's concern here is not to knock down a theory but to absorb and incorporate its insight into an ever-widening vision, a theory that aims only to devise methods of falsification is one-sided and misses out one of the crucial dimensions of social and political debate.

Popper's theory of criticism needs to be modified in another respect as well. We saw earlier how social and political thought is integrally tied up with interests, values, prejudices. The civil climate of criticism that presupposes the willingness to expose oneself to others' relentless probing and to learn from their criticisms can hardly be sustained in a society where participants are involved in a ruthless struggle for survival or supremacy. Since social and political theory inevitably has, or can be seen to have, *some* practical implications, its discussion inevitably arouses fears and suspicions and introduces into calm academic discussion the all too familiar urgency of the market place. Marx is right that in a society characterized by clashes of sectional interests, the tendency to distort ideas is likely to be great. Mannheim's point that participants in a debate can better understand each other the greater the similarity of their experiences, is also appropriate here. In other words the pursuit of objectivity and truth requires the creation of a society from which violent clashes of interest have been eliminated, where there is less acute division of labour and specialization of thought so that people have the disposition and the ability to view their disciplines in a wider context, where there is considerable social mobility so that individuals have a chance to see their society and life from different perspectives, where there is equality of educational opportunity so that no intellectual inquiry is dominated by people sharing a uniform life-style. This is indeed the basic lesson we can learn from ideologists, that just as ideas are closely tied up with individual interests and values, so also is the search for truth and objectivity tied up with the creation of a humane society.

By criticism and sympathetic imagination social and political theories can be improved. But we need to be careful how we describe the process of improvement. Popper himself and many others have described it as getting closer to the truth, implying that one day we might reach the truth, the absolute truth as Popper calls it.[19] Now because social and political thought is necessarily partial, selective, culture-bound, the idea of absolute truth does not make sense. An absolutely true theory would be one that can *never* be faulted, that accounts for the total diversity of relevant experience without distorting or over-looking *any* element in it, that uses concepts with which *no one* can quarrel, that rests on *no* assumptions that the theorist has not clearly articulated and defended. It is difficult to imagine what such a theory can even look like. Since values enter into the theorist's interpretation and explanation of his subject matter, an absolutely true social theory is possible only if we have an absolutely true moral theory, a set of absolutely true moral values; but such a moral theory is not available for obvious reasons. Just as the notion of absolute truth does not make sense, the notion of progressive approximation to it has to be rejected as well for the simple reason that there is nothing *towards* which one can be said to be moving or to which one can be said to be getting closer. The spatial metaphor carries the danger of inducing the belief that if we keep trying hard we would one day get to the truth. In other words it conveys the mistaken notion that the pursuit of truth is a journey that has a terminus, a destination that will one day be reached. It was this imagery that probably led Mill, Hegel, Marx and others to believe that progress will or must one day reach perfection. Theories, like society, can certainly be improved; but as they can *always* be improved, there is no terminus where improvement can be assumed to come to an end. Even as there cannot be an absolutely perfect society, a society in which there are no deficiencies whatsoever, for somewhat different reasons there cannot be an absolutely objective or absolutely true social theory either.

Because no theory about human behaviour can ever pretend to absolute truth and objectivity, there is no theory that cannot be criticized.[20] But precisely because *every* social theory can be criticized and shown to be partial, culture-bound and narrow-based, no social theory can be rejected simply because it is open to criticism; otherwise no social theory would ever deserve acceptance. Since *no* theory can be absolutely true, one can only judge it in *comparative* terms, that theory being better which is less open to criticism than its rivals. To continue with our analogy, theories are like societies; if one demanded to live only in a society that was flawless, one would never find a society worth living in. One must be content to judge a society as better or worse than others that exist or are practically possible. Similarly, one theory is better than another and deserves acceptance if it is less partial, less discretionary, less culture-bound than its rivals.

A choice between social and political theories however is not always as clear-cut as this. Of a social theory, as of any other theory, we make a number of demands. It should not ignore any relevant fact; it should not distort facts; it should define its concepts clearly; it should be internally consistent; it should be imaginative and open up fruitful lines of inquiry; it should be structurally neat and tidy. Like moral ideals that cannot all be achieved, these demands cannot all be met. In tightening up its concepts or in achieving comprehensiveness, a theory may lose in empirical richness. In trying to be 'absolutely accurate', it might become as chaotic as the reality itself, losing in coherence what it gains in suggestiveness. As no theory possesses all the qualities one ideally expects in it, beyond a certain point the choice between them is a matter of individual discretion. There is also another point. Extreme and one-sided theories have often contributed far more to the growth of knowledge than those prosaic and balanced theories that see all sides of the question and never manage to rise above the level of common sense. Their uncompromising intransigence and unconcealed and fierce partiality force other practitioners of the discipline to re-assess their assumptions, and stimulate and raise the level of intellectual debate. Objectivity, therefore, is not the only or even always the highest virtue in a theory. If a discipline is dominated by a single body of assumptions that its professionally socialized practitioners unconsciously assume to be self-evidently true, there is much to be said for advancing or accepting an extreme theory in order to stir them into critical self-examination and to encourage a radical reappraisal of the conceptual tools of the discipline. Since objectivity and impartiality are achieved as a result of the clash of subjectivity and partiality, falsehood and extremism often make most worthwhile contributions to the discovery of truth.

NOTES AND REFERENCES

1. For a discussion of the nature of active reason in Aristotle, see Sir David Ross, *Aristotle* (London, Methuen, 1964), p. 148 ff.

2. In the following paragraphs I am much indebted to George Lichtheim's 'The Concept of Ideology', *History and Theory*, IV (2) (1965).

3. See Ernst Cassirer, *The Philosophy of the Enlightenment* (Boston, Beacon Press, 1962), p. 105 f.

4. K. Mannheim, *Ideology and Utopia* (London, Routledge, 1960). All page references are to this edition.

5. Merton draws a suggestive parallel between Mannheim's intellectuals and Marx's proletariat. Both are recruited from all classes of the population; both are believed to have an 'unimpaired' aptitude for theory; and both are exempt from the virus infecting other members of their society. *Social Theory and Social Structure* (New York, Free Press, 1968), p. 561.

6. Richard Rudner, 'The Scientist *qua* Scientist makes Value Judgments', *Philosophy of Science*, 20 (1) (1953).

7. Christoph Steding, *Politik und Wissenschaft bei Max Weber* (Breslau, Korn, 1932). Also *Das Reich und die Krankheit der europäischen Kultur* (Hamburg, Hanseatische Verlagsanstalt, 1938).

8. For an informative account of this and other types of criticism of Weber, see Guenther Roth, 'Political Critiques of Max Weber: Some Implications for Political Sociology', *American Sociological Review* (1965).

9. Hans Kohn, *The Mind of Germany* (New York, Scribner, 1960), pp. 269 and 278-87. Also Wolfgang Mommsen, *Max Weber und die Deutsche Politik, 1890-1920*, (Tubingen, Mohr, 1959).

10. Felix Kaufmann, *The Methodology of the Social Sciences* (New York, Humanities Press; London, Faber, 1949), p. 19. Also p. 38 and 13.

11. Quoted in J. P. Mayer, *Max Weber and German Politics* (London, Faber, 1956), pp. 127-28.

12. *Religion and Economic Action: A Critique of Max Weber* (London, Harper Torchbook, 1964).

13. 'Social Disorganization: The Conflict of Normative and Empirical Approaches' in *Modern Sociological Theory*, Howard Becker and Alvin Boskoff (eds.) (Dryden Press, Hinsdale, Ill., 1957).

14. 'Historical Trends in Personality Research' in *Perspectives in Personality Research*, Henry David and J. C. Brenglemann (eds.) (London, Crosby Lockwood & Son, 1960). Also David McClelland, 'Toward a Science of Personality Psychology', and Gordon Allport, 'European and American Theories of Personality', in *Perspectives in Personality Theory*, David and Helmut von Bracken (eds.) (New York, Basic Books, 1957).

15. 'Neutrality and Political Science' in *Philosophy, Politics and Society*, Laslett and Runciman (eds.), Third series (Oxford, Blackwells, 1967).

16. 'The Interpretation of Pueblo Culture: A Question of Values', *Southwestern Journal of Anthropology*, 2 (4) (winter 1946).

17. I have argued this point in detail in my 'Scholarship and Ideology', *Cross Currents* (fall 1970). Reprinted in *Perspectives*, 3 (1), Western Michigan University.

18. Karl Popper, *The Open Society and its Enemies*, Chs. 22, 23 and 24, and *Conjectures and Refutations*, Ch. 10 (Routledge & Kegan Paul, 1963). I am all too aware that this paragraph raises a number of intricate questions concerning the nature, presuppositions and limits of criticism, but we cannot pursue them here.

19. *Conjectures and Refutations*, op. cit., p. 224.

20. Here and in what follows I am indebted to Kuhn's stimulating remarks in *Criticism and the Growth of Knowledge*, Imre Lakatos and Alan Musgrave (eds.) (Cambridge University Press, 1970), p. 259ff. As will be seen I do not accept Kuhn's paradigmatic relativism.

The Marxian Concept of
Bourgeois Ideology:
Some Aspects and Perspectives

R. N. BERKI

I

The concept of bourgeois ideology in Marxian thought seems to be inevitably tied up with the notions of 'falsehood' and 'false consciousness'. While 'ideology' in general in Marxian usage (especially from Lenin onwards) has clearly a number of different senses, the adjective 'bourgeois' considerably reduces, if not totally eliminates, all ambiguity. Bourgeois ideology, so the doctrine runs, consists of ideas and beliefs that distort or 'disguise' reality, in particular social and political reality. The disguise is functional. Bourgeois society is based on the antagonism of social classes, one of which is the ruling class, the others being either the totally oppressed (the proletariat) or those on the borderline, such as the peasantry or the *petit bourgeoisie*. This antagonistic social reality can only be upheld if the antagonism contained in it is disguised, and the members of society, both the oppressed and the rulers, are fed on ideas and beliefs which give them a false identity or consciousness. In other words, bourgeois ideology represents a conflict-ridden, oppressive world as though it was something good, desirable, or at least inevitable, a world which it is one's privilege or good fortune to live in, or one to which one has at least to reconcile oneself. To this world of false beliefs and ideas Marxian thought contrasts its own categories, which, *ex hypothesi*, represent the 'true' or a 'higher consciousness', one which makes the oppressed realize that the bourgeois world can, ought to, and will be overthrown, and the antagonism of classes replaced by the

88

unity and harmony of classless society. Now this is a considerably simplified account of the Marxian doctrine, but certainly one which contains its crux—or, at any rate, one which puts into words its more widely known, more conspicuous form of appearance. The very least it tells us about the Marxian doctrine is that it appears to have an unredeemingly hostile view of bourgeois beliefs and ideas. The attitude it articulates is *combative* and highly militant: bourgeois ideology is not afforded any sympathy, any quarters, any possibility of its being able to change, improve, rise above its functional limitations; it is not afforded any *value*. To this attitude on the level of political confrontation corresponds, on the level of philosophical or theoretical analysis, a doctrine which could be variously described as *positivist* or *metaphysical*. Since these terms are used here in a technical sense, a brief word of explanation might be necessary. The Marxian view of bourgeois ideology could thus be characterized as 'positivist' or at least as one containing a large dose of positivism, in so far as it presupposes a sharp and unbridgeable dividing line between ideas and beliefs pertaining to a false consciousness and those comprising the true one. This view also appears 'metaphysical' inasmuch as it operates with abstract, unchanging entities, that is, in this case, 'bourgeois ideology' as such on the one hand and Marxian thought on the other. (This meaning of the term 'metaphysical' derives from Hegel and was adopted by Marx and Engels when dealing with adversaries.)

However, the question we shall be asking here is whether or not the combative and positivist appearance of the Marxian view[1] is the only one evidenced by a careful reading of the Marxian texts, or indeed the only one which it is logical and/or advantageous for Marx and the Marxists to hold. Hence, questions relating to the ultimate validity of the Marxian doctrine as a whole will have to be disregarded. Our problem here is a limited one. It is to decide in precisely what sense bourgeois ideology can be said to be 'false': is it, for example, the case that the ideas and beliefs employed to bolster up bourgeois society are erroneous and invalid in themselves, or is it that they acquire their false, ideological character only in the specific context of this society? Does bourgeois ideology falsely represent earth as heaven, or does it conjure up a false, non-existing heaven? Is bourgeois ideology like alcohol, dimming the senses and creating a euphoria which is itself opaque, ephemeral and counter-productive? Or is it like some psychedelic substance which (allegedly) enables its user to experience more 'authentic' being and to perceive more remote but realizable human potentialities? To what extent, if any, can bourgeois ideas be taken as being at least approximations or prefigurations of ideas that pertain to a higher consciousness?

It is clear that the proper appreciation of questions of this kind—and these questions are pertinent as well as interesting—requires an attitude on the part of Marx and Marxism, which is vastly different from those adumbrated above. It is our contention, however, that Marxian thought does contain elements or aspects, which reveal a stance opposed to the militant, combative positivism commonly associated with Marx's concept of bourgeois ideology. This alternative view or attitude, to some extent complementing but at one point also conflicting with the other one, has been at various times, and often in a muted, apologetic manner, subscribed to by a number of Marxist thinkers. To get the flavour of this alternative, suffice it here to quote three short passages from the works of three well-known Marxist thinkers. First, it is Henri Lefebvre's opinion that Marxism:

> retains one essential philosophical contribution: emergent truth is always mixed up with illusion and error. The theory discards the view that error, illusion, falsity, stand off in sharp and obvious distinction from knowledge, truth, certainty. There is continual two-way dialectical movement between the true and the false, which transcends the historical situation that gave rise to these representations.[2]

Antonio Gramsci writes thus:

> To judge the whole philosophical past as madness and folly is not only an anti-historical error, since it contains the anachronistic pretence that in the past they should have thought like today, but it is a truly genuine hangover of metaphysics, since it supposes a dogmatic thought valid at all times and in all countries, by whose standard one should judge all the past.[3]

And Roger Garaudy:

> ... Marxism would be the poorer if St. Paul and St. Augustine, St. Theresa of Avila, Pascal and Claudel, the Christian meaning of transcendence of love were to become foreign to it.[4]

Differences notwithstanding, it appears that these sentiments all articulate a position which is germane to Marx's own way of thinking, and which, in spite of superficial appearances, has its rationale in the very basis of the Marxian doctrine. Yet, from the political angle, the attitude displayed here is not combative and militant but *accommodating*; it does not turn away from bourgeois ideas and beliefs in undisguised and undiluted hostility but is prepared to afford them a certain kind of *value*. From the philosophical angle, again, the view here presented is not positivist and metaphysical but *historical* and *dialectical*: what it assumes is not hard and fast abstract categories, but dynamic historical processes.

The Marxian dialectical conception is, of course, different from those idealist and abstract materialist systems of thought which otherwise share its position *vis à vis* the notion of falsehood or falsity. Hegel, for example, and Feuerbach, in different ways, would also deny that there is a sharp distinction between truth and falsity, and would rather talk in terms of 'imperfect' representations of the truth, for example, art and religion as abstractly representing philosophy in Hegel's case, and Christian theology erroneously attributing true and existing properties to a non-existent divinity, as Feuerbach asserts. The point is that these thinkers (and others, like Bradley) can *afford* to show such a sophisticated and essentially accommodating attitude towards falsity or imperfect representations of the truth; because being 'philosophers' in the traditional and non-positivist sense, they have a conception of an underlying, enduring, timeless category of 'truth', in terms of which all other ideas, however absurd or remote they might appear at first, can be called 'approximations'. But this road is not open to Marx, since he unreservedly rejects the idea of a timeless truth pertaining to concrete social reality. As he pungently puts it: 'The abstraction, the category taken as such, i.e. apart from men and their material activities, is of course immortal, unchangeable, unmoved; it is only one form of the being of pure reason; which is only another way of saying that the abstraction as such is abstract. An admirable tautology!'[5] Marx's meaning, clearly, is that although it is quite possible philosophically to conceive of permanent categories, it is the very 'permanence' of the categories that renders them useless, irrelevant and misleading in endeavours to explain concretely the way human societies are and the manner of their transformation. But then if this is taken to be the basic Marxian position, it might appear to exclude any possibility of ascribing an 'accommodating' attitude to Marx: if truth is not a timeless category, then the beliefs and ideas comprising bourgeois ideology cannot be regarded as even 'imperfectly' representing a realm which in some sense lies behind or beyond them; in this case they appear as nothing but distortions occasioned by and *coeval with* bourgeois society.

Yet there might be a way out. The Marxian dialectic is historical: it dispenses with the idea of an eternal truth, but it retains, in Lefebvre's words, a philosophical element which looks upon truth as something 'emerging' out of falsity. Now, if anything, this must signify a conception of the relationship between truth and falsity that is in basic opposition to the hard-and-fast positivist view. 'Emerging', in the very least, has to convey the meaning of a gradual, smooth, evolutionary process, a dynamic state of affairs within the framework of which emerging truth has a close, internal relationship to the 'falsehood' which gives rise to it in the first place. Dialectical emergence, furthermore, means that in the transformation of falsity into truth, the former is not simply denied and as a consequence totally liquidated without a trace, but on the contrary 'preserved' and transvalued and thus essentially retained in the emerging truth itself. To put it more concretely and in accord with the Marxian categories, dialectical emergence should mean that there is an unbroken historical continuum between false or distorted beliefs and ideas, those belonging to bourgeois ideology on the one hand, and true or higher beliefs and ideas on the other. To go yet a step further, the dialectical conception of change also suggests that in principle it ought to be possible for an observer, an observer at any rate who occupies the vantage point of a higher consciousness, to perceive certain points on the continuum—perhaps single ideas or more or less idiosyncratic articulations of beliefs which are otherwise easily classifiable as being either true or false—where the distinction between false and true is so blurred as to render judgement difficult. Conceivably, an out-and-out dialectician would be tempted to say that at least at one point on the historical continuum one should be able to put one's finger on something that is *both* true and false, a 'moment' in which truth and falsity are united and identical. But this heady extremism might run into difficulties of various kinds, so we might as well not pursue it any further. Minimally, however, we ought certainly to be able to assert, on the strength of the dialectical conception, that in some instances on the historical continuum it must and will be *problematic* to ascribe either truth or falsity to ideas: some notions and beliefs will, inevitably, appear as containing light and darkness in an equal measure and so blended as to make conceptual disentanglement a hopeless task. Now, while we would not want to assert that the evidence here, textual and logical, is in any way conclusive, certain aspects of the Marxian doctrine of bourgeois ideology strongly suggest that there may indeed be found a few blurred and problematic spots situated in the border area between truth and falsehood, a few cases where bourgeois ideas can be validly regarded as being approximations or prefigurations of ideas of a higher consciousness.

To comment briefly on an apparent stumbling-block, before we turn to a consideration of the topics relevant in this connection. It might be thought at first glance that the materialist conception of history, the very backbone of the Marxian doctrine, *eo ipso* denies the possibility that ideas can 'prefigure' anything that is not in the material, i.e. socio-economic, reality of which they are a reflection. (Whether or not they are purely 'reflections' in the passive sense, or also 'projections' in the sense of issuing out of human sentiments and aspirations, is an interesting question but irrelevant to the present context.) But in actual fact there is no incompatibility here at all. When asserting that ideas can prefigure the future, we do not assert that they are also, on that account 'primary' and hence *causally* responsible for future occurrences. We might hold with Marx—or with Freud, for that matter, whose view on this score appears rather similar—that consciously held ideas and beliefs are merely the emanations or rationalizations of subconsciously operating 'forces' in society, be they contradictions between productive forces and productive relations, or repressed instinctual energy. In this case, we might entertain the possibility that ideas and beliefs can tell us something interesting, important, amounting even to valid predictions, about possible future occurrences. But even if we accept the value of the information thus gained, we are still at liberty, if we so wish, to attribute changes not to the ideas themselves, but to the subconsciously operating forces which called them into being in the first place.

It appears, to return to the actual subject of our investigation, that the judging of the relative importance or emphasis afforded in Marxian thought respectively to the positivist or dialectical approaches to the question of bourgeois ideology is governed by two kinds of considerations. The first concentrates on the nature of the subject matter under investigation. Here all depends on whether we look upon bourgeois ideology as an abstract whole or as a spectrum consisting of and analysable into related but detachable elements. The second concentrates on the nature of the actor or observer: here judgement is dependent upon whether we consider Marxian thought itself as a once-and-for-all revelation or as an evolving, maturing system of ideas. In Section II we shall address ourselves to some problems connected with the first consideration; in Section III an attempt will be made to draw some wider implications of our view, here taking the nature of our 'observer', Marxian thought itself, into account.

II

It would be less than reasonable to expect Marx to judge bourgeois ideology an abstract whole, and to extend his hostility in an equal measure to all the sundry beliefs and ideas it comprises, since Marx does not consider bourgeois *society*, the world which generates and is nourished by ideology, an abstract whole either. Though on the surface most devastatingly critical of what might at first appear to be 'all' aspects of the bourgeois world, in truth Marx's pronouncements contain a great deal more than ridicule and denunciation. His stance is predominantly critical, but behind this the total conception also contains a commendatory element. In this, it may be added here, Marx differs significantly from more romantically-minded revolutionaries—some of his contemporaries among them—whose revolutionary vision assumed the radical, total overthrow and elimination of all parts and facets, the social, political as well as productive system, of bourgeois society. The total criticism that Marx advocates is of a rather different character. It does not prevent Marx from registering his approval, even admiration, where he thinks these are due. Indeed, though this may appear something of an exaggeration, the Marxian attitude to the bourgeois world is not unlike a love-hate relationship. Marx's picture of bourgeois society is like a kaleidoscope with vividly contrasted but intermingling colours, or one whose perception involves an unexpected Gestalt switch: the wizened, wicked, old-witch-countenance of bourgeois society suddenly becomes the face of an attractive young maiden, and then back again. Marx's well-known predilection for obstetric metaphors when describing the overthrow and transformation of bourgeois society is suggestive here. Marx believes that the society of the future, since it 'emerges' from capitalist, bourgeois society, 'is thus in every aspect, economically, morally and intellectually, still stamped with the birthmarks of the old society from whose womb it emerges'.[6] It would be foolish to read too much into metaphors like this, but one should not belittle their significance, since their well-nigh constant employment would certainly not be consistent with the combative attitude and the romantic, extreme kind of revolutionism which tend often to be attributed to Marx. In his case, one might venture to say, recourse to the birth-metaphor signifies something more than mere literary taste or the influence of the intellectual environment of the age, rampant with biological and evolutionary speculation. The new, in Marx's terms, thus resembles the old in many important respects, especially during the former's infancy, while its very birth, of course, presupposes the being of its parent and predecessor.

Bourgeois society, though beset with oppression and antagonism, is something special, a form of society that is unique on account of the nature of the contradictions it contains. As the *Communist Manifesto* declares, 'everlasting uncertainty and agitation distinguish the bourgeois epoch from all earlier ones'. Now 'man is at last compelled to face with sober senses his real conditions of life, and his relations with his kind'.[7] We are treading on the threshold between truth and falsity. It is Marx's view that the 'mystical veil' (ideology) over the truth about the life-process of society does not finally disappear until 'it is treated as production by freely associated men'. This, however, presupposes a 'material groundwork',[8] which, Marx argues, is the particular achievement of a stage of social development compared to which earlier stages appear as mere local developments of mankind and as mere idolatry of nature.[9] Only now does nature become a pure object for man, a thing purely for utilization; it ceases to be recognized as a power on its own right '. . . [Capital] shows itself destructive of [nature worship] and is a perpetually revolutionizing agency, breaking down all the barriers which inhibit the development of productive forces, the extension of needs, the manysidedness of production, exploitation and the exchange of natural and spiritual powers.'[10]

In the first place then, we might be inclined to construe Marx's views on the bourgeois epoch as tending to employ two different sets of perspectives, these perspectives being also the criteria for the judging of this world. There is a limited, narrower perspective which turns the limelight on the *internal* features of bourgeois society, with attention focused exclusively to what happens 'inside' as it were, that is, to the totality of *inter-human* relationships that compose this world. In this perspective—and only here—the bourgeois epoch is then meted out a judgement that is wholly adverse, wholly critical, wholly denunciatory. There is, however, a larger and in some sense higher perspective that focuses on the *external* characteristics of the bourgeois epoch, with attention fastened on the totality of its human relationships *to nature*. (Perhaps it would be appropriate, if not too pedantic, to use the term 'society' to refer to the first perspective and 'epoch' to refer to the second.) It is in this larger perspective, with the emphasis on the 'material groundwork', production, the liberation and extension of productive forces, that Marx's views become distinctly more favourable. It is not the case, of course, that Marx wholeheartedly approves of the way in which nature is utilized, 'exploited' in the bourgeois epoch. Neither, however, is he a modern environmentalist who would abhor 'growth' and denigrate production as a worthy human goal. Thus even if we could not infer from his views that he regards the bourgeois epoch as being already beyond the watershed dividing 'history' from 'prehistory', we are at least entitled to argue that in one perspective, the external, he affords qualified yet wholehearted approval of what this epoch, as a whole, is doing.

Now there is obviously a lot more to be said on this score, and no one could deny that an interpretation of Marx's thought along these lines is open to further queries, but we have to move on. If it is accepted that in the Marxian view at least some aspects of bourgeois society stand nearer to the future than others, even though, morally speaking, they still fall short of what is desired, then it might seem to follow that at least some aspects of bourgeois ideology are also more deserving and more truthful than others. In more concrete terms, if it is the case that in its external relationship to nature the bourgeois epoch shows itself decidedly more progressive than in respect of its social, interhuman characteristics, then bourgeois beliefs pertaining to the human relationship to nature will probably also display features more akin to the 'truth' than their counterparts dealing with the other dimension. On the whole, it seems, such an hypothesis would be borne out by the Marxian pronouncements. It is interesting to note in this connection the very marked distinction in the attitude Marx shows towards *religion* on the one hand, and towards natural science and certain kinds of bourgeois philosophy on the other. Religion is dismissed unceremoniously. Its progressive *function* might be noted from time to time,[11] but approval is never extended to its *content* or indeed to 'religion' as a category of human experience. Religious ideas might be explained in terms of valid human aspirations, but this does not make the ideas themselves in any way valid.[12] Marx regarded religion as the expression of a wholly abstract contradiction (with both sides being invalid), 'an inverted attitude to an inverted world',[13] a spirit which 'can never really be secularized'.[14] Wherever they may be, the blurred and problematic spots between bourgeois ideology and the higher consciousness are certainly not to be found here.

With bourgeois *rationalism* the situation is entirely different. Rationalism is the appropriate faith of the human being, who, as the *Manifesto* states, is at last in the bourgeois epoch

97

compelled to face the world 'with sober senses'. Marx's whole-hearted endorsement of the achievements of natural science in the bourgeois epoch must, of course, be mentioned in this connection, though strictly speaking this is irrelevant here, since neither Marx nor Engels would regard natural science as being 'ideological' anyway. More significance, however, is to be attached to the Marxian attitude towards Marx's greatest 'bourgeois' intellectual predecessors, in particular Hegel and Ricardo. Both Hegel's philosophy and Ricardo's economic science were accepted by Marx as constituting the bases for real, solid knowledge. They were certainly not 'ideological' in the sense of error, falsehood or illusion, otherwise Marx would not have spent so much time and energy studying them. It is Marx himself who insists that in the case of Hegel his own task was to find the 'rational kernel within the mystical shell',[15] while in the case of the Ricardian science of political economy, his main contribution appeared to him to have lain in drawing the proper historical inferences and spelling out the implications in socio-moral terms. And Marx, of course, did not think that either Ricardo or Hegel just stumbled upon the truth by accident, but on the contrary ascribed their individual achievements to the triumph of bourgeois thought as such (though not denying individual genius). Moreover, Marx finds valid pre-figurations of a higher consciousness even in the case of earlier bourgeois thinkers, with special reference to the 'atheism'[16] and 'materialism' of the French eighteenth-century philosophers.[17]

But we can go even further than this. It is not merely the case that the bourgeois epoch is revealed to us containing a fundamental contradiction between its 'external' and 'internal' aspects, the former being judged qualitatively different and 'progressive' and the latter denounced as the arena of misery, interhuman strife and oppression. This basic contradiction is, as it were, further reflected, concretized, in the shape of lesser contradictions *within* the less progressive part, in the very heart of bourgeois society considered in relation to its purely 'internal', i.e. social and political, aspects. In this narrower perspective also, it appears, Marx looks upon bourgeois society, again, not as though it composed a dumb, abstract whole, but in terms of a *spectrum*. It is here, indeed, that Marx's thought reveals its genuinely historical character. Whereas the former distinction revealed the spectrum of the bourgeois epoch merely in spatial terms, here it assumes a temporal, historical character. Marx, in other words, draws a distinction between the more and the less progressive internal elements of bourgeois society, the respective weight of which is governed by the passing of time and the historical consolidation of the epoch.

The justification for this reading of Marx comes mainly from the work in which the concept of 'ideology' is discussed at greatest length by him and by Engels, a work which, incidentally, contains the only discussion of ideology in general 'sociological' terms, as opposed to the concreteness and historical specificity with which the Marxian arguments are usually presented. This is, of course, the first part of the *German Ideology*. Here, amongst other things, Marx puts forward an explanation concerning the historical ascendancy of social classes. Although the theory advanced by Marx has general implications (as well as a general intent?), particular attention is of course on the bourgeoisie. Now the point relevant to our purposes concerns Marx's way of accounting for the fact that the bourgeoisie during its ascendancy, in the seventeenth and eighteenth centuries, succeeded in gaining approval for its bid to obtain power and to overthrow the monarchical and aristocratic establishment. It even managed to secure the active support of other groups of the population. One important way in which this success was achieved was through the possession and employment by the bourgeoisie of 'universal' notions, ideas couched in terms of a 'public realm' or 'common interest'. Marx makes the point that the bourgeoisie was 'compelled' at this stage to 'appear' as the 'whole mass of society' 'representing' 'its interest as the common interest'. Now it is precisely at this point that one can go astray and succumb to a metaphysical, positivist interpretation of Marx's meaning. Does Marx really mean that the bourgeoisie was merely engaged in a gigantic exercise of mass deception (possibly including self-deception)? Did it advance a falsehood as though it were the truth? What Marx actually says right after the passages cited above gives an entirely different impression. Talking about the class in ascendancy, he says that the new class 'can do this [i.e. represent its interest as the common interest] because, to start with, its interest really is more connected with the common interest of all

99

other non-ruling classes, because under the pressure of hitherto existing conditions its interest has not yet been able to develop as the particular interest of a particular class.'[18]

It is not the case, in other words, that the 'emergence' of the bourgeoisie is exactly contemporaneous with the emergence of its antagonism with the proletariat. In the period of its ascendancy the bourgeoisie does not merely make itself out to be the representative of the whole mass of society, but it truly *is* that representative. It is not, properly speaking, a 'class' at this stage at all, since, on the one hand, it has not developed its specific class consciousness,[19] and on the other it has not yet rigidified its particular, antagonistic interest opposing it to a new group, one which it itself generates. The bourgeoisie here rather appears as a progressive 'elite' leading the 'people', one might even be tempted to say the people's 'vanguard'. The modern class struggle makes its historical appearance only later, developing gradually as a consequence of further changes in the mode of production.

The inference we have to draw from this, however, is that the progressive historical role of the bourgeoisie can reasonably be expected to mean also the presence of genuinely progressive, forward-pointing ideas in the armoury of bourgeois ideology, now of course with direct reference to the social and political scene. If the bourgeoisie really *was*, at one time, the leading progressive force in society, it follows that at least some of the beliefs that made their appearance at this stage, or indeed all those deriving their general appeal from ideas connected with the period of ascendancy, must be afforded a considerably higher status than would be the lot of actual lies or mere prejudices and illusions. A few of these ideas might even deserve to be looked upon as prefigurations of a higher consciousness. As Habermas puts it: 'Even bourgeois ideologies could be traced back to a basic pattern of just interactions, free of domination and mutually satisfactory.'[20] And elsewhere he affirms that the 'public view' advanced by the bourgeoisie 'had to agree objectively with the common interest at least to the extent that it was [articulated] in argument, [and] accepted as public and rational'.[21] We may yet even go further and surmise that, at least in a large part, the subsequent rigidification of bourgeois society, with its pattern of oppressive class antagonism, must represent a relative decline in bourgeois *practice*, as distinguished from the devaluation of bourgeois ideas, and furthermore, it is a decline which is actually *measured* in terms of the very same bourgeois ideas. Again, too much should not be made of this, and below we shall have further opportunities to comment on the point. In general terms, however, it would be difficult not to agree with Marcuse's view as being a correct interpretation of Marx: 'Whereas during the period of the militant rise of the new society all of these ideas had a progressive character by pointing beyond the attained organization of existence, they entered increasingly into the service of the suppression of the discontented masses and of mere self-justifying exaltation, once bourgeois rule began to be stabilized . . .'[22]

Marx's differential attitude towards the various beliefs constituting bourgeois ideology in the largest perspective is duplicated here on a smaller scale. We have seen that whereas Marx unreservedly rejects religion he displays a more accomodating attitude towards bourgeois rationalism. Much the same is true of his views regarding bourgeois social and political ideas, though admittedly here the picture is not so clear, Marx's attitude being characterized by a certain amount of ambiguity. As regards some typical bourgeois notions in this sphere, we should have no serious problem in trying to disentangle and interpret the Marxian position. The cherished idea of 'freedom', for example, receives only contemptuous dismissal. Marx does not mince his words in denouncing the 'freedom' of the liberal philosophers, as an ideal which assumes conditions of total human alienation. Liberal freedom, Marx argues in the piece which must be seen as one of his very best, *On The Jewish Question*, boils down to the demand that the human 'individual' should be free from other individuals, and it erects boundaries between human beings instead of uniting them in society. This freedom, in Marx's view, only *appears* as though it were referring to the human being; really it refers to man's alienated social powers. Liberals demand the freedom *of* property and the freedom *of* religion, instead, as Marx would wish, freedom *from* property and religion. Associated terms, such as 'rights' and 'the individual', are treated by Marx in essentially the same way, sometimes with venom, sometimes with ridicule, but never even the faintest sign of approval. Now it is quite true that Marx also

talks about 'freedom' as a worthy and valid ideal, and sometimes even about 'individuality', but it is important to note that
here the similarity between the bourgeois and the Marxian
concepts is merely verbal. On analysis they are revealed to be
opposites, contraries, rather than being the extensions of one
another or even displaying 'family resemblances'. Here at least,
it seems, one must pay due regard to the acuteness of positivist
approaches to the history of ideas, which, of course, imply an
a priori denial of any kind of prefiguration.

We encounter, however, an entirely different situation regarding another basic political notion of the bourgeois epoch,
the ideal or principle of 'equality'. Here the Marxian position
appears markedly more heterogeneous and ambivalent, and
there is none of the unredeeming hostility and intransigence we
see in connection with Marx's critique of bourgeois 'freedom'.
With equality we are just about to reach the blurred, problematic area between truth and falsity, the dawn separating
darkness from light. The important point to note is that Marx's
critical remarks on the ideal of equality fall into two groups,
only one of which resembles his aforementioned denunciation
of the liberal concept of freedom. On the one hand, the principle of equality is rejected by him wholly and categorically,
but only as it is understood in bourgeois society, in so far, that
is, as the concept is disfigured and arrested through its conceptual association with other bourgeois notions. Marx thus
unreservedly rejects the notion of 'equal rights' since, like its
sister-notions—bourgeois freedom and individuality—it takes
for granted the existence of alienated—fragmented and selfish—
individuals. Equal rights in the conditions of bourgeois society,
Marx says, provide merely a 'narrow horizon' which will be
transcended only in the future phase of communism. Likewise,
Marx pours scorn on the notion of equality as it appears in the
context of the exchange-relationship between capital and labour
in bourgeois society. But this is only one side of Marx's critique.
He also criticizes—and this is more to the point here—the bourgeois system of the division of labour which is responsible for the
actual differences between human beings. In bourgeois society
the ideal of equality is destined to remain only an empty aspiration, not to be realized as long as the division of labour is there.
In other words, Marx's critique here is directed more to bour-

geois *practice* and less to the idea in terms of which the practice is justified. Equality, that is, appears as a more or less valid human aspiration, even though one-sided and inadequate. At this point the contradiction Marx seems to notice is between 'a universal form' and a 'partial content',[23] and, most significantly, he fails to condemn the form. On the contrary, at the time when he was already dismissing bourgeois freedom and other similar notions as being 'religious' (always a term of abuse with him), he also wrote: 'Equality as the basis of communism is its political justification.'[24] He also regarded equality as the French expression 'for the unity of human essence, for man's consciousness of his species and his attitude toward his species, for the practical identity of man with man, i.e. for the social or human relation of man to man.'[25]

The rationale for Marx's position is easy to see. While bourgeois freedom as an ideal goes directly against his own vision of a future classless society where man achieves unity with the 'species', bourgeois equality appears as an inadequate approximation as well as a *presupposition* of this Marxian goal. Marx's vision of a world where there is a 'practical identity of man with man', where one can fish in the morning and criticize after dinner, where human beings are in almost a literal sense substitutable for one another, is a vision whose realization assumes the fullest development of equality. Thus equality is truly a 'dawn concept'. Indeed, the Marxian ambivalence is almost exactly matched by the apparent unease, the constant modifications and hedging with which the notion of equality is treated by all but the most radical of liberal political philosophers. Locke, Mill and T. H. Green, for example, all find it most difficult to combine 'moral' egalitarianism with the socioeconomic reality of the bourgeois world. Liberalism as bourgeois ideology, we might say, upholds but cannot come to terms with the idea of equality. Marxian thought, as the negation of bourgeois ideology and the successor to liberalism, rejects and at the same time adopts the idea of equality, doing both with a less than completely clear conscience.

It may also be of some interest to note briefly Marx's views on radical, egalitarian democracy, that is, the progressive bourgeois 'idea' of the state. (It is important to note the distinction, drawn implicitly by Marx, between this 'idea' of the state and the bourgeois state in actual fact. The latter, of course, Marx rejects without much ado.) But consider, for example, the following, taken from *On The Jewish Question*:

> The perfected political state is by its nature the species-life of man in opposition to his material life . . . man leads a double life, a heavenly one and an earthly one . . . He has a life both in the political community, where he is valued as a communal being, and in civil society where he is active as a private individual. . . . The political state has just as spiritual an attitude to civil society as heaven has to earth . . . In the state . . . where man counts as a species-being . . .[26]

This passage shows a curious discrepancy between two sides of the Marxian critique. As Avineri puts it, 'for Marx the being of the state attests to the existence of a tension between the actual and the ideal, between the existing particularistic, interest-oriented social forces and the postulate of universality'[27] Very similarly to the case of equality, here again we are confronted with a contradiction of bourgeois society which involves an ideal, the 'postulate of universality', which Marx does not seem to want to denounce wholeheartedly. Quite clearly, Marx looks upon the 'earthly heaven' of the state as being something rather different from the religious heaven. This earthly heaven, we may be inclined to suggest here, is one which goes very near indeed to Marx's own vision of future society, at least as regards the latter's expected infancy. The idea of the bourgeois state— this is the point—'values man as a communal being'. It comes near to expressing a state of (theoretical) existence which appears almost to melt into the realm of being which, in Marxian terms, signifies the fulfilment of man's species-essence. Marx, in the passage quoted above, seems mainly to lament over the fact that this, in itself valid and worthy, idea of the bourgeois state is contradicted, frustrated, thwarted by its infernal opposite, the 'earthly' realm of civil society and the private sphere. His complaint rings true and genuine when he says that 'the sphere in which man behaves as a communal being is degraded below the sphere in which man behaves as a partial being . . .'[28]

Is this then an instance of prefiguration, the radical democratic state being another 'dawn concept'? The point, alas, is by no means amenable to an easy solution. It does indeed appear to be the case that Marx abandoned the idea of 'radical democracy' in his youth—it may even be true that, for all obvious intents and purposes, he never really was a radical democrat.[29] Yet doubts remain. For one thing, even his more mature writings show frequent lapses into, if not a predilection for, the language of bourgeois democratic philosophy, and Marx by no means always condemns bourgeois democratic institutions, even though they fall, in idea as well as in fact, far short of the desirable. The Paris Commune provides an interesting example. It was, of course, seen by Marx to be non-socialist in character,[30] yet he welcomed it as a step forward in the right direction. He regarded it, further, as a radical democratic republic, and singularly failed to condemn it on that account. The Paris movement expressed, Marx says, vague aspiration after a republic that was not only to supersede the monarchical form of class-rule, but class-rule itself. 'The Commune was the positive form of that republic.'[31] And then: 'Its special measures could but betoken the tendency of a government of the people by the people.'[32] Does the gap then between Lincoln and Marx appear to be an unbridgeable one?

In the *Critique of the Gotha Program* Marx again castigates the ideas of the 'free state' in no uncertain terms. He is, indeed, at his most contemptuous and vituperative when ridiculing the German Social Democratic Party theoreticians' preoccupation with the 'democratic litany' of the free state, equal rights, etc. The democratic republic, he says, 'is precisely this last form of state of bourgeois society that the class struggle has to be fought out to a conclusion'.[33] Are we, however, not entitled to read some significance into the fact that, according to Marx, this form of state is to be the 'last' one before the transformation? Marx also says, in the same work, that the desired transformation will be followed immediately by a 'political transition period in which the state can be nothing but the revolutionary dictatorship of the proletariat'.[34] Now it is a well-known (and justifiably lamented) fact that Marx makes hardly any reference to the 'dictatorship of the proletariat' in his whole vast literary output, and of course he nowhere says what precise form this 'political' transition period is likely or ought to take. At any rate, the word 'political' used in this context is itself suggestive. Engels, for his part, asserts quite unambiguously in his critique of a later Social Democratic programme that the democratic republic 'is even the specific form for the dictatorship of the proletariat'.[35] The interpretive significance of this statement may be lessened by the fact that it was Engels, and not Marx, who wrote it, and that he wrote it after Marx's death—while the fact that the Marx-Engels Institute of the USSR thought it proper to print the two critiques in one volume might serve only to bring home a fine dialectical point in a pedestrian form. Yet it appears at least arguable that in the idea of radical democracy we are again presented with one of those problematic and blurred spots occupying the continuum between ideological falsehood and the truth of a higher consciousness. The old goes out with what the new comes in, the form remains while substance changes, and the substantial change is itself partially determined by the remaining form. The tension, uncertainty, ambivalence and occasional acute controversy surrounding the concept of radical democracy in Marxian thought right down to the present day—see especially such notions as 'socialist democratism' and 'socialist legality'—only go to provide running illustration for the truth of the dialectical conception.

We might want to append a few concluding remarks to this whole section. As we have seen, it does make sense to interpret the Marxian doctrine of bourgeois ideology in such a way as to allow for a more accommodating attitude on Marx's part to come to light, and to present his view in what appears a more plausibly historical, dialectical form. Might then we not put forward the suggestion that, rightly understood, Marx's doctrine is meant to be *evolutionary* as far as the historical change of ideas is concerned? Marx, undoubtedly, talks about a 'radical rupture'[36] in both institutions and ideas, but it would not be too far-fetched to contend that this 'rupture' means something wholly different in praxis from what it means in idea. It is in the realm of praxis: institutions of property, legal relations and the structure of the state, and in this realm only, that one can meaningfully talk about 'revolutionary' transformations, and it is with reference to this sphere that Marx wished to distinguish himself, his doctrine and his movement, from gradualist and reformist socialism. Only in praxis do confrontation and struggle mean actual hostility, fight, the erection of barricades, and the like. Only here does it make sense to talk about an 'irreconcilable conflict' in society. But the realm of ideas is different. Marx did indeed claim that his thought, his doctrine itself was 'revolutionary'. But what did he mean by it? He meant, clearly, that the *necessity* of solving the problems and riddles of the intellectual sphere by *revolutionizing praxis* was first stated in his doctrine. But the doctrine is not revolutionary in the sense of it being *in idea* an entirely novel departure, a completely clean break with ideas of the past. It builds on, grows out of, and further develops bourgeois thought—as Marx himself was always ready to acknowledge. In this connection it is instructive to recall that the whole point of the *German Ideology* is to expose the false revolutionism of radical Left Hegelian thinkers, who, especially Stirner, were mistaking verbal extremism and intellectual avantgardism for what Marx regarded as the real thing. Communism, he claimed, was a 'real movement'. Revolution in action and evolution in thought thus compose a perfect dialectical unity in his world of ideas.

III

The interpretation we are advancing here appears in some degree capable of extension and adaptation to the problems besetting Marxian thought and the Marxist movement in the present age, a hundred and odd years after their inception and in a state of maturity. Here, alas, lack of space makes it imperative that the following remarks be stated in a sketchy and somewhat speculative manner. Whatever Marx himself may have meant by revolution in praxis, and however sanguine his expectations regarding its imminence may have been, there is one basic and inobliterable fact which his latter-day followers and developers of his thought have to face, and this is the continuing, enduring presence and apparent vigour of the 'bourgeois epoch'. It is this objective fact which has brought about the gradual, halting, painful yet inescapable change of heart and mind on the part of the majority, the 'mainstream', of Marxists, issuing in the global attitude of 'peaceful coexistence'. It is, as far as the Marxists themselves are concerned, basically an involuntary state of existence, though its complex roots permit several and widely differing explanations. Broadly speaking, the causes of the phenomenon of peaceful coexistence can be searched for in three main directions. First, taking the line most favourable to Marx, it can be argued that the worldwide Marxist movement is so strong today, having not only a politico-military power-base but also the overwhelming predominance and attraction of its ideas, that Marxists can afford to wait patiently, and, to employ the Marxian metaphor, look towards the natural birth of the new epoch and dispense with the surgeon's knife. The second and ideologically more neutral explanation would argue in terms of technological overdevelopment: whatever the rights and wrongs involved, and whatever the real, ultimate power-positions of the two opposing systems of society, the possibility of nuclear war and mass destruction makes anything but peaceful confrontation too dangerous to be worth while. Thirdly and most damagingly to Marx, it could be argued that bourgeois institutions, and in the final analysis bourgeois ideas and ideology in general, have proved much stronger and more resilient than they were expected to be in the nineteenth and even in the first half of the twentieth centuries. But whichever line one would wish to take—and there are other possibilities—one thing becomes clear: peaceful coexistence signifies first of all the most exclusive ideological confrontation between Marxists and their opponents. And this redefines the whole vexed problem of deciding on the correct attitude towards bourgeois ideology. But what is actually happening?

Peaceful coexistence, of course, is primarily a Stalinist-inspired concept, its utility having been looked for, and found, in the sphere of diplomatic and trade relations between Marxist and non-Marxist states. And here we can remark on a curious discrepancy. The Stalinist concept is based on a sharp distinction between institutions and ideas: it argues for the necessity of peaceful relations between socialist and capitalist states, at the same time insisting on continued hostility and intransigence in the ideological field. Now one would not (this side of the lunatic fringes anyway) wish to deny the desirability of the first, but it is more than reasonable to question the validity, and indeed the wisdom, of the second. What is the rationale of attempting to keep Marxism pure white, in a condition of innocent chastity? Though the idea gains some support from a number of Marx's own pronouncements couched in the more combative idiom, it really has no justification in the proper dialectical perspective. If 'revolution' is the wrong category to employ in the realm of ideas, then so is the notion of 'fighting' or 'confronting' ideas by excluding them from one's circle of vision, by denying them any legitimacy and status as reflections of objective reality projected by the human mind. Ideas cannot be fought or conquered by silence or incantation or the gnashing of teeth. They can only be dealt with dialectically, by a process of criticism, transvaluation and absorption. The natural vehicle for this is open and genuine debate, the greatest possible amount of interaction between opposed beliefs and systems of thought. Shutting itself away from the wind of ideas, Marxism stands in danger of the fate befalling many an old maiden in similar situations; it atrophies, withers away, while vainly and spleenishly expostulating against suitors who ungratefully pass by. It is in order to add at this point that this basically Stalinist-inspired attitude is by no means confined to 'Stalinists' in the narrower sense, i.e. party hacks and official theoreticians whose concern is to maintain a power-political status quo. The same attitude, though more inexplicably, is displayed by those Western Marxist intellectuals whose vast literary erudition and enviable powers of reasoning and expression lead them merely to the esoteric and scholastic parlour-game of internecine, tribal disputes, in complete and disdainful oblivion of advances in 'bourgeois' culture and scholarship.

Marxian thought has reached the stage of maturity, and at least in one important respect, it seems, the original doctrine of bourgeois ideology has to undergo major revision. The dialectical streak in Marx's own thought allows for an accommodating attitude, attributing some value and a degree of validity to a variety of progressive bourgeois ideas, with special reference to Hegelian philosophy, economic science and some principles of liberalism. The rationale for this is Marx's recognition that his own conceptions are heavily indebted to these bourgeois formulations; in other words, their validity derives from their historical anticipation of the Marxian doctrine itself. The corollary of this is that once Marxism, as the expression of a higher consciousness, appears on the scene, even the most progressive of bourgeois ideas become, as it were, anachronistic and valueless. But what happens in a situation of protracted stalemate, with Marxism locked in combat with a supposed invalid who refuses to lie down? What Marxists have to face up to is the fact of the continuing development of bourgeois ideology—something which is not and could not be foreseen by Marx. Bourgeois thought, indeed, can in some sense be said to have benefited from Marxian thought itself; it has learnt directly from Marxian ideas, and indirectly it has been forced to achieve greater clarity, coherence and even self-confidence as a result of it having so long been on the defensive. Gramsci for one, among modern Marxist thinkers, writes about Marxism which is 'so productive of new truths that the old world resorts to it to furnish its arsenal with the most modern and effective arms'.[37] Lukács, too, has thought that such late advances in bourgeois thinking as the adoption of economic planning signify 'the capitulation of the class consciousness of the bourgeoisie before that of the proletariat'.[38] But of course it is not merely in economic ideas that the influence of Marxism on bourgeois thought has evoked a positive response from the latter: the influence is there also in philosophy, aesthetics, literature, even theology. Hence when Marxism refuses to listen to voices outside, it really foregoes the possibility of learning from itself, its own worth as well as its past mistakes and onesidedness.

The impasse, however, shows some signs of losing its erstwhile rigidity. We may end this investigation by commenting briefly on two major developments in Marxism which should augur well for the future—a future to be valued by Marxists and non-Marxists alike. The first such development is what has come to be known by the term, *dialogue*. It has meant, not merely conversation with some representatives of the churches—though this is what has gained greatest publicity—but also an increasing willingness on the part of Marxists to pay attention to scientific and cultural advances in the non-Marxist world, to open up their learned journals and academies to foreign scholars, to attend conferences on subjects even as hopelessly 'ideological' as sociology and political science, to receive and utilize in their own fields the more solid achievements of Western learning. Needless to say, a dialogue needs two partners, and the Marxist overtures have had to be matched by the good will and learning zeal of the other side. Only that in the latter's case one would not make a sensation out of finding a rationale; at least as far as liberalism is concerned, it has always professed a belief in the desirability of a free flow and creative exchange of ideas. It is through the dialogue that Marxism can really show its vigour—and perhaps in the long run even its superiority—as an ideal, intellectual force, as the dialectical negation of bourgeois ideology.

The second development concerns the alleged 'deradicalization' of large segments of the Marxist movement in opposition, particularly in advanced industrial society, but also to some extent in the countries of the developing world. This has been accompanied by the emergence of a new radical movement on the left flank of Marxism, feeding mainly on the ideas of anarchism, romanticism, oriental inwardness and passivity, and the neo-Freudian 'sexual revolution'. Its intellectual spokesmen have not been slow to take Marxists to account for this alleged deviation from the radical path, and although the primary target has been present-day Marxist parties and thinkers (amidst repeated attempts to 'rescue' Marx from his disciples), sometimes the waves of criticism reach Marx himself, and the very basis of his doctrines is renounced on account of being too 'political'.[39] Now the issues involved are extremely complex, and it would amount to the greatest injustice to all sides if an attempt was made here to pass judgement in a few sentences. *Possibly* the New Left charges have considerable weight behind them, possibly Marx's thought needs to be updated in the way suggested by such critics as Fromm, Reich and Marcuse, possibly the deradicalization of Marxist parties is a sign of *embourgeoisement*, leading to an intellectual and political *cul de sac*. But there may be some valid considerations on the other side. Deradicalization means, among other things (and these 'other things' may be very important indeed), the increasing tendency of Marxists to ally themselves with such radical though unmistakably bourgeois movements as civil rights associations, national and anti-colonial movements, campaigns against racial discrimination, not to mention industrial disputes. Also, and more interestingly in this connection, Marxists have shown a growing predilection for the employment of bourgeois terms, the categories and principles of liberal political philosophy, in their writings and speeches. Do not such notions as 'equality', 'equal rights', 'rights of the citizen', 'civil liberties', 'democratic constitution' smack, in Marxian terms, of 'bourgeois ideology'?

They do but, in the dialectical perspective, this is no reason for wanting to discard and ridicule them, in an attempt to soar high and above into the realm of a 'higher consciousness'. On the contrary, Marxists may well prove their maturity precisely by concentrating on the 'dawn area', by criticizing bourgeois society first from the standpoint of the latter's own most progressive principles, by taking their cue from beliefs and ideas which, though being integral parts of 'bourgeois ideology' constitute *also* the dialectical meeting-point between bourgeois thought and Marxism itself.

NOTES AND REFERENCES

1. It is this combative view which we find illustrated in the shorter and more polemical works of Marx and Engels, in particular the *Manifesto*, the *Poverty of Philosophy*, the *Eighteenth Brumaire* and *Ludwig Feuerbach*. There is a hard tone also to Lenin's *Materialism and Empiro-Criticism* and Stalin's *Concerning Marxism in Linguistics*. There seems to be a surprising shortage of non-Marxist academic works devoted to a study of Marx's concept of bourgeois ideology, though the topic is touched on in most commentaries. Such accounts as have been found particularly useful will be referred to further on. G. Lichtheim's article, 'The Concept of Ideology' ('*History and Theory*', Vol. 4, 1964-5), makes some interesting points, and Z. A. Jordan's *The Evolution of Dialectical Materialism* (New York, St Martins Press, 1967) contains a useful account.

2. Henri Lefebvre, *The Sociology of Marx*, tr. by Norbert Guterman (London, Allen Lane, 1968), p. 85.

3. Antonio Gramsci, *The Modern Prince and Other Writings*, tr. by Louis Marks (New York, Int. Pub. Co., 1957), p. 109.

4. Roger Garaudy, *From Anathema to Dialogue: The Challenge of Marxist-Christian Cooperation* (London, Collins, 1967), p. 77.

5. Letter to Annenkov, December 28, 1846, reprinted in Karl Marx, *The Poverty of Philosophy* (Moscow, n.d.), p. 181.

6. Karl Marx, *Critique of the Gotha Program* (Moscow, n.d.), p. 20.

7. Karl Marx and Frederick Engels, *Manifesto of the Communist Party*, tr. by S. Moore (Moscow, n.d.), p. 48.

8. Karl Marx, *Capital*, tr. by S. Moore and E. Aveling (Moscow, 1961), Vol. I, p. 80.

9. Ibid. Vol. III, p. 254. *The Manifesto*, though understandably its tone is angrier than that of the *German Ideology* and the *Grundrisse*, does nevertheless go into generous detail listing the most spectacular achievements of the bourgeois epoch, mentioning also, most significantly, its triumphs in 'intellectual production' (p. 49).

10. Karl Marx, *Grundrisse der Kritik der politischen Oekonomie (Rohentwurf)* (Berlin, 1953), p. 313.

11. Engels seems to have been more favourably disposed to religion, on account of the latter's progressive function, than was Marx, as witness his remarks in the *History of Early Christianity* (1895). On this, see Herbert Aptheker, 'Marxism, Religion and Revolution', *Cross Currents*, Vol. XVIII, No. 2, spring 1968.

12. A. C. MacIntyre's view, to the effect that for Marx religion 'plays at least partly a progressive role in that it gives the common people some idea of what a

better order would be' (*Marxism and Christianity*, London, Duckworth, 1968, p. 80), appears somewhat exaggerated. For Marx, on the present interpretation, religion does not give any such 'idea' of the future.

13. *Towards a Critique of Hegel's Philosophy of Right: Introduction* in Karl Marx, *Early Texts*, tr. and ed. by D. McLellan (Oxford, Blackwell, 1971), p. 115.

14. *On The Jewish Question*, ibid., p. 99.

15. *Capital*, Vol. I, p. 20.

16. Karl Marx, *Economic-Philosophic Manuscripts 1844*, tr. by M. Milligan (Moscow, 1961), p. 136.

17. Karl Marx and Frederick Engels, *The Holy Family or Critique of Critical Critique*, tr. by R. Dixon (Moscow, 1956), pp. 175-6.

18. Karl Marx and Frederick Engels, *The German Ideology* (London, Lawrence & Wishart, 1965), p. 62. The original clearly brings out the indicative sense: '*Sie kann dies, weil im Anfange ihr Interesse wirklich noch mehr mit dem gemeinschaftlichen Interesse aller übrigen nichtherrschenden Klassen zusammenhängt . . .*'. Marx's marginal remark on the manuscript is also significant: '. . . *der Illusion der gemeinschaftlichen Interessen (im Anfang diese Illusion wahr)*'. Karl Marx-Frederick Engels, *Werke* (Berlin, 1962), Band 3, p. 48.

19. Cf. E. J. Hobsbawm, 'Class Consciousness in History' in I. Mészáros (ed.), *Aspects of History and Class Consciousness* (London, Routledge, 1971).

20. Jürgen Habermas, *Toward a Rational Society*, tr. by Jeremy J. Shapiro (London, Heinemann Educ., 1971), p. 111.

21. Jürgen Habermas, *Strukturwandel der Öffentlichkeit: Untersuchungen zu einer Kategorie der bürgerlichen Gesellschaft* (Neuwied am Rhein, 1965), p. 100.

22. Herbert Marcuse, *Negations* (London, Allen Lane, 1968), p. 98.

23. Cf. I. Mészáros, *Marx's Theory of Alienation* (London, Merlin Press, 1970), p. 136.

24. *Economic-Philosophic Manuscripts*, op. cit., p. 154.

25. *Holy Family*, op. cit., p. 56.

26. *Early Texts*, op. cit., pp. 93-4.

27. Shlomo Avineri, *The Social and Political Thought of Karl Marx* (Cambridge University Press, 1968), p. 203.

28. *Early Texts*, op. cit., p. 104.

29. Avineri, op. cit., pp. 33-8 takes this line. It is, however, arguable that the decisive shift in Marx's position regarding this point occurs between the two critiques of Hegel and the *Manuscripts*. Cf. R. N. Berki, 'Perspectives in the Marxian Critique of Hegel's Political Philosophy', in Z. A. Pelczynski (ed.), *Hegel's Political Philosophy* (Cambridge University Press, 1971), pp. 207-8.

30. Cf. Avineri, op. cit., p. 200.

31. Karl Marx, *The Civil War in France*, with an Introduction by Frederick Engels (London, 1933), p. 40.

32. Ibid., p. 48.

33. *Critique of the Gotha Program*, op. cit., p. 33.

34. Ibid., p. 31.

35. Ibid., p. 58.

36. Cf. 'The Communist revolution is the most radical rupture with traditional property relations: no wonder that its development involves the most radical rupture with traditional ideas.' *Manifesto*, p. 79.

37. Gramsci, op. cit., p. 117.

38. Georg Lukács, *History and Class Consciousness: Studies in Marxist Dialectics*, tr. by Rodney Livingstone (London, Merlin Press, 1971), p. 67. This is not to say, of course, that Lukács' tone in this classic work is very 'accommodating', though later writings of his show a mellowing of disposition. Leszek Kolakowski's book on

Positivist Philosophy, on the other hand, is a work of constructive and accommodating criticism (tr. by Norman Guterman (Harmondsworth, Penguin, 1972, *passim.*))

39. Such an attack is mounted by Theodore Roszak in *The Making of a Counter Culture: Reflections on the Technocratic Society and its Youthful Opposition* (London, Faber, 1970), Ch. III.

Ideology and Intellectuals

ANTHONY ARBLASTER

Most conceptions of ideology are implicitly or explicitly hostile or derogatory. Thus, both from the point of view of orthodox Marxists and from that of the would-be anti-ideological empiricists who, in the late 1950s, proclaimed 'the end of ideology', ideology is seen as a veil that stands between men and reality, something that obscures and distorts facts rather than revealing them. Whether someone is consciously committed to a particular ideological position, or whether his/her beliefs unconsciously reflect an established ideology, the implication is the same: an ideological position is a partisan position, non-neutral and non-objective.

Given these assumptions about ideology, certain fundamental questions about the behaviour and the proper role of intellectuals immediately arise. Can the intellectual, who is supposed to have a special and perhaps professional concern with truth,[1] escape from or rise above the partiality and distortions of ideology? Is the intellectual especially well qualified, or well placed, to do this? And if the answer to this question is 'no', should not the intellectual at least make the attempt to be 'objective' and 'impartial', if he is seriously committed to the pursuit of truth? Then there are the empirical questions that must be closely connected with these normative ones. Do intellectuals as a group in fact rise above ideology? If not, why not? From one angle these are questions about the proper and the actual roles of intellectuals, and about the appropriateness or otherwise of commitment and detachment, partiality and neutrality, in the intellectual life. From another angle they are questions about truth, how it is to be reached, and by whom. Obviously such large questions do not have definitive and final answers to them, and this essay is inevitably intended only as a contribution to what is, or ought to be, a constant process of self-questioning among thoughtful people, and in particular among those who are professionally concerned with ideas.

It is appropriate to start with Karl Mannheim, since it is he who is most readily identified with the distinctly unfashionable thesis that intellectuals, or the intelligentsia—Mannheim uses both terms more or less interchangeably—are the particular group that is uniquely well equipped to escape from the toils of partisan ideologies and, borne on the wings of scholarship, soar towards the sun of truth. (It would be inadvisable to press the image of Icarus any further.) Mannheim, starting from a very thorough grasp of the extent to which *all* thought is saturated with 'ontological, metaphysical, and ethical pre-suppositions',[2] which may reflect a particular social structure or the position of a particular social class, goes on to ask the central question in any discussion of ideology: 'Which social standpoint *vis-à-vis* of history offers the best chance for reaching an optimum of truth?'[3] (He asks it, unfortunately, in the excruciating English into which *Ideology and Utopia* was translated—which may very well reflect an equally excruciating German.)

Mannheim begins to answer his own question by pointing optimistically to the development of the theory of ideology itself. This theory, by 'unmasking' hitherto unnoticed deter-minants of thought, itself marks a sizeable step in the direction of truth: 'Perhaps it is precisely when the hitherto concealed dependence of thought on group existence and its rootedness in action becomes visible that it really becomes possible for the first time, through becoming aware of them, to attain a new mode of control over previously uncontrolled factors in thought,'[4] he writes at the beginning of the book. Later on he claims, confidently and more specifically, that the capacity to perceive the socially rooted character of various modes of thought is precisely what makes 'politics as a science [is] for the first time possible'.[5] This comprehensive understanding gener-ates a natural urge towards a synthesis that will incorporate what is best in these opposing ideologies in a new ideology, itself to be transcended at a later historical stage. But the theory of ideology itself requires that 'the tendency towards a total synthesis must be embodied in the will of some social group'.[6] This group needs to be 'a relatively classless stratum which is not too firmly situated in the social order', and Mannheim identifies this 'unanchored, *relatively* classless stratum' as the 'socially unattached intelligentsia'[7].

In Mannheim's view the intelligentsia does not form a class. It is 'to a large degree unattached to any social class'.[8] It is a heterogeneous group which is 'recruited from an increasingly inclusive area of social life',[9] and forms a kind of crucible, or focus of the various social interests within a society. Thus the intelligentsia is open, both intellectually and socially, and non-attached. In other words Mannheim puts forward sociological reasons for holding that intellectuals, as a group, have a particularly good chance of escaping from the trap of ideology; and it is therefore on sociological ground that we must meet his arguments.

First, Mannheim, writing in the late 1920s, nowhere mentions the institutionalization of intellectual life. For a sociologist this is surely astonishing. Mannheim writes as if the intelligentsia was what it perhaps was in the France of the Enlightenment, or England in the nineteenth century, a stratum of economically self-supporting, non-incorporated people, of whom some lived on their writing, some relied on private wealth, a few occupied sinecures in the Civil Service, and many occupied sinecures in the somnolent universities. In connection with this type of intellectual, the type of Montesquieu and Voltaire, Bentham, Coleridge, de Tocqueville, John Stuart Mill and George Eliot, it is just possible to conceive of the intelligentsia as an 'unanchored' and 'socially unattached' group even though, given the benefit of historical perspective, we do not find much difficulty in locating them within the class structure and class struggles of their times.

But, with certain conspicuous exceptions such as Bernard Shaw and Bertrand Russell,[10] both of whom came to maturity in the nineteenth century, today's equivalents of Voltaire and Coleridge and Mill—if figures of comparable stature can be found at all—are virtually all teacher-academics. The pattern of social change has produced, among other results, the wholesale

117

incorporation of intellectuals into the educational system. I do not mean to imply by this that all the intellect of contemporary society is concentrated in educational institutions, for I do not accept Mannheim's sharp distinction between the intelligentsia and the rest, who, he appears to imply, are *not* 'in a position to have intellectual convictions'.[11] Gramsci makes the more accurate (and more humane) distinction when he says that 'all men are intellectuals . . . but all men do not have the function of intellectuals in society'.[12] It is in respect of those who have that function, those whose primary or professional concern is with matters of the mind and the imagination, that this incorporation has taken place. It has placed them in an obviously dependent position, and this dependence has inevitably reduced the social detachment which Mannheim saw as one of the conditions that enabled them to surpass current ideology. And academics, so far from being outside the class structure, are very clearly concerned with their status within that structure, and with obtaining the kind of (grossly inflated) incomes they see as commensurate with that status.

Mannheim's picture of the social non-attachment of the intelligentsia is further weakened by the obviously bourgeois atmosphere of the institutions to which they now generally belong. Admittedly, to many of those inside these institutions it is *not* obvious that their predominant ethos and customs have this class character, but this is a product of social myopia. To the working-class student the contrast is very clear indeed. Richard Hoggart's account of his relationship, as an exceptionally talented but also 'raw and uncertain' working-class student at Leeds University, with his stylish Professor of English, Bonamy Dobrée, makes this abundantly plain.[13] But if we are used to a certain ethos, a certain style, it requires imagination to appreciate how class-bound it may appear to someone approaching it from 'outside'.

The thesis of non-attachment is also undermined by the fact that Mannheim, like so many other complacent contemporary commentators, overestimated the speed at which the class character of the intelligentsia would give way to social openness. Equality of educational opportunity, regardless of social class, remains an ideal which is far from being completely attained, and when access to that minority of the educated who fulfil the function of the intelligentsia is considered, the position is correspondingly far worse.

If it be accepted that Mannheim was mistaken, or at least extremely over-sanguine about the likely social non-attachment of the intellectuals, we must consider also the actual performance of intellectuals. Do they live up to Mannheim's expectations? Do they move beyond established ideologies to create a synthesis of thought which opens up an intellectual path into the future? But first, who, precisely, are the intellectuals?

So far we have not gone beyond speaking of 'those whose primary or professional concern is with matters of the mind and the imagination'. This is vague, and could be understood to include all those who teach, and research, and a large number of those who live by writing and speaking in the media. Yet the normal tendency is to define an intellectual not by his occupation or professional role, but according to a less tangible judgement of his or her intellectual preoccupations and activities. We are more likely to describe people as intellectuals on the basis of their conversation than their occupation. The intellectual is thought of not as someone who displays great mental or imaginative ability in his or her particular field, but as someone who applies those abilities in more general areas, the areas of religion and philosophy, and social and political questions. Thus, in thinking of intellectuals, the names of Coleridge and Thomas Huxley might readily occur to us, but not those of Wordsworth or Charles Darwin; or in our own time the names of W. H. Auden and Sir Peter Medawar, but not those of Robert Graves or Lord Rutherford. It is the involvement in general debate and controversy outside a specialism that is normally taken as the hallmark of an intellectual. But this is to make being an intellectual a matter of choice, of self-definition, and although this may correspond to ordinary usage, it is hardly satisfactory when it comes to discussion of what the role of the intellectual ought to be, of what his responsibilities are. For in such a discussion it may very well be that one criticism many people would make of academics is that by retreating into their specialisms they are defaulting on their obligations as intellectuals—obligations to be aware of the social and political context in which their work is done, and the uses to which it may be put. Such a criticism cannot accept that these people simply choose not to be intellectuals in the normal sense, and that such a choice is a morally neutral one. So it may be that a definition of the intellectual in terms of his or her occupation rather than in terms of his or her choice to step beyond the bounds of a specialism is in fact more satisfactory than the conventional conception, however bizarre some of the results of such a broad definition may seem. Thus, in turning now to the actual performance of intellectuals in relation to ideology, we have to consider first the positive performance of those who accept the role of the intellectual and offer a commentary upon the major public issues of the day, but also the negative performance of the much larger number of intellectuals by profession who do not accept that role.

It is not so many years since it was common among many Western intellectuals to proclaim the arrival of what Edward Shils was perhaps the first to call 'the end of ideology',[14] and at first glance this might have seemed like the case *par excellence* of intellectuals escaping from ideology. They demonstrated their emancipation by denouncing the delusion that they had cast off, or to which, perhaps, they had never fallen prey. Yet with the passage of time it has become clear even to many who could not see it then that this ostensibly anti-ideological position was itself very markedly ideological. For one thing the conception of ideology current among these writers was an extremely tendentious one. Bernard Crick wrote that 'totalitarian ideology presents a clear contrast to politics',[15] in a chapter devoted to defending politics against ideology, without giving any indication that there might be such a thing as non-totalitarian ideology. In the same vein Daniel Bell identified ideology with 'apocalyptic beliefs that refuse to specify the costs and consequences of the changes they envision'.[16] A much less sophisticated disciple of this school, Irving Kristol, for five years an editor of *Encounter*, brought the latent anti-Communist anti-Left bias of this conception of ideology right out into the open when, reporting on the teach-ins of 1965, he wrote that 'within the "teach-in" movement there are many unreasonable ideological types—pro-Castro, pro-Viet Cong, pro-Mao, anti-American'.[17] To be anti-Castro and pro-American would not, apparently, have been to be either unreasonable or even ideological.

The ideology whose end was so prematurely announced was, essentially, the ideology of socialism, and the recommended alternative to it was political empiricism. An effective critique of empiricism, philosophical or political, lies well beyond the scope of this essay. It must be sufficient to note here that even so resolute an opponent of ideological politics as Michael Oakeshott has argued that purely empirical politics are a strict impossibility,[18] and that empiricism, despite the claims that its supporters make for it, is not generally thought of as a neutral and non-ideological political prescription. Empiricism, which eschews programmes for wholesale social and political change, and commits itself to the piecemeal approach, implies acceptance of the existing overall social structure. It is therefore an essentially conservative prescription, and has usually been recognized as such. It is only in relation to the wholly tendentious conception of ideology referred to above that such a prescription could possibly be thought of as non-ideological. Whoever may have escaped from the ideology trap, it certainly wasn't Daniel Bell or Irving Kristol, both of them perfectly recognizable specimens of a common species, the Cold War conservative-liberal.

If we now turn to consider the behaviour of contemporary intellectuals in a more general way, it soon becomes clear how far they are, as a collectivity, from realizing Mannheim's ideal. So far from providing the pattern of detachment which was his ideal, many intellectuals have committed themselves quite consciously and voluntarily to a variety of partisan viewpoints. But if partisanship can be defended, servility cannot. And many intellectuals, perhaps the majority, have kept silent or explicitly acquiesced when brute force has been used by many different regimes to punish dissent and crush free expression, while, what is perhaps worst of all, many have, often without thinking about it or even perhaps being aware of it at all, allowed themselves to become the tools and agents of government and established orthodoxies.

It was in the 1920s that Julien Benda coined the now famous phrase, the *trahison des clercs*. He would not in the subsequent decades have found any reason to withdraw it. The forms of this treason that have attracted most attention, and condemnation, in the West, have been those that occur *outside* the West, above all in Communist countries and among left-wing intellectuals generally. Much of the comment on the career of Jean-Paul Sartre has been of this type, and some of the obituary notices for Georg Lukács were in the same vein. Conor Cruise O'Brien has defended Sartre, in my view effectively, against this kind of criticism.[19] Lukács's is certainly a more difficult case. But the many cases of compliance and the rare cases of defiance among East European and Communist intellectuals never go without notice in the West, for obvious reasons. It is more appropriate for Western intellectuals to examine their own record, and set their own house in order. For, as O'Brien has remarked, 'Clerks can betray in more than one way, and in our culture the Communist way is neither the most tempting nor the most rewarding.'[20]

In fact the period of the Cold War saw a great many Western intellectuals putting their talents at the service of the great anti-Communist crusade, in which the CIA is now known to have played a far larger part than any 'reasonable', moderate, Guardian-reading intellectual would have been prepared to admit was possible only a decade ago. From the English point of view the most sensational example of this involvement was, of course, the magazine Encounter. O'Brien, John Saville and others[21] have documented Encounter's record amply enough to establish that the journal's claim in its first editorial, that 'Encounter seeks to promote no line . . .'[22] was belied by that and every subsequent issue, since it has in fact consistently promoted for almost twenty years a strongly anti-Communist and, more recently, anti-New Left line. The journal's rather feeble attempts to conceal its partisanship are, however, much less objectionable from the point of view of our present concerns than the dishonest selectivity that accompanied this commitment. Encounter was thought to be upholding liberal values, and many of its contributors saw themselves as doing the same. But it was Communist and other left-wing regimes that were made the almost exclusive target of this supposedly liberal attack, while other equally illiberal regimes, such as Battista's Cuba (but not Castro's, of course) and South Africa, were simply ignored or even made the subject of bland apologetics.[23] A commitment to cultural freedom requires that one attacks tyranny and intolerance impartially, wherever they occur. *Encounter* and the intellectuals associated with it did not honour that commitment. In fact they betrayed it.

It has been the Vietnam war, in all its ramifications, that has provided the most dreadful and disturbing demonstration of the subservience of intellectuals in the West. This has been documented in abundant detail by Noam Chomsky,[24] who points to the contrast between the traditional role of the intellectual, 'or at least his self-image', as 'a dispassionate critic',[25] and 'the . . . natural tendency of significant segments of the American intellectual community to offer their allegiance, not to truth and justice, but to power and the effective exercise of power.'[26] What is perhaps most astonishing and disturbing is not that there are so many intellectuals who will, without question or demur, place their abilities and specialist knowledge at the service of any governmental enterprise, however brutal or futile, but that there are some who even welcome the prospect of the intellectual losing or renouncing the traditional role of which Chomsky spoke. One such is the prophet of the so-called technetronic age, Zbigniew Brzerzinski. In his article 'America in the Technetronic Age', which appeared, inevitably, in *Encounter*, he sees the United States moving into an age in which 'knowledge becomes a tool of power' and a university ceases to be 'an aloof ivory tower' and becomes instead 'an intensely involved *think-tank*, the source of much sustained political planning and social innovation'.[27] Brzerzinski recognizes that

A profound change in the intellectual community itself is inherent in this development. The largely humanist-oriented, occasionally ideologically-minded intellectual dissenter, who saw his role largely in terms of proferring social critiques, is rapidly being displaced either by experts and specialists, who become involved in special government undertakings, or by the generalist-integrators, who become house-ideologues for those in power, providing overall intellectual integration for disparate actions.[28]

It is depressing enough that intellectuals should be willing to accept the roles which Brzerzinski foresees for them—'specialists . . . involved . . . in government undertakings' and 'house-ideologues for those in power'. But the subordination of intellectuals to the state and its requirements does not occur only at the individual level. There is a strengthening tendency for the institutions within which, as has been suggested, most intellectuals now work, also to be shaped according to the particular political priorities of particular governments. Increasingly, public funds are made available to educational institutions, not for them to dispose of according to their own academic priorities, but for specific purposes decided on at government level. Recently, in the English university system, town planning and management studies have been favoured in this way. It is unlikely that less obviously 'useful' or profitable studies, like the bulk of the arts and social sciences, will receive similar encouragement, whatever their intellectual merits. The owners and controllers of private industry also play their part in determining the general pattern of study and research, for they too will be willing to support such dubious academic enterprises as management and business studies, while they are unlikely, to put it mildly, to be prepared to 'waste' their money on such unprofitable activities as archaeology, or drama, or philosophy. It is hardly necessary to spell out the effects of these institutionalized pressures on the individual scholar or intellectual.[29] Crudely, he who pays the piper calls the tune.

It would be misleading to present a monolithic picture, and indeed the very fact that outstanding intellectuals such as O'Brien and Chomsky can be quoted as critics of the developments I have been discussing, would contradict such an interpretation. The tendency towards the integration of the academy, and so of intellectuals, into the structure of corporate state capitalism has not gone unnoticed or unchallenged. There has been articulate and eloquent opposition. But articulacy and eloquence are not a substitute for power, and the opposition remains an opposition to what are the dominant trends. Generally speaking the evidence of the actual performance of intellectuals does not support Mannheim's view of their independence and their capacity to escape from the established ideologies. What is more, it might well be added that figures like Chomsky and O'Brien are as strongly committed to their particular ideological positions as the Cold War intellectuals who have been the principal object of this critique.

But this last point does not really affect Mannheim's thesis. On the contrary, the diversity of ideological positions lends

support to the belief that there is at least a potential for independence of mind among intellectuals as a group. Widespread
lip-service is paid to the principle that education is intended to
teach people to think for themselves. We need not take this too
seriously, since it is clear that much formal education does not,
in practice, have any such aim in view. Nevertheless, the continuous simmering of discontent and criticism among students,
and more recently among school-students as well, which occasionally erupts into significant institutional crises, must owe
something at least to the fact that students have, by some means
or other, acquired the ability to form their own opinions. I am
suggesting that contemporary Western education, with all its
inadequacies, is not simply a process of indoctrination, that to
some extent it provides people with the means to independent
thought, and, further, that almost any educational system which
is not relentlessly monolithic is likely to do this to some degree.
There is thus some evidence to support Mannheim's belief that
education may enable at least some of those who get it to move
beyond the limits of the orthodox and established belief
systems.[30]

To say this, however, is not to suggest that they can escape
from ideology altogether. But perhaps Mannheim is not wanting to suggest that—we saw earlier that he emphasizes the degree
to which all thought is based upon 'ontological, metaphysical,
and ethical presuppositions'. And perhaps even if he did want
to suggest it, it is simply not possible. It is possible for intellectuals to some degree to stand outside the *prevailing* ideology,
even if most of them do not in fact do so. But to suggest that they
can escape from ideology altogether into a world of objectivity
to which they alone have privileged access is to go a good deal
further than that. Objectivity is a goal of scholarship as truth is
a goal of argument, and frequent claims are made by academics
and intellectuals to be in possession of one or both of these
coveted prizes. But any survey of the worlds of the mind is more
likely to reveal conflict and competition between different
ideological interpretations of the world than any simple contrast
between objectivity on the one hand and bias and distortion
on the other. However, this only pushes the problem a stage
further back. How do we choose between competing ideologies?
Any criteria we are likely to use, whether we operate a simple

test of correspondence to reality, or whether we speak of their explanatory power or their comprehensiveness, carries with it a necessary, ineliminable reference to truth or reality. Whatever its difficulties, the use of some concept of truth or fact or reality as a touchstone is a necessary part of the whole intellectual enterprise.

What then does the traditional commitment of the intellectual to truth imply so far as his relationship to ideology is concerned? I would argue that it should involve both commitment and detachment, and that there is a constant dialectical tension between these two demands. There must be a degree of detachment *from* ideology. The intellectual, whatever his commitment, must always be prepared to test the hypotheses of ideology against indisputable (as opposed to disputable) realities. He must also be committed to certain minimal standards of honesty, accuracy and objectivity. And this is not a banal demand, since it is undoubtedly the case that much ideologically motivated work, often of great merit considered as interpretation, does not conform to these standards. Further, the intellectual has the obligation to become aware of the ideological assumptions that underpin and, normally, set definite limits to his area of study, even though it is so easy for the specialist within that area to pursue his work unconscious that such assumptions and such limits even exist. The commitment to truth does, in my view, require the systematic development of this kind of self-awareness on the part of intellectuals. It is this that the appropriate degree of detachment from ideology requires, and not, as so many academics crudely suppose, a philistine determination to ignore ideology altogether. It is a serious condemnation of the irresponsibility as well as the parochialism of so many academics in particular that they do not even ask themselves the relevant questions in this context—that they do not ask themselves, for example, whether they are not, albeit inadvertently, helping to sustain some ideological approach to reality which is obscuring or neglecting important truths even though it may bring to light some trivial ones. The British Society for Social Responsibility in Science is an example of a step towards this kind of self-awareness, by its insistence that scientists think about what happens to their work when it falls into the hands of government and industry.

There needs also to be detachment at the institutional level. Intellectuals, whatever their personal political orientation, ought to view with repugnance the increasing subordination of organized intellectual activity to the requirements of state and government. They ought not to accept that any government should be in a position to regulate the flow of knowledge and argument in society, or to determine into what channels research and inquiry should be directed. Nor should such power be in the hands of non-accountable private conglomerations of economic power. These tendencies, together with the tendency among educational authorities themselves not to tolerate the presence in their institutions of the educationally radical teacher, constitute a serious threat to the ideological openness of intellectual institutions, and that openness is a necessary condition of a healthily independent intellectual life within a society.

To talk of the ideological openness of institutions implies that within those institutions it is legitimate for individuals to hold to particular ideological commitments. I would go further, and argue that such commitments are not merely legitimate; they are both unavoidable and desirable. We have already seen how implausible claims to ideological detachment usually are. Whatever degree of neutrality may in principle be possible, it is evident that it is seldom attained. Therefore intellectuals, and particularly teaching intellectuals, do better to admit freely their ideological biases, and operate on a basis of open, rather than ill-concealed, partisanship.

In any case it is very doubtful whether the effort to achieve ideological neutrality brings one nearer to the truth than frank partisanship. More illumination is usually obtained through the clash of opposed ideological interpretations of reality than by attempts at impartial surveys of the battlefield from a would-be God-like vantage point. The 'neutral' survey usually ends up as dull and uninspired, representing both sides far less persuasively and passionately than they would themselves. Trotsky once wrote that 'only a participant can be a profound spectator'.[31] There is a sense in which the idea of detachment, in some ways a necessary virtue, as has been suggested, is also a tempting trap for the intellectual for, in many circumstances, to remain outside, uncommitted, is a guarantee of incomprehension as well as mere dullness. It is rare to find an intellectual like John Stuart Mill who can feel the force of more than one ideological position (as his essays on Bentham and Coleridge demonstrate), and yet also have something positive to say. Most of those who have made a significant contribution to human thought have been ardently partisan and one-sided, and it is precisely this 'biased' non-neutral character that gives their work its forceful and perennially stimulating character.

To suggest that intellectuals *do* rise above ideology is obviously implausible. To argue, as Mannheim does, that they are especially well qualified to be *able* to do so, also appears over-optimistic in most respects. (If they can, why don't they?) When, finally, we consider whether they *should* try to free themselves from ideology, a simple and unqualified answer is clearly not possible. Explicit commitment is preferable, for several reasons, to bogus neutrality. But truth is an indispensable touchstone, and detachment in some respects a necessary virtue.

The proper role of intellectuals is one that combines detachment and commitment. Their function ought in any society to be a critical, questioning one. So far from allowing themselves to become incorporated in the processes of government or to perform the role of 'house-ideologues for those in power', they ought to form a kind of permanent potential opposition, always ready to subject the established ideology to examination and to ask questions and raise issues which those in power would prefer to bury or to forget. As Marcuse has argued, they have the duty of trying to prevent the development of a one-dimensional culture, by keeping alive ideas which constitute a vital critique of existing society.[32] This is itself a commitment, but it is a commitment to detachment, detachment from orthodoxy.

NOTES AND REFERENCES

1. 'It is the responsibility of intellectuals to speak the truth and to expose lies.' Noam Chomsky, 'The Responsibility of Intellectuals' in *American Power and the New Mandarins* (Harmondsworth, Penguin, 1970), p. 257.

2. Karl Mannheim, *Ideology and Utopia* (London, Routledge, 1960), p. 79.

3. Ibid., p. 71.

4. Ibid., p. 4.

5. Ibid., p. 132.

6. Ibid., p. 136.

7. Ibid., p. 137.

8. Ibid., p. 139.

9. Ibid., p. 139.

10. See Stuart Hampshire in *Modern Writers and Other Essays* (London, Chatto, 1969), pp. 111-12.

11. Mannheim, op. cit., p. 142.

12. Antonio Gramsci, 'The Formation of Intellectuals' in *The Modern Prince* (London, Lawrence & Wishart, 1957), p. 121.

13. Richard Hoggart, 'Teaching with Style' in *Speaking to Each Other*, Vol. II, (London, Chatto, 1970), pp. 201-17.

14. Edward Shils, 'The End of Ideology?', *Encounter* (November 1955).

15. Bernard Crick, *In Defence of Politics* (London, Weidenfeld, 1962), p. 42.

16. Daniel Bell in *Commentary* (October 1964), p. 70.

17. Irving Kristol, 'Letter from New York', *Encounter* (August 1965), p. 70.

18. Michael Oakeshott, 'Political Education' in *Rationalism in Politics* (London, Methuen, 1962), pp. 114-15.

19. See *Writers and Politics* (London, Chatto, 1965), p. 82.

20. Ibid., p. 170.

21. See O'Brien, pp. 169-73; John Saville, 'The Politics of *Encounter*' in *The Socialist Register 1964* (London, Merlin, 1964), pp. 192-207; and Christopher Lasch, 'The Cultural Cold War' in *The Agony of the American Left* (New York, Knopf, 1969), pp. 61-114.

22. *Encounter* (October 1953), p. 1.

23. O'Brien, op. cit., pp. 172 and 173.

24. In Chomsky, op. cit.

25. Ibid., p. 251.

26. Ibid., p. 249.

27. Zbigniew Brzerzinski, 'America in the Technetronic Age', *Encounter* (January 1968), p. 18.

28. Ibid., p. 22.

29. This has been done by Conor Cruise O'Brien in his essay in M. Black (ed.), *The Morality of Scholarship* (Cornell University Press, 1968).

30. See the account given by Roger Poole in *Towards Deep Subjectivity* (London, Allen Lane, 1972), Ch. 1.

31. Leon Trotsky, *Trotsky's Diary in Exile, 1935* (London, Faber, 1959), p. 48.

32. See Herbert Marcuse, *One Dimensional Man* (London, Sphere, 1968), pp. 58-62.

Politics Without Ideology:
The Perimeters of Pluralism

ROBERT BENEWICK

I

It has been asserted that 'as the exclusively proper way of ordering and explaining public life, it [political pluralism] remains the heart of the liberal ideology of the western world'. It has also been asserted that 'political pluralism as an ideology has lost most of its explicit apologists and only lingers quietly as a submerged, inarticulate ingredient of Western liberalism'. In this fashion Henry S. Kariel introduces and concludes his authoritative contribution to the *International Encyclopedia of the Social Sciences*.[1] It would appear that in the space of five pages Kariel has laid pluralism to rest. Alas, this is not the intention and Kariel has written elsewhere at length and with eloquence on his subject.[2] The two quotations reflect, whether intentional or not, a debate in the United States which has attracted little attention in Great Britain.[3] This suggests that the first quotation is applicable to the United States and the second to Britain. It will be shown that pluralist doctrine is alive but not very well in Britain.

Political pluralism is seen as a way in which power is ordered in a liberal, democratic political system. Importance is placed on freely organized groups which compete with each other to promote their interests. In the United States where the institutional arrangements have been designed to disperse power, competition among groups is seen as a further democratic diffusion of power. In Britain where the political system is more centralized the group process is seen as a channel for participation. In both systems pressure groups function as supplements to the electoral and legislative processes.

The emphasis on the promotion of interests discounts ideology and blunts ideological conflict. Yet political pluralism is accepted as a justification of political arrangements, an explanation of political behaviour and as a democratic prescription. As such, it is incorporated into the conventional wisdom of political discourse and political science. At its most sophisticated level, as one critic argues: 'Interest-group liberalism seems closer to being the established operative ideology of the American elite than any other body of doctrine.'[4] In less subtle contexts elitist critiques of liberal institutions are countered, inequities and irrationalities in voting behaviour are rectified and Western democracy stands in marked contrast to the totalitarian model.

In this essay the pluralist debate in the United States will be briefly summarized. The degree to which pluralism is an operative ideology contributing to the underpinning of the British political system and influencing its study will then be assessed. Finally an attempt will be made to develop a model of the British pressure group world to suggest some of the consequences of the pluralist view. Pluralism has engendered distinctive forms according to the differences in the political culture, political development and political arrangements of the two countries. This is an advantage for analysis in so far as two liberal democratic models are provided—a presidential and a parliamentary system of government. Since the American system is constructed on a principle of dispersion of power, the applicability of pluralist critiques to Britain, where institutional power is more concentrated, may be instructive. If not, understanding of the more elusive variables, political culture and political development, may be enhanced.

The focus will be on the world of pressure groups. The assumption is that in liberal democracies pressure groups play similar roles subject to the constraints cited above. The differences are mainly ones of technique and points and degrees of access. America's institutional pluralism may provide more effective targets, but granted this, it is not uncommon to talk of administrative pluralism in Britain. In the United States the pluralist debate encompasses the formal institutional arrangements and the methodological assumptions and findings of the community power studies. The substance of these controversies are also to be found in the pressure group studies. Where the debate has evolved into one between the pluralist model and the elitist model, they both tend to suffer from self-validating assumptions. At best, as Theodore Lowi has noted: 'The pluralist approach suggests what to look for and the elitist model perhaps what not to look for.'[5] No attempt will be made to pronounce on the merits of one approach *vis à vis* the other for the task in regard to Britain is more immediate. That is, how the ideological bias of the pressure group world affects the position of important but disadvantaged sectors of society.

Three main arguments underlie this essay. First, pluralism may be an essential component of a democratic political system but it does not necessarily function democratically. Second, in so far as there is an explicit or implicit pressure group world ideology in Britain, pluralism is the conventional view. Third, pluralism rather than promoting group visibility has tended to obscure it.

II

In the United States the pre-eminence of pluralist ideology can be credited to a number of considerations. Pluralism does not even occupy the minor place in American political theory that it does in British political thought. Moreover, it has a specialized meaning. As traditionally formulated in terms of democratic theory, the institutions and associations within society are distinguished and separated from the political—i.e. the state. The concern is to insulate institutions and associations and thereby the individuals that compose them from the possibilities of state control and domination. With the acceptance of the need for state regulation and the positive role of the state, government has become a target for associations. Pluralist doctrine has been adjusted accordingly. Yet pluralism can be seen to be rooted in the mainstream of American political thought in so far as it is accepted as a reaffirmation of the Madisonian and Jeffersonian traditions of democracy and of de Tocqueville's justifications of American society. *The Federalist Papers*, particularly No. 10, which expressed the primacy of factions, government neutrality, and the requirement for dispersing power, serves as a point of departure for both the pluralists and their critics.[6] The Jeffersonian conception stresses small groups, decentralization and also the dispersion of power while de Tocqueville emphasized political participation and intermediate associations.[7] The celebration of these themes imparts a continuity, assurance and wisdom to American political development.

Pluralism is a recognition if not an acceptance of one of America's leading myths, the melting pot. Social pluralism is thereby accounted for in the political system. The pluralist position corresponds to some of the realities of American society and the exercise of power in so far as the political system is decentralized, power diffused and fragmented, and group activity encouraged. That group conflict exists, that excesses have been checked and rewards shared, however unequally, is apparent to all but the most severe critics.

The notion of a market place in which the public interest is furthered by freely competing groups with government as a neutral referee transplants the economic model and with it the capitalist ethos to the political arena. As roles have changed in the market place, there have been corresponding changes in the political system. If classical liberalism no longer pertains, concentrations and abuses of power are held in check by 'countervailing' powers or 'veto groups'.[8] The economic model also places a high priority on bargaining which is in accord with the traditional belief in pragmatism.

For the purpose of analysis the pluralist framework, although also mechanistic, supplies a more searching approach to American society than the Marxist critique of the state. It is not surprising then that political science has made its contribution—what Lowi describes as elevating 'the pressure group system from power to virtue'.[9] The revival of interest in Arthur Bentley's *The Process of Government*, with its group determinism and dominance and its plea for a scientific approach, found influential support in David Truman's *The Government Process* and Earl Lathan's 'The Group Basis of Politics'.[10] Pluralist studies achieved particular prominence as rebuttals to elite analysis. Titles like C. Wright Mills' *The Power Elite* and Robert Dahl's *Who Governs?* are indicative of the controversy.[11] As if to confirm the wisdom of pluralist writers, critics joined in as 'countervailing forces'.[12] This social science pluralism should not convey a false impression if only because of the time dimension involved. Pluralist theory places a high value on interests as distinct from ideas. So it may not be entirely fortuitous that it peaked at a time when ideology was devalued, politics interpreted as administration, consensus and technocracy venerated.

Pluralism became something of a doctrinal showpiece reflecting a desire, if not need, to reassert American values and institutions.[13] Pluralist democracy stood for the antithesis of a totalitarian ordering of society and the bulwark against the evils of mass society.[14] It was one response to the traumas of World War II, the Cold War, McCarthyism and rapid social and technological change.[15] A focus on the accommodation of interests also fits well with a devaluation of ideas and the glossing over of divisive forces.[16] An emphasis on stability emerged with the condition becoming confused with the value. Peter Bachrach has forcefully drawn attention to another of the ideological uses of pluralism. Contemporary democratic theory supported by empirical research displays a marked loss of faith in the common man. Elites have replaced the common man as the custodians of democratic ideals with a concomitant stress on maintaining political equilibrium.[17] Elite pluralism helps to reconcile elitist behaviour with democratic theory.

In assessing the ideological uses of pluralism there is a danger of fusing a descriptive material with its application. This question is tackled in other essays in this volume. In the present context, however, an ideological spill-over into both American and British political discourse can be detected.

These considerations and others underpin an explicit formulation of an American pluralism based on the following propositions: periodic elections determine the general direction of policy; between elections views and interests are or can be articulated by organized groups; as in elections this is a competitive process with each group attempting to maximize its influence and counter any undue advantages that may accrue to its competitors; government is both an accessible and legitimate target for it tenders rewards in terms of allocating resources and is a referee insuring against an imbalance of influence and unchecked concentrations of power; ideally, the end product will be policies customed to the benefit of all parties and a political system more or less in balance.[18]

Pluralist theorists, whether writing about institutions or groups at the national or local levels, recognize that this characterization represents American pluralism in its ideal form.[19] It assumes an equality of resources among competing groups and that they are representative of their constituencies and subject to democratic control. They argue, in effect, that no group or coalition of groups has *so much power or influence* as to comprise a monolithic power elite. It is further granted that within the respective groups there is elite control. Yet these elite groups or their leaders are competitive precisely because their resources differ and because their spheres of influence are limited or defined. Finally, in the event that imbalance occurs a democratically elected government can act as a countervailing force.[20]

This elite pluralism can be seen to be ideological in so far that its version of reality is accepted as an approximation of the democratic ideal.[21] The critics whose arguments are relevant in the present context dispute whether pluralist interpretations accord to everyone's reality and vision of the ideal. In general, they seek to expose elitism and create conditions that will promote pluralism in its more democratic form. This may not be merely a matter of closing the gap.

Their main criticisms can be briefly summarized. The most frequent charge levelled at the pressure group system is its unrepresentative nature.[22] It is a highly exclusive world favouring narrowly based constituencies which in turn are skewed towards the more successful and prosperous. Another approach recognizes the barriers to achieving legitimacy and to gaining access to the decision-making process.[23] Groups with specific demands and well-defined claims gain preference over groups claiming to represent a wider constituency or a more diffuse public. Since the process is geared to the former, a stigma may attach to the latter. One consequence is that issue saliency is not necessarily a criterion for determining the priorities for processing demands. Legitimacy may be established by possessing the resources for bargaining. Information is a common one but it may not be enough for the test of merit is often one of acceptability.[24] Not only are certain types of groups favoured but so are certain types of demands and policies. It follows that the established, the known and the tried are preferred to the new, the experimental and the radical.

Group legitimacy raises the questions of accountability and the government's role as referee or balancer. Grant McConnell has described a parcelling-out process amounting to 'usurpation' where a 'substantial part of government has come under the influence and control of narrowly based and largely autonomous elites'.[25] McConnell is not describing a monolith nor elite competition for the command posts of the United States. Instead elite autonomy almost seems conditional on respect for autonomous concerns within sharply defined boundaries.

Elite pluralism not only bestows advantages but may further endow those so blessed with sanctions. If a recognized interest opposes a new or unrecognized one, it can conceivably mobilize its superior resources including accredited access to exclude the challenger. Its preferential position is thereby further entrenched.[26] There are also sanctions on members in that a group's status makes membership virtually mandatory and assumes loyalty to the leaders.[27] Finally legitimacy *per se* may be a sanction if it discourages the articulation of new demands. Not only could this weaken the pluralist process but it could act as an encouragement to direct action.

Closely allied to these problems is what could be described as 'qualitative legitimacy'. Access does not necessarily ensure influence or results. What may be decisive is the position to select the issues, draw up the agenda and set the terms of reference.[28] Pluralist theory, even as set out by the revisionists, tends to justify such pre-emptions often by not distinguishing between issues and by not specifying the areas where an elite may be dominant. The denial of a monolithic elite does not mean that there is an equality between competing elites. Finally confrontation does not always take place and when it does there is no guarantee of a balanced outcome. Accommodation is a likely result, but accommodation that minimizes consideration of unrepresented interests which may include the public.

In sum, the critics point to an operational bias which ranks groups and issues, establishes preferences, and influences the allocation of rewards. This operational bias is supported by an ideological one which shapes legitimacy and acceptability. The debate between the pluralists and the critics has been unsatisfactory in so far as the two sides talk past one another and empirical investigation is hindered by ideological predispositions. The critical focus, however, has drawn attention to the disadvantaged and in doing so encouraged the promotion of a more democratic pluralism as well as the search for alternatives. This in turn has raised questions fundamental to democratic theory and practice.

The American critics have prepared a formidable list of indictments some of which are familiar to the student of British pressure groups. Nevertheless, British theory remains unrevised and unchallenged with at least one consequence: there has been little attempt to take into account a new world of pressure groups that has arisen in the last decade.

III

It was in Britain that political pluralism received elaborate theoretical expression and more explicit advocacy. Recently a prominent British sociologist claimed that 'pluralism was the dominant mode of thought of left and right between about 1900 and 1925, wherever people speculated about politics and society'.[29] Pluralist ideas, as was only fitting, resembled the many-headed hydra. To stretch the analogy, a difficulty with pluralist thought is that it goes on increasing as it is combatted. Among the proponents of its many variations were F. W. Maitland, J. N. Figgis, Harold Laski, R. H. Tawney, A. D. Lindsay, Ernest Barker, G. D. H. Cole, A. J. Penty, S. G. Hobson, and A. R. Orage. Reacting against both nineteenth-century individualism and idealism as ideological justifications of industrialization, a theory of society was fashioned where the state was viewed as one of many associations. Concomitant with this analysis was a demand for functional representation which was manifested in the Guild Socialist movement.

The impact of these currents on British political development and contemporary practice is assessed differently in two influential essays on British politics written in the 1960s. A. H. Birch in *Representative and Responsible Government* and Samuel H. Beer in *Modern British Politics* note the antecedents to pluralism in British political thought.[30] These are traced more fully by Beer who develops the notion of a 'persistent corporatism'.[31] In attempting to justify pluralism's current relevancy he also undertakes an examination of the political culture. What is important is that whereas Birch tends to dismiss pluralism as a period piece, Beer sees it as basic to modern collectivist politics and describes the interaction between pressure groups and Whitehall as 'administrative pluralism'.

Groups are instrumental in both the American and British versions. Where, in the United States, group competition and confrontation is accented, in Britain the emphasis is placed on representation, responsiveness and participation, ideally of functional constituencies. Competition takes place less between groups than within them. This also has the advantage of muting confrontation with the government. A sponsor-client relationship between the relevant government department and group designates a high degree of legitimacy for the latter. The role of the Civil Service emerges as somewhat ambiguous. Where interests clash or overlap the department concerned represents its clients in bargaining for preference among government priorities, thereby furthering administrative pluralism. The Civil Service is also seen as representative of the public interest and neutral in itself; a status neither worthy of nor convincing for men of public affairs and power.

A few observations are in order at this juncture. Criteria, tangible and intangible, exist for establishing recognition and legitimacy. The close relationship between a government department and a group is facilitated by the representative nature of the group. Representativeness is used in two senses. One is functional in that a group is recognized or even created as an 'affected interest'. The other is that the group is accepted as the aggregate voice of its clientele.[32] Allen Potter discerns two more criteria—relevancy and responsibility. Both function to admit some groups and exclude others. According to Potter the test of a responsible group is its past behaviour, its adherence to the rules of the game and its style of leadership.[33] To the extent then that responsibility is an operative criterion it rests in large part on ideological grounds.

There is, given the differences in political culture, what could be described as cooperative farming or farming-out rather than parcelling out as in the United States. Agriculture affords a blatant, although by no means exclusive, example.[34] There has not been a group takeover but distinctions between private and public government and administration have been blurred.

Efficacious pressure groups are also said to subscribe to the notion of a public interest. The difficulties here are not only what is meant by the public interest but also that there may be at least three versions represented by a 'neutral' Civil Service, a partisan government and a constrained parliament. Administrative pluralism or, more generally, pressure group legitimacy has ideological consequences for other sectors and interests in society.

Only one dimension of British pluralism has been emphasized. The pressure group world is now recognized as an integral part of the political system. W. J. M. Mackenzie refers to it as one of the three worlds comprising the structure of British government.[35] S. E. Finer has written of a new constitutional trinity.[36] Potter, cognizant of the problem of legitimacy, states that the political organization of Britain consists 'in one sense of governmental bodies, political parties and organized groups and in another of "gentlemen and players" '.[37] J. D. Stewart concludes that pressure groups have become a fifth estate while Beer develops his collectivist theory of representation with its major theme of party government and minor theme of functional representation.[38] In a recent study of the Confederation of British Industry, W. P. Grant and D. Marsh argue that 'the notion that the traditional constitutional trinity of King, Lords and Commons has been replaced by a new trinity of Whitehall, CBI and TUC has a certain credence, even if it is somewhat exaggerated'.[39]

Judging from the number of surveys and case studies undertaken the pressure group world is well charted. A pattern emerges and it is familiar enough. The most effective point of pressure is the executive or more specifically the Civil Service. Groups in possession of requisite resources, for example, information, skills, organization, numbers, 'friends', economic and political sanctions, and that meet the more ideological requirements for legitimacy are likely to gain entry into the Whitehall departments. Much depends on the ability to demonstrate reciprocal benefits and needs. Since most of the consultations and negotiations are over matters of detail and are routine, concern over undue advantage or influence is not exaggerated. Where a powerful group is involved, for example, the CBI, whose brief covers a wide range of government policy, constraints are imposed by the government's own priorities, other pressure groups and public opinion.[40] Moreover, there are other points of access not only for those who enjoy close relations with Whitehall but for those groups that do not. The importance of parliament, the political parties and public opinion as pressure group targets cannot be discounted.

In order to describe the pressure group world political scientists have devised vertical categorizations: interest and promotional groups (Finer, Birch); spokesmen and promotional groups (Potter); sectional and cause groups (Stewart); producer and consumer groups (Beer); protective and promotional groups (Blondel); formal role and promotional role groups (Moodie and Studdert-Kennedy).[41] The interest-orientated groups in the former categories tend to possess better if not more resources than the issue-orientated groups in the latter categories. They are also more likely to qualify as legitimate. At the same time these are not rigid dichotomies and there is considerable overlapping with groups in either category attempting to exert pressure at various target points in the political system.

The British studies are far from complacent. Finer warns of a 'closed circle', Potter of an 'inner circle',[42] Mackenzie of a 'new medievalism', and Blondel of the development of a 'corporate' state. The pluralist approach qualifies these views however. R. T. McKenzie reasons that 'it would be foolish to ignore evidence of a trend in this direction; equally foolish to ignore the countervailing forces'.[43] The concern is primarily with the groups that are included rather than those excluded. Typical of what passes for conventional wisdom is the following assessment: 'Most major groups have obtained not only recognition but by now their main objectives, usually as a result of political action over a period of time. Groups now direct their efforts largely towards day-to-day adjustments of their relations with government. . . .'[44] It is here that prevailing ideology both influences and limits description so it is necessary to look at the explanations and justifications of the pressure group world. This invites a less cautious approach than is the norm in British studies but it may be rewarding in so far as different aspects of the pressure group world are highlighted. The early empirical work was both inspired and inhibited by the secrecy that surrounds much of the workings of British politics. Moreover they made no pretence at being timeless.

Political scientists, let alone politicians, seldom describe the political process in terms of democratic pluralism and the label may even be consciously avoided because of the historical associations in Britain and its American connotations. Yet pluralist analyses and justifications are not difficult to uncover and are used in a number of ways. In the first place, notwithstanding the preceding remarks, the political system is increasingly viewed in a pluralist perspective. According to Richard Rose, 'The processes of policy are plural; in effect, government is a composite of political and social institutions.'[45] S. A. Walkland acknowledges the fragmentation as well as the integration of political power.[46] Beer's pluralist characterization of British politics is not restricted to the administrative process, while Peter Self, proceeding along similar lines, draws attention to the growing legitimacy of pluralist principles.[47]

In the second place, critical assessments of the pressure group world underscore the alternatives and counterbalances that act upon it. For W. J. M. Mackenzie there is the government determined to use its majority: 'it is this that still gives primacy to the party system and to the traditional doctrines of the constitution'.[48] Finer sees the pressure group world as an imperfect one where conflicting pressures and influences do occur but unequally. At the same time the sum of institutions, procedures and values acts as a corrective and counterbalance.[49] Where Finer is alarmed by secrecy Harry Eckstein is complacent for the democratic process supplies counterweights and countervailing forces. These will be activated where there is a concrete public interest: 'That, in any possible world, is all one can reasonably expect democratic machinery to do.'[50] Graeme Moodie and Gerald Studdert-Kennedy are more guarded. Within the pressure group world there is a plurality of groups and overlapping memberships but they recognize the limitations. More important are the restraints imposed by the political culture and the system of government.[51]

In the third place, as already mentioned, pluralism or

corporatism is invoked to describe the sponsor-client relationships between groups and government departments. Pluralist doctrine is not confined solely to that aspect of the pressure group world, however. Stewart, in his study of pressure at the parliamentary level, notes that a group exists in a world of groups and that 'the most powerful argument for or against a group is the attitude of another group'.[52] More explicit is the introduction to a special issue of *The Political Quarterly* (1958) devoted to pressure group studies which concludes: 'In short, groups give us today a genuinely pluralist society in all spheres and levels of government. And without pluralism we should indeed be helpless before the Great Leviathan'.[53]

Finally pluralism has been used as a democratic justification of the political system. John Plamenatz provides an outstanding example:

In a country which has been democratic for a considerable time and where there is general literacy, every section of the people is spoken for by some organization or other. The voice of the people is heard everlastingly, between elections much more even than at them, through these spokesmen; and their demands are not vague but precise. It is because there are elections from time to time that the precise demands continually made on the people's behalf are always listened to.[54]

The pluralist view of the pressure group world has been reinforced by changes in the political and ideological climate. The proliferation of pressure groups in post-war Britain is credited to the managed economy and the growth of the welfare state. Not only did this increase the need for sections of society to deal directly with the government but the government in turn became increasingly reliant upon organized interests for advice and cooperation. With the acceptance of a managed economy and the extension of the welfare state, the ideological divisions were seen to be narrowing. Politics was viewed as being more about interests and administration and less about principles and issues. This provided an ideological prop for administrative pluralism, or bluntly stated: 'Anyhow, who would take much interest in these transactions?'[55] It should be clear that this was not a denial of a conflict theory of politics as is sometimes claimed, for conflict is implicit in pressure group theory. Rather it was the substance of political conflict that was held to have changed, promoting some groups at the expense of others.

The growing faith in technocracy was equally reassuring. The technological means and knowledge were seen as available to plan for growth, prosperity, security and to mop up the marginal areas of deprivation. Again there was empirical evidence to support this version of consensus. The events of the late 1960s, with the increase in political militancy and direct action, were said to have 'shattered' consensus. Nothing so dramatic occurred. What was shattered was an ideologically biased view of consensus.[56] This was affirmed rather than negated by the further growth of pressure groups extending the range of issues formally articulated.

Perspective on the pressure group world is also shaped by the nature of research. Much of the work on British pressure groups was undertaken in the 1950s and suggests the influence of American political science. The study of American groups was well advanced both in theory and method and although the British work was hardly derivative it did draw on American experience. More directly there are the important contributions by American scholars. In so far as group theory has been discounted, it has been superseded by organizational theory which also encourages pluralist analysis. The more recent critiques do not seem to have made a similar impact. Instead radical critics have preferred class or elite analyses. This approach either relegates pressure groups to the periphery of political power or assumes that they are incorporated into a circle of influentials. The point is that the pressure group world is not treated as an entity so that the traditional justification, 'it works', stands fundamentally unchallenged.[57]

IV

The pressure group system works as long as the government and the political parties perceive and accept issues, but what is perceived and accepted may be influenced by ideological considerations. In other words, it works for some and not for others or it works better for some than for others in that access alone does not guarantee success but provides a head start. Moreover an issue and its resolution may not be accepted because the group that articulates it is unacceptable, that is, it fails to fulfil the more ideological criteria of legitimacy. The National Council for Civil Liberties, for example, is an organization which has progressively placed a high premium on hard research in order to gain legitimacy and thereby continuous access. Yet since their inception in the 1930s they have been regarded with hostility.[58] The situation is compounded by the NCCL's watchdog role and the need to remain representative of its clientele.[59] It is not just that the problems of legitimacy and access remain unresolved but that it has become crucial as the range of issues has increased. And these issues relate to those sections of the population whose resources, electoral and organizational, are limited.

One way of drawing attention to the problem would be to refine or replace the conventional pressure group typologies. The present vertical dichotomies of the pressure group world imply opportunity for access and influence for all groups. Pluralism is thereby vindicated. Efficacy is a matter of resources so that even if elite pluralism is undesirable from some standpoints, it is at least defensible on rational grounds. Moreover, the conventional model is proving inadequate to cope with the increasing number of articulated demands and the changes in political styles where the distinctions between political movements and pressure groups are becoming blurred. Granted that the prevailing vertical dichotomies were never intended to establish clear demarcations, the new groupings are hybrid in character. The action groups, service groups, welfare groups, minority groups, tenants' associations, buffer organizations, defence organizations, and dissident groups within established clienteles cannot comfortably be slotted into the sectional or promotional categories. More fundamentally they really do not slot in until issue recognition occurs and group status is achieved in terms of the accepted frame of reference. The issues raised may be more than matters of adjustment yet adjustments may have important political consequences.

One alternative would be to superimpose a horizontal stratification upon the vertical categories. This approach would focus on the elitist elements and indicate the extent to which the pressure group world like the broader one is one of privilege. For example, administrative pluralism would be seen more properly as a form of elite pluralism. At the same time it would convey the impression of a system that is more static and rigid than is actually the case. Where would Shelter be placed? Moreover, problems inherent in the vertical classification schemes would not be resolved. How would Shelter relate to the London Squatters campaign? If mobility is assumed it may be possible to chart how groups succeed or fail to gain legitimacy, what kinds of issues are accepted and on what basis, and what effect the process has on the nature and character of the groups.

Perhaps a more fruitful approach would modify both the macro and micro views of pressure groups. In place of a pressure group world commonly divided into two not very precise categorizations of clusterings of groups, a model based on three or possibly four worlds could be developed. Rather than viewing the pressure group world as one of three worlds of government a more complex universe would emerge where the patterns of power are more readily discernible. In other words, the exercise would be to locate the extent to which each world is plugged into the political system. What is lost in terms of precision as in the case of the three worlds of nations is gained in visibility.

The parallels that can be drawn with the system of international stratification are limited but suggestive. Three worlds do not imply associations or alliances nor do they imply uniformity or parity among groups. Within each world are groups whose relationships with the power structure, kinds of resources and world views are markedly similar. It is thereby possible to sketch the character of each world.

First world groups are interested in maintaining a balance of power while second world groups are not fundamentally concerned with altering it. There is no power struggle as exists between the first and second worlds. The nature of the third world of groups is more ambivalent. As with the third world it is more difficult to define. It is an expanding and transitional world. There is a populist element in that whether a group is representative rather than simply representing its clientele has consequences for third world groups. In this sense a group may have to demonstrate its legitimacy to its clientele as well as to the government and the criteria may well differ. A common denominator is the acceptance of the group process, however much the political system and the prevailing ideology is being challenged. Some groups strive for world pre-eminence which, in the present context, means membership in the first or second worlds. Success may transfer a group to another world but this does not have to be the case. Others neither aspire to first or second world status, demanding recognition in their own right. Consequently, there are groups that reject the power structure yet are dependent upon it and those that attempt to maintain a strict independence. Another clustering of groups could be described as colonial in so far as they are used by the government as buffer organizations. Within the first and second worlds there are groups with third world affinities. These include what could be described as guerilla movements operative within recognized groups where they may challenge the latter's legitimacy.

The first world, then, includes groups, whether interest or promotional, whose access to the decision-makers is continuous, resources impressive, legitimacy established, and whose demands are considered to be mainly routine. Some can, and indeed do, impose commanding constraints but when acting as pressure groups it is in their interests to maintain rather than to disturb the balance of power. The CBI and the TUC are outstanding examples.

For second world groups access is more or less accepted although it is likely to be intermittent. Resources are varied yet limited relative to first world groups. They tend to be issue-orientated and engender opposition but the balance of power is only marginally affected. Second world groups accept and further consensus. Examples are to be found among the social reform groups which experienced considerable success when the Labour Party was in office in the 1960s.[60] Some of the groups establish sponsor-client relations and more properly belong in the first world while others are successful in mobilizing support at the parliamentary level. Considerable attention has been devoted to these groups which may be less important politically than some of those in the third world.

The third world, as already indicated, is more amorphous. The degree to which these groups are recognized varies widely and access is likely to be sporadic. At the same time the groups tend to be highly active and at different levels of the political system. Many cannot meet the requisites for legitimacy and even when they do they remain suspect. Consequently, militancy is an important resource. It is not just a matter of issue recognition, poverty is not denied for example, but of establishing its priority and promoting its resolution. Since the ultimate satisfaction of their demands may involve a radical re-structuring of society and the re-ordering of priorities they challenge or threaten the balance of power. An atlas would be needed to chart the range of issues, forms and activities of third world groups.

There is a propensity for third world groups to be radical in ideology and militant in tactics. Neither social protest nor social service is new to British political development nor restricted to the third world. The recent burgeoning of issues and groups is as much the product of modernization, the welfare state and their ideological justifications as are the first and second world groups. The third world is also a response to the political universe and the other pressure group worlds. It is less a matter that demands are inadequately articulated or on occasion violently expressed than why this is the case.

The model pays tribute to the plurality of groups but this cannot be equated with democratic pluralism. There exists a third world separate and unequal and the gaps between the worlds may well increase. Beyond this it may be worth while to include a fourth world of unarticulated demands and for that matter articulated but unsuccessful claims to account for third world drop-outs. The model can be used to draw attention to the degrees of exclusion and exclusiveness, privilege and underprivilege and to a universe that is defensive and resistant. In the final analysis it is not the model that counts but the power structure and its ideological underpinnings.

NOTES AND REFERENCES

1. Vol. 12 (New York, Macmillan and the Free Press, 1968), pp. 164-8.

2. *The Decline of American Pluralism* (Stanford, Calif., Stanford University Press, 1961); *The Promise of Politics* (Englewood Cliffs, New Jersey, Prentice-Hall, 1966).

3. An outstanding exception is Trevor Smith, *Anti-Politics* (London, Charles Knight, 1972); British writers have tended to treat the pluralist debate as one of

industrial society more generally or pertaining more particularly to the United States. See T. B. Bottomore, *Elites and Society* (Harmondsworth, Penguin, 1966); Ralph Miliband, *The State in Capitalist Society* (London, Weidenfeld, 1969); Frank Parkin, *Class Inequality and Political Order* (London, MacGibbon & Kee, 1971); Geraint Parry, *Political Elites* (London, Allen & Unwin, 1969).

4. Theodore J. Lowi, *The End of Liberalism* (New York, Norton, 1969), p. 84.

5. 'American Business, Public Policy, Case-Studies, and Political Theory', *World Politics*, Vol. XVI, No. 4 (July 1964), p. 686; see also William E. Connolly, *Political Science and Ideology* (New York, 1967), p. 30; Peter Bachrach and Morton R. Baratz, 'The Two Faces of Power', *American Political Science Review*, Vol. XVI, No. 4 (December 1962), p. 947; W. J. M. Mackenzie, *Politics and Social Science* (Harmondsworth, Penguin, 1967), pp. 231-4.

6. Robert A. Dahl, *A Preface to Democratic Theory* (University of Chicago Press, 1963) represents perhaps the most interesting example because of its celebrations and reservations; for a discussion and critique of the contemporary influence of No. 10 see George D. Beam, *Usual Politics* (New York, Holt, Rinehart, 1970).

7. For a discussion of the influence of Alexis de Tocqueville see William E. Connolly, 'The Challenge to Pluralist Theory' in William E. Connolly (ed.), *The Bias of Pluralism* (New York, Aldine, 1969), pp. 3-34; British writers have drawn attention to John C. Calhoun's *Disquisition on Government*. See A. H. Birch, *Representation* (London, Macmillan, 1971), pp. 84-6; S. E. Finer, *Anonymous Empire*, 2nd edn. (London, Pall Mall Press, 1966).

8. For the countervailing power model see John Kenneth Galbraith, *American Capitalism* (Harmondsworth, Penguin, 1963); for veto groups see David Reisman *et al.*, *The Lonely Crowd* (New Haven, Yale University Press, 1950, 1953).

9. Lowi, *The End of Liberalism*, op. cit., p. 74.

10. Reprinted (Bloomington, Indiana, Principia Press, 1949; New York, 1951); *American Political Science Review*, Vol. XLVI, No. 2 (June 1952), pp. 376-97.

11. C. Wright Mills, *The Power Elite* (Oxford University Press, 1956); Robert Dahl, *Who Governs?* (New Haven, Yale University Press, 1961).

12. See the more radical critiques in Philip Green and Sanford Levinson (eds), *Power and Community* (New York, Pantheon, 1970) and Marvin Surkin and Alan Wolfe (eds), *An End to Political Science* (New York, Basic Books, 1970).

13. See the citation for the Woodrow Wilson Foundation award for *Who Governs?* Quoted in Kariel, *The Promise of Politics*, op. cit., p. 109.

14. See William Kornhauser, *The Politics of Mass Society* (London, Routledge, 1960); Arnold Rose, *The Power Structure* (Oxford University Press, 1967).

15. See Zbigniew Brzezinski and Samuel P. Huntington, *Political Power: U.S.A./U.S.S.R.* (New York, Viking Press, 1966).

16. 'It is amazing and distressing how many 1930s left-wing liberals have become 1960s interest group liberals out of a concern for instability.' Theodore Lowi, 'The Public Philosophy: Interest-Group Liberalism', *American Political Science Review*, Vol. LXI, No. 1 (March 1967), p. 24.

17. *The Theory of Democratic Elitism* (University of London Press, 1967), p. 32; see also Grant McConnell, *Private Power and American Democracy* (New York, Knopf, 1966), pp. 352-3; Parry, op. cit., p. 152; Democracy and elites have been squared on other grounds. See Bottomore, op. cit., p. 113.

18. The most prestigious proponent has been Robert Dahl. In addition to the works already cited see his introductory text, *Pluralist Democracy in the United States* (Chicago, Rand McNally, 1967). As W. J. M. Mackenzie notes the introductory course at many American universities is seen as part of the process of citizenship training. *The Study of Political Science Today* (London, Macmillan, 1971), p. 32.

19. Truman's group analysis is also an interpretation of American democracy.

See *The Process of Government*, op. cit. and 'The American System in Crisis', *Political Science Quarterly*, Vol. 74, No. 4 (December 1959), pp. 481-97.

20. See Robert A. Dahl, *A Preface to Democratic Theory* (Chicago, Phoenix, 1956, 1963); N. W. Polsby, *Community Power and Political Theory* (New Haven, Yale University Press, 1963).

21. Truman gives the game away when he revises his position to emphasize the guardian role of elites, 'The American System in Crisis', op. cit. The events of March 1968 when members of the liberal establishment intervened to curtail plans to escalate the Vietnam War add credibility to Truman's thesis if the view of one observer is correct. Townsend Hoopes, *The Limits of Intervention* (New York, McKay, 1969).

22. Perhaps the most eloquent as well as the most often cited expression of this criticism is found in E. E. Schattschneider's *The Semi-Sovereign People* (New York, Holt, Rinehart, 1960), pp. 30, 35.

23. For example, Robert Paul Wolff, 'Beyond Tolerance' in Robert Paul Wolff, Barrington Moore, Jr. and Herbert Marcuse, *A Critique of Pure Tolerance* (Boston, Beacon Press, 1965), pp. 43-6; Wayne A. R. Leys, 'Ethics in American Business and Government: The Confused Issues', *The Annals of the American Academy of Political and Social Science*, Vol. 378 (July 1968), pp. 34-44; Kariel, *The Promise of Politics*, op. cit.

24. See Philip Green, 'Science, Government, and the Case of Rand—A Singular Pluralism', *World Politics*, Vol. XX, No. 2 (1968), pp. 301-26; *Deadly Logic* (Ohio State University Press, 1966), Ch. 7.

25. McConnell, op. cit.; See also John Kenneth Galbraith, *The New Industrial State* (Harmondsworth, Penguin Books, 1969).

26. See Theodore Lowi's 'The Iron Law of Decadence', *The Politics of Disorder* (New York, Basic Books, 1971); see also Donald A. Schon, *Beyond the Stable State* (London, Temple Smith, 1971).

27. Lowi provides one of the most sophisticated statements of this position. *The End of Liberalism*, op. cit., p. 88.

28. Ibid., Ch. 3; 'American Business, Public Policy, Case-Studies, and Political Theory', op. cit., p. 681; Robert S. Lynd, 'Power in American Society as Resource and Problem' in Arthur Kornhauser (ed.), *Problems of American Democracy* (Detroit, 1957), p. 30. There are also various cultural and psychological barriers. Schattschneider refers to these as the 'mobilization of bias', op. cit., p. 71; Bachrach and Baratz recognize them as a 'face of power', op. cit., pp. 47-52; see also Parry, op. cit., p. 130. These may also act as restraints on legitimated groups.

29. D. G. MacRae, '1843 and All That', *New Society* (25 November 1971).

30. A. H. Birch, *Representative and Responsible Government* (London, Allen & Unwin, 1964); Samuel Beer, *Modern British Politics*, 2nd edn. (London, Faber, 1969).

31. See also Harry Eckstein, *Pressure Group Politics* (London, 1960), p. 24.

32. This may be more apparent than real not only in the trade union movement but on the industry side. See Beer, op. cit., pp. 421-4 or read the newspaper.

33. *Organized Groups in British National Politics* (London, 1961), Chs. 11, 12.

34. Peter Self and Herbert J. Storing describe the National Farmers Union as functioning almost as 'an arm of the state', *The State and the Farmer* (London, Allen & Unwin, 1962); S. E. Finer remarks that 'a close relationship tends to become a closed one', *Anonymous Empire*, op. cit.; see also Eckstein, op. cit.

35. 'Pressure Groups in British Government', *British Journal of Sociology*, Vol. VI, No. 2 (June 1955), p. 218.

36. Finer, op. cit.

37. Potter, op. cit., p. 241.

38. *British Pressure Groups* (Oxford University Press, 1958), p. 244; Beer, op. cit., p. 70.

39. 'The Confederation of British Industry', *Political Studies*, Vol. XIV, No. 4 (December 1971), p. 415.

40. Ibid., p. 409; see also S. E. Finer, 'The Federation of British Industries', *Political Studies*, Vol. 4, No. 1 (February 1956), pp. 61-84.

41. J. Blondel, *Voters, Parties, and Leaders* (Harmondsworth, Penguin, 1963), Ch. 6; Graeme C. Moodie and Gerald Studdert-Kennedy, *Opinions, Publics and Pressure Groups* (London, Allen & Unwin, 1970), Ch. 5; R. T. McKenzie divides groups into three vertical categories: sectional, promotional and all other groups. 'Parties, Pressure Groups and the British Political Process', revised for Robert Benewick and Robert E. Dowse, *Readings on British Politics and Government* (University of London Press, 1968), pp. 144-5.

42. 'British Pressure Groups', *Parliamentary Affairs*, Vol. IX, No. 4 (autumn 1956), p. 422.

43. R. T. McKenzie, op. cit., p. 149.

44. S. A. Walkland, *The Legislative Process in Britain* (London, Allen & Unwin, 1968), p. 35.

45. Richard Rose, *Politics in England* (London, Faber, 1965), p. 213.

46. Walkland, op. cit.

47. Beer, op. cit., Chs. XI, XII; 'Administrative Democracy', *New Society* (24 February 1972), pp. 389-91.

48. 'Pressure Groups in British Government', op. cit., p. 146; see also R. T. McKenzie, op. cit., pp. 149-50.

49. *Anonymous Empire*, op. cit., p. 111 and Ch. 9.

50. Eckstein, op. cit., p. 161.

51. Moodie and Studdert-Kennedy, op. cit., p. 72.

52. Stewart, op. cit., p. 43.

53. 'Pressure Groups in Britain' in *The Political Quarterly*, Vol. 29, No. 1 (January-March 1958), p. 4.

54. 'Electoral Studies and Democratic Theory. I. A British View', *Political Studies*, Vol. VI, No. 1 (February 1958), p. 9.

55. Eckstein, op. cit., p. 158.

56. See Robert Benewick and Trevor Smith (eds.), *Direct Action and Democratic Politics* (London, Allen & Unwin, 1972).

57. 'The justification for trade associations acting in a representative capacity is that, on the whole, it works.' Sir Norman Kipling, Director General of the FBI, 'Letter', *The Times* (15 January 1953). Kariel cites a similar justification for American pluralism, *The Promise of Politics*, op. cit.

58. Compare police submissions to the Cabinet in the 1930s (Mepol. 2/3089. Public Records Office) with a review of Michael King, *Bail or Custody* (Cobden Trust, 1971), quoted in *NCCL Bulletin*, January 1972, No. 1, p. 6 or the attitudes of the Northumberland Constabulary, *The Times* (17 June 1972).

59. The problem is being studied in depth in a forthcoming history of the NCCL by Robert Benewick.

60. See especially Peter G. Richards, *Parliament and Conscience* (London, Allen & Unwin, 1970).

Against Federalism

PRESTON KING

INTRODUCTION

It happens surprisingly frequently that a writer elaborates upon extracts from others, entirely refutes them, and then reaches a conclusion which he or she supposes to be startlingly contrary to the view confuted, and which yet, in all essentials, remains the same. Ernest Barker turned against corporatism or pluralism; what he turned to he called polyarchism. M. P. Follet turned against pluralism; what she turned to was 'federalism'. But pluralism, polyarchism and federalism, taken as ideologies, are in essentials much the same. Follet slightly exaggerated the pluralist position, and then came to a conclusion which she shared with traditional pluralists.

'The political pluralists,' Follet wrote, 'believing that a collective and distributive sovereignty cannot exist together, throw overboard collective sovereignty. [But] when they accept the compounding of consciousness taught by their own master, James, they will see that true Hegelianism finds its actualized form in federalism.'[1] Most writers whom we might designate as pluralists, however, do not 'throw overboard collective sovereignty'. Further, they all tend to espouse federalism as the magical institutionalization of the many-in-one.

It is as easy (or as difficult) to call writers like Otto von Gierke, J. N. Figgis, Hugo Knabbe and H. J. Laski federalists as it is to call any of them pluralists. The counter-argument to the doctrine of sovereignty, in the practical sphere, was usually assumed to consist in the fact that federal states were tenable, were 'working' propositions: they displayed an effective authority that was highly diffused. The advocates of federalism, including individuals as diverse as Alexis de Tocqueville, Pierre-Joseph Proudhon, John Calhoun, James Bryce, Edward Freeman, and Sobei Mogi, usually did not understand it only as a constitutional mechanism, but also as an end; not merely as a practical (and sometimes the only possible) means of achieving unity, but sometimes as the ideal means of realizing liberty in order. These statements, clearly, will not hold in equal degree for each writer cited, but they are generally accurate. What they are intended to suggest is that the favour which was and is frequently bestowed upon an abstract understanding of federalism, derives from the supposition that federalism, as such, is good, the embodiment of institutional liberty, and is thus to be attained for itself alone. Seen in this light, federalism assumes an ideological character quite like pluralism or liberalism (or, as in different families of ideas, like conservatism, fascism or communism); in this form it projects not merely statements of fact, but a universally desirable state of being.

The Federalist Papers (1788) start less as a doctrine than as a technique to achieve a specific end; if they are universalist the universalism is mute (at least) to the point of being moot. But by the time we reach Proudhon's *Le principe fédératif* (1863), we are afloat in very different waters; Proudhon has swept us out into a sea of doctrine. He is discussing federalism, not federation. And he promotes it as Plato promotes 'forms' or More 'Utopia' or Moore the 'Good'. There is, it need scarcely be said, a strict affiliation between the ideal of political federalism and that of economic federalism; and between both of these and philosophical pluralism. If we were arbitrarily to divide the latter into political, economic, and legal aspects, the most convenient terms we could apply to them would probably be federalism, syndicalism, and 'pluralism' (in that order). Thus, federalist ideology need not be seen as being *different* from pluralism, but merely as relating to a distinct aspect of pluralism. In what follows we shall treat federalism as a form of pluralism, the evolution of which we shall try to set against the history of institutional fact which emerges out of and interacts with federal ideology; not to demonstrate the validity of a puratively universal federal principle, but to show something of the quite limited and time-bound conditions underlying the principle; not so much to elaborate upon *federalism* as upon *federation*.

The influence of federalism (as a pluralism) justifies a brief attempt to portray it as a historical phenomenon rather than as a philosophical panacea, a synonym for justice and liberty (liberty itself being often mistaken for justice). Although federalism is (and rightly) associated in general with certain liberal assumptions, federation, despite this, is historically nothing more in itself than an institutional device, which (like all such devices) may be used as a means indifferent to ends, or as a means which promotes the wrong ends. The historical roots of federation go considerably deeper than the American Revolution; as a principle, it can be made to transcend the notion of co-ordinate spheres of power. Federation might best be understood in terms of the problems to which it has constituted a set of historically varying answers.

If we understand the problems, the understanding of structure more clearly follows. The governments of the United States, Switzerland, Canada, Australia and South Africa were all established (in that order) as federations, but they all differ significantly in structure. If we start from their problems, we can understand why the Swiss paid little attention to the separation of powers theory, by contrast with the Americans who were most attentive thereto; why Canada became fairly highly centralized, and South Africa far more so—by contrast with Australia, which is still characterized by considerable local autonomy.

Although Professor Greaves is right in suggesting that federal states should not be regarded 'as a mere stage in the growth of a unitary state',[2] and thus that they are not necessarily evanescent, it is nevertheless true that they have tended to evolve (where they have survived) towards increasing integration. The facts support Henry Sidgwick's observation that 'federalism arising from historical causes is likely to be in many cases a transitional stage through which a composite society passes on the way to completer union', although his explanation of this phenomenon, which he gives as follows, is not particularly incisive: 'As time goes on, and mutual intercourse grows, the narrower, patriotic sentiments that were originally a bar to full political union tend to diminish, while the inconvenience of a diversity of laws is more keenly felt, especially in a continuous territory.'³ What he says is often true, but not always (as Sidgwick admits by his qualification: in *many* cases); and where it is true, it is not the whole truth. Switzerland does not appear to be dramatically moving away from her federal structure; thus it would be difficult to refer to this structure as a recognizably transitional stage to something different. In the United States, further, as in Nigeria, it was most significantly a civil war—rather than a gradual wearing down of patriotic sentiments, etc.—which forced upon local or statist separatism the character of a transitional stage toward 'completer union'. It remains true, nevertheless, not only that federation has been a transitional stage toward an integrated polity in many cases, but that (where the federal structure has survived) it has been so in most cases.

Although federations have often been formed as aspects of the disintegration of a larger union (as, for example, the British Empire), their evolution (or at least their establishment) is in itself integrative as well as disintegrative. The establishment of a federation in itself represents an attempt at union, in some fashion, at some level, and in regard to certain purposes. Once established, and on the assumption that other things remain equal (which is a purely formal assumption that may not be justified in any given set of circumstances) the tendency has been (and probably will be) for federations to move toward greater integration, conceived in terms of an extension of central authority. But there is nothing in the nature of things to prevent the collapse of a federation; the only relevant point being that such a collapse must run wholly contrary to what the proponents of the federation initially sought to achieve. Finally, the expression 'completer union' has no specific content; or, to put it differently, its content is variable, depending on the degree of unity with which the federation begins. To extend the territorial authority of the central government does not mean that a polity is moving toward an abstract ideal (or ordeal) of 'unity'; for this extension may merely prove to be a compensatory measure to cope with the increasing technological and industrial complexities (involving a vast proliferation of quasi-independent authorities) that are characteristic of modern life and that affirm the relative absence of anything that even approximates to 'total' central control. The essential historical point about federations is that, in the classical cases of formation, they have involved (from the perspective of the new federal centre) an attempt to establish (not to weaken) some degree of unity between *territorial* units which would otherwise be regarded as mutually independent (except perhaps from a broader, imperial point of view).

CONTRACT: GOVERNMENTAL AND SOCIAL

Federal government is usually conceived to be democratic government. It is thought to respond to a demand for particularity and individuality. It is often conceived as a means of inhibiting the growth of power, and even occasionally as a means of destroying power. It may be conceived as a means of making order compatible with power's destruction; or as a means of reconciling as little government as possible with as much autonomy as possible.

Behind such notions as these lies the idea of social contract, which implies rationality, good will, an ultimate principle of Natural Law; that the people must, of their own accord, agree to bind themselves together; that harmony results from reason, which has made the compact possible.

Natural-Law theory, in so far as embodied in the work of Languet, Locke, Harrington and Sydney, *inter alia*, really served to promote a revolutionary cause. It served to establish the right of the people (at least the merchant and industrial classes) to participate in government. It also, quite significantly, sanctioned (usually) the protection of property from governmental confiscation, and suggested that government's essential purpose lay in securing the rights of property-owners. Following this theory, when such 'rights' were violated, as, for example, by excessive or arbitrary taxation, government lost its title to office and could be justifiably removed. The essence of politics, the purpose of government, was to protect interests.

Contract theory has a long history. But as Ernest Barker has suggested, it is with St Thomas Aquinas 'that the theory of Contract is finally hatched'.[4] Aquinas serves as a support to the Divine Hooker. And the latter's influence upon Locke is direct. Contract Theory has been used equally, of course, by 'absolutists' (such as Hobbes) as well as by 'pluralists' and 'liberals'. Historically, however, it has been the distinctive weapon in the liberal-pluralist arsenal; it has been the primary instrument, however blunt and unwieldy, used against the abuse of power. It was used by Languet in the *Vindiciae contra Tyrannos* (1579) in defending the Huguenots. It was used by Althusius in the *Politica methodice digesta* (1603); by the Jesuits Suarez (*Tractatus de legibus*, 1613) and Mariana (*De rege et regis institutione*, 1599); by Natural Law theorists from Grotius and Pufendorf to Fichte and Kant; by Proudhon, Renouvier (*Science de la Morale*, 1869), Spencer (*Man versus the State*, 1884) and numberless others.

The compact may be considered in two ways:

1. As a means of establishing society generally.
2. As a means of establishing government in particular.

The history of contract in modern times starts in the sixteenth century. It does not appear, first, as a social contract, and next as a contract of government; the historical order of these two forms of contract—as is well known—is reversed. The later *social* contract presupposes a state of nature (as in Hobbes and Rousseau) in which persons confront one another as strict individuals and out of which they create a social order.

The earlier contract of government merely asserts that government is established by a community (already existent) and that, where the government violates recognized rules of conduct, it can legitimately be removed by the community. All theories of contract, however, cannot be decisively sorted out into these categories, and many writers, like Locke, use both.

FEDERALISM QUA CONTRACTUALISM

The theory or doctrine of federalism grows out of both types of contract. In contract theory, whether governmental or social, one begins either from an individual, or from a community, who represent or constitute certain interests. If the contract is governmental, the assumption is that certain rights naturally attach to the people (which may be understood as a mass of individuals or as distinct groups, like the church or family and so on) and that the established government has a duty to protect these rights; indeed, that the purpose envisaged by the 'people' in granting authority to government is that it should protect these rights (whether to life, civil liberty, property, or otherwise). Thus, protection of one kind or another constitutes the popular interest in government, and to the extent that it is provided (and not withdrawn), to that extent is the government legitimate (i.e. really based upon popular consent 'originally' or implicitly given). If the contract is social—which it will tend to become (as in Hobbes) when the corporate structure of society (or the view of society as being so structured) deteriorates, so that the basic social unit comes increasingly to be viewed as the individual rather than the group (such as the family, etc.)— then it is no longer the 'people' as a corporate unit, or as a plurality of corporate units, that is conceived to bear an interest, or interests, or to have attached to it a right or rights: it is merely the individual who bears rights, and whose interests are ultimate and irrevocable. Thus, the difference between social and governmental contracts primarily relates to the different loci of interests or rights involved. If we have a contract where groups are considered as bearers of rights, then the protection of their interests is ultimate; and where the interest of groups is ultimate, this must imply relative autonomy and self-containment *vis-à-vis* other groups within the society, including the state as the protective agency. Where individuals, however, come to be viewed as possessing ultimate rights, the rights of groups as such tend to disappear, for they can only be legitimated by reference to the more ultimate rights possessed by individuals.

Federal theory relates to both governmental and social contracts, since both dictate a hard core (whether the individual, church, province or otherwise) of interest and of right to be protected. The individual or the group yields a certain degree of autonomy in order to acquire a certain degree of protection; each concedes obedience to government in return for protection of certain rights and interests. Federalism is more intimately related to the earlier (the governmental) than to the later (the social) theory of contract in so far as it assumes that the basic, interest-bearing units within the federation are territorial (the states, provinces or whatever): the interests of these units could be represented (as in the USA) in a separate deliberative chamber (e.g. the Senate). At the same time, federalism is more intimately related to the social than to the governmental contract in the degree that it assumes that individuals are the ultimate right- and interest-bearing units in so far as the direct operations of the federal (central) government are concerned. (This means that a federal government, while operating within its sphere, deals directly—in taxation, imprisonment, etc.— with all individuals where their activities fall under its control, rather than with them through their state or provincial legislatures.) One can construe federal arrangements to mean that both individuals and groups have—within the federal polity— specific rights and interests, which it is the duty of this polity to protect. In contract theory generally, where private rights (individual or group) are infringed, the duty of obedience—at some indeterminate point—ceases to be binding. The difficulty with federal (or any other) forms of government is that if the *individual* protests (an infringement of his civil rights, for example) he cannot effectively withstand the government *qua* individual, except, perhaps, by flight. The further difficulty specific to federal arrangements is that if the *group* (i.e. state or province) protests (an infringement of some aspect of its legitimate autonomy), it, too, is unlikely to be able to stand up to the central government, except, perhaps, by secession. But if it secedes, such secession makes it simultaneously impossible for federal citizens (i.e. those resident in the defector zone) to perform their specific duties of obedience to the central government.

Contract theory arises out of a situation where law is highly respected, even revered. The theory is convenient, despite many logical and historical defects, because it permits men (who are not content with the *status quo*) to contend that in breaking an actual law they are really upholding an original law—the law of contract. But contract theory is not supposed in fact to be an actual part of the law by those who appeal to it, but to be *implicit* in the law. Thus the overthrow of a tyrant is legal in so far as his tyranny is illegal—in so far as he has done the contrary of, or has merely omitted to do what by implication was, his duty. In federal systems, however, an attempt is made to reduce the range of these implications and to state precisely what the rights and duties of individual, local, and central units are to be. Thus the formal importance of a document (which is almost intended to represent Natural Law) that stands above and defines the spheres of operation of the machinery of government. This document will generally advance the rights of individuals and the duties either of the central or of the local government. If the document states the duties of the central government, it will generally be contended that all remaining or residual duties rebound to the local governments; if local government duties are stated, it may be contended that all residual duties redound to the central government. There may, of course, be compromises between these two positions. But the basic assumption, whatever the compromise position, would be that both individual and *territorial* units (as opposed, for example, to the merely professional or functional units in corporatism) constitute vested interests which, beyond some point, cannot be infringed. If the individual rebels, in consequence of a violation of his rights, there is little chance that he will succeed; in any event, his rebellion, even if successful, need not prejudice the continuation of the local-central relationship. If the territorial unit rebels, however, there may be a greater chance of success; and the rebellion, if successful, automatically puts an end to the relationship between the central government and the citizens of the rebellious territory.

Thus, if federalism truly represents *co-ordinate* spheres of authority, with the central government autonomously operating within one jurisdiction and the local governments within another, this must imply that each has final say in regard to what is done under its own separate sphere of control. (1) If the central government can, in fact, overrule the local governments; or (2) if the local governments can secede from the central government; then in neither case does one espy truly co-ordinate spheres of authority. In the first case, this is obvious. But it is also true in the second case; for here, secession means not merely that the local government has overruled the central government's control over the local territorial unit; it has equally voided the possibility of the central government exercising any control over the citizen-members of that unit. The central government would no longer control the local government in any respect—thus losing one leg of its power—

and it would also no longer control the citizens of the local (non-central) government in any respect; and this would be the only leg of central power left standing.

If federal government were based on the assumption that local and central governments were equally supreme and final *within their respective spheres*, then this would entail that the union was merely a treaty arrangement, i.e. a confederation. The reason why federal governments are generally not regarded as confederations is only because they have generally not admitted in practice any right of local secession, which is really the only ultimate weapon of self-protection that an independent territorial unit can have. Further, this right cannot logically be admitted in so far as the central government claims not only to be dealing with interest-bearing territorial units, but also with interest- and right-bearing individual units. The central government may conceivably admit of a right of a local unit within a certain sphere to have final say; but if there is a dispute and the effectiveness of the local decision can only be affirmed through secession, this automatically leads to conflict over the control of citizens. Thus, given the possibility of a dispute over jurisdiction (which is always present) the central government can never logically concede to local governments a truly final say within some broad sphere of interest, without at the same time conceding to them the ultimate right of secession; and to concede that right is to grant that a local unit may unilaterally void the allegiance of the central government's citizens (or subjects).

Thus, federal structures may be loosely built, but they are not built so loosely as to incorporate a *right* of secession. Instead, it will be enjoined that disputes be adjudicated by a central judicial body; and where that happens, the ultimate, formal right of decision-making lies with a federal court, and inasmuch as that is so, even ultimate control of its allotted sphere cannot be viewed as a matter of purely local prerogative. Here, then, the doctrine of federalism conflicts with the fact of federation. Federalism, as a derivative (like corporatism and syndicalism) of contract theory, often asserts the indefensibility of rights possessed both by individuals and by territorial groups. But federation, while admitting (sometimes) the theoretical validity of this position, at the same time secures that the ultimate decisions about what these rights are, and how they are to be interpreted, lies with an organ of the central government.

This fact of federal supremacy does not leave much room for an effective theory of balance. Of course, no central government anywhere has total power. The entire idea (as I have suggested elsewhere) may, indeed, be logically self-contradictory (i.e. how can a limited agent wield unlimited control?). Some central governments have much, others little, some virtually no power. The result of the contrary pulling of diverse individuals, groups, and interests may, of course, be viewed in terms of a balance. But this is to play fast and loose with language. A balance may imply a harmony, not only between equals, but also between unequals. One may have a 'natural harmony' between supply and demand when there is a great deal of the first and little of the second (and vice versa). One may find the same when there is much political power at the centre or virtually none. 'Harmony', 'balance', etc. not only obtain between one 'free' man and another, but also between master and slave. To say that a federal structure involves a balance of power may, in some tautological sense, be true. But to the extent that this is true of federal governments it is true of all governments. If 'balance of power' implies any effective equality between central and local governments then this is rarely true of working federations anywhere. In the notion of balance, we confront again something of the difference between the theory of federalism and the fact of federation.

In later versions of the theory of social contract—as in Herbert Spencer—the individual is canonized, The idea of the good is perfect liberty; evil is subjection to central or governmental authority. Such views of contract, whether evoked on the political left or right, suggest (given the mushrooming evils which fall out from power) that the ideal government is one where a minimum of authority is reconciled to a sufficiency of social justice. From the notion that Natural Law places a moral limit on the uses of power, we evolve toward the notion (given the demise of Natural Law) that protection against authority only resides in the division and balance of groups (so that the limits placed upon the abuse of power become more institutional than moral). Natural Law may not effectively place a check upon the abuse of power (since it merely constitutes a moral principle that may be readily violated); but the non-existence of power itself, or at least the reduction and division of it, is assumed necessarily to diminish *pari passu* the possibility of its abuse. Thus we approach the notion that there must be little power, and that what there is must be spread out. The balance between *individual* representation (e.g. the U.S. House of Representatives) and territorial *corporate* representation (e.g. the U.S. Senate); and the balance between the legislature, executive and judiciary may be interpreted, and were in a degree intended, to demonstrate or embody some ideal notion of a division or balance of power. The effort to diminish power results in some notion of countervailing forces. One force checks another. The power of one legal corporation places a limit upon the extent of power of another. In Montesquieu's interpretation of the English Constitution, we find the first significant statement of a separation of powers theory, ante-dating the American constitution. Other, but usually less famed, writers, such as Althusius, Grotius, Pufendorf and Locke, offered much the same kind of political analysis of balance long before 1748 and *The Spirit of the Laws*. Most of them presented some notion of overlapping associations, all fairly independent of one another and based on consent, as a clue both to how society or government *was* organized and as to how it *should be* organized.

Federalism, then, constitutes essentially an ideology of political pluralism sometimes conceived not merely on a geographical basis, but more generally in regard to political function. What is basic to it is the belief that power is evil, that protection against it is only to be found in a notion of balance, of division, of the reduction of power to smaller corporate units or to individuals. This doctrine of balance, it is clear, together with the practical experience of popular rule, had a considerable influence upon the American experiment.

FEDERATION QUA EVOLVING TECHNIQUE

For the federal constitution-makers of 1787, the idea of balance was doubtless fairly important. But the institutions which they concocted were scarcely copied from the ideal represented by this notion. Their negotiations did, of course, betray ample reasonableness and compromise. The American Constitution, in fact, was a result of compromise straight down the line, on the question of representation and its character (resulting in a bicameral legislative network), on the question of civil rights (involving the later addition of a Bill of Rights to the original Constitution), on the question of the western territories (resulting in their surrender to the central government, the latter to assume responsibility for their settlement), on the questions of slavery and presidential powers. These compromises, although partly intended (both consciously and unconsciously) to serve as an institutional expression of liberal doctrines, were also, and quite directly, intended to resolve certain outstanding difficulties which the looser confederal arrangements (established immediately following the close of the war against Britain) had been unable to meet. The most crucial of these difficulties involved, naturally, external defence and internal order (troubled by events like Shay's rebellion) as well as fiscal and other problems. Federation, in short, was a novel technique adopted with a view to making a stronger central government compatible with the retention of considerable independence by the component state units. American federation, from a 'pluralistic' point of view, was only really novel by virtue of its establishment, within the central government, of a strict division between the executive and the legislature, and the establishment of a separate representative body for the territorial state units.

The constitutional structure of federations has tended to be rigid. This is partly explained by their contractualist foundations. Federations generally demand (sometimes legitimately) a complicated legal structure; but these may be occasionally intended in an obvious way as an *a priori* defence against the power of government and even as an obstacle to its expansion; so that the mode of transforming the structure of government to suit the changing and expanding needs of the citizenry may become difficult and roundabout; from which derives the very great importance of judicial review in federal constitutions, of judge-made law, in short, and the never-ceasing dispute about the appropriateness of it.

Federal structures have often leaned toward a cramping legalism. In this connection, it is appropriate to speak primarily

of federation in America, because the American was the first
significant experiment of a federal as opposed to a confederal
kind, and set an example for the Swiss (1848) and for later
experiments. In so far as federation was, or may today be
intended, to promote particular liberal ends (federalism), and
in so far as it was or is intended to make consent in government
viable (by creating impossible complications in the governing
process), it may easily defeat these very ends. American bi-
cameralism and the duality of presidential and congressional
roles have often created tremendous difficulties (although
decreasingly) for a stable policy and for the promulgation
of one which might be made meaningful to a national electorate.

American federation, however, was not a complete expression
of federalism, of doctrine. Far from it. Charles Beard's work[5]
provides a sharp corrective for those who tend to view federalism
idealistically. His work is not without its faults and many regard
it as excessively economic in its interpretation of the American
Constitution. But the minimal point of importance, which
Beard conclusively affirmed, was that the American federal
structure represents more of a response to specific interests and
problems than it does a general ideological desire to achieve an
abstract balance or liberty. Nevertheless, the federal structure
would, of course, tend to be defended doctrinally to the extent
that interests (as, for example, Southern interests) were pre-
judiced by the subsequent tightening of the federal structure
(thus the doctrine of states' rights).

The Americans had first, in 1781, tried confederation. This
was an ordinary kind of arrangement that was usual enough
and as ineffective as it was usual. But confederation, which
implied contractual agreements between heads of state, or
simply between states, as opposed to their members, was the
kind of political order which theorists who were interested
in governmental pluralism had written about prior to the
American experiment. The Federalist Papers created a new
interest.[6] About 100,000 out of 160,000 voters approved the
new constitution which these essays were written to defend.
The Constitution was based upon a modified conception of co-
ordinate spheres of government, one local, the other central,
both 'equally' sovereign and independent, but performing

different functions, demanding allegiance from all members of the federal community when these entered either or both governments' sphere of jurisdiction.

This separation of central and local, with the expansion of industry, the development of rapid communication and transport, the tremendous increase of population and specialization, has become more and more unreal. In recognition of this unreality, the central government, both by legislation and by action of the judiciary, has gone far toward dismantling the geographical particularism characteristic of the federation during its earlier stages. The conventional, doctrinal response to these central initiatives has been couched in terms of a defence of the 'American way of life' and of states' rights. It is correctly indicated that the present line of federal evolution was not envisaged by the signatories to the Constitution. An apt response has been that such foresight would in any event have been impossible. Increasingly, concern appears to have shifted from what the signatories would have (probably) desired to the question regarding what appears to be in the interest of the country as a whole.

The federal system is scarcely accepted as a fetish today. Nothing has done more to alter it in the United States than the introduction of the income tax by the federal government in 1913. War and depression and racial injustice demanded extensive reorganization. But the basic alteration in tax structure was essential to any substantial increase in federal expenditure, and consequently it affected vitally the ability of the central government to act significantly in a number of different spheres. American government today only entails in a limited degree real co-ordination, and none in the sense that this implies truly separate spheres of control.

Other nations that have accepted a federal structure have also tended to modify it (conceiving the original American system as a model) in significant ways. The Canadians, for example, virtually jettisoned the notion of provincial residual powers in drawing up a series of proposals for a federal government at the Quebec Conference of 1864; which was to dilute the hard contractualist core of federalism; for the direct implication was that much power devolved from the central authority, rather than having been partly yielded up to it by the provincial

governments. Thus, virtually no legal limit, besides the enu-
meration of certain local powers (which, however, have not
been much encroached upon) was really placed upon the scope
of the central government's sphere of action. The point was to
avoid a Canadian civil war. Although it is easy to overstate the
case, it is clear that the Canadians were less concerned with the
underlying doctrine of contract. This is not to suggest that there
is no important distinction between local and central authorities
in Canadian government. It is to say that the distinction tends
more to be viewed as a matter of practical necessity than of any
doctrinal deductions. Even in the case of Australia, notably
fundamentalist in the Pantheon of federal states, Geoffrey
Sawer was prepared to predict 'that as the economy develops,
the courts will expand the federal commerce power'; Sawer
accurately concluded that 'they will not lack dicta from which
to draw assurance in doing so'.[7]

Still other nations, in adopting a federal-style government,
have frankly used its organizational form as a convenience in
order to accommodate various linguistic or racial groups.
Yugoslavia is an interesting example of an attempt to federate
Serbo-Croats, Slovenians, Macedonians and other linguistic
groups. The Russian administrative system is even organized
along federalist lines.[8] In this way the federal technique has
been extended to one-party states. But its doctrinal form, its
'principle' (conceived as the institutionalization of liberty) has
not been accepted, but rather a variant of its legal form, which
serves to guarantee the reasonably efficient governance of a vast
land mass while catering to the particularistic sentiments (and
needs) of many disparate peoples.

Thus, federalism can be viewed both as a doctrine and as a
technique. When viewed as a doctrine, it seems to acquire the
character of an 'essence'. The mixture of doctrine and of an
adaptable, modifiable, legal form, in which mixture federalism
often consists, tends to confuse writers such as Wheare. He tends
to ask, in vital earnestness: What is the *true* definition of federal
government? He concludes that federal government *is* federal
government 'by the principle of the general and regional
governments being co-ordinate and independent in their
respective spheres.'[9] But even this minimal definition is not
extensively valid for those countries to which he applies it, and

America is his prime example. It is obvious that the relation between the central and local governments in America is not one of equality, and many of the constitution-makers never really meant it to be. State legislation must always dovetail with federal legislation. State power is always inferior to federal power. State social services have in large degree to meet federal standards and the finances which support them largely derive from federal sources. The power of the purse—and of withdrawing it—constitutes a real sanction. Moreover, the courts can always, by virtue of broad construction and use of the general welfare and similar clauses, extend the jurisdiction of the central government. The point is that final decisions about the matter of jurisdiction and about the utilization of force in the enforcement of such decisions ultimately lie with the central government.

Professor Wheare may well argue that 'once granted that a government is acting within its allotted sphere, that government is not subordinate to any other government in the United States.'[10] The difficulty about this argument, however, is that it will equally apply to any government whatever, where there is a formal delegation of power to inferior bodies (as to county councils, etc.). Once granted that a city or county council or a board or a nationalized industry (or whatever) is operating within its allotted sphere, it operates independently *within that sphere*. What we recognize on reflection, however, is that such a parcelling out of competences is necessary to any large-scale administration of human affairs. The competences assigned may be more or less rigidly held. But the ultimate question is: who decides disputes regarding what is the appropriate sphere of authority of a corporation, or board or inferior territorial unit? If it is not the inferior unit itself, but an organ of the central government, then one is dealing with a political or legal structure that ultimately requires the centralized co-ordination of separate authorities. If secession is not legally envisaged then all disputes must be settled within the union. This usually means that they must be referred to the central judiciary. Either the final decisions of this judiciary must be binding, or the inferior units possess a right (or are permitted a right) of secession. If there is no right of secession, the central judiciary's decisions must be binding, and where they are disregarded, the

167

corporation or group or unit which does so must be viewed legally as in a state of rebellion. This is true of the USA and of the USSR.

A RESPONSE TO PROBLEMS

Hamilton, one of the chief authors of the American Constitution and the principal writer of the federalist papers, was interested in some concept of balance of powers, but this had basically to do with the classic executive, legislative and judicial functions. He was absolutely opposed to local particularism. In his view, 'a dangerous ambition more often lurks behind the specious mask of zeal for the rights of the people, than under the forbidding appearances of zeal for the firmness and efficiency of government.' Hamilton argued that demonstrative clamouring for local and popular rights constituted 'a much more certain road to despotism' than the demand for order and efficiency; he argued against local tyrannies, in short, and for a strong, central government to hold the balance against them.[11] Speaking at the Philadelphia Convention of 1787, Hamilton supported the establishment of a central and completely sovereign national government, one which would 'annihilate the state distinctions and state operations'. Hamilton, in fact, appeared to envisage only two possible results of constitutional equivocation: 'The general power whatever be its form, if it preserves itself, must swallow up the state powers. Otherwise it will be swallowed up by them.'[12] He preferred the former to the latter possibility. The general feeling among the delegates was that he overstated his case. James Wilson, of Pennsylvania, admitted the need for a stronger central government and, equally, the importance of preserving the state governments, which were variant manifestations of the need for local administration (present in all governments). Hamilton then concurred, in regard to state authority: 'he admitted the necessity of leaving in them, subordinate jurisdictions'.[13] Rufus King, of Massachusetts, finally made the decisive point that what the union was *called* was ultimately unimportant. 'The States were not sovereign in the sense contended by some.' At the same time: 'He doubted much the practicability of annihilating the States. . . .'[14] Thus, a union of the States would necessarily impose upon all citizens a national character, and at the same time leave to the States, because of their size, diversity, and the lack of rapid communications between them, a large measure of local independence. King, in short, went straight to the heart of the matter. The American federal result represented a compromise arrived at between disparate governmental units which sought to effect a beneficial and enduring unity.[15]

This is the history of most subsequent federations. It is true of Switzerland, and—in a smaller degree—of Canada, Australia, India and Nigeria, for example. The difference with these last is that federalism was imposed as well as negotiated. This is to say that the purpose of negotiations was two-pronged: (1) to establish independence from a colonial power; (2) to establish indigenous unity between formerly colonized territories (or to retain unity within one such territory). Federalism could be imposed in the sense that the colonial power might require the acceptance of an internal structure as a condition for independence. This might be done in order to secure a 'democratic' order (pluralism, balance, etc.) or in order, through weakness, to retain dependence at a higher, 'neo-colonial' level—or in order to do both. Under these conditions, federalism represents (not 'promotes') that degree of unity which seems compatible with the attainment of independence. Provided that such a federation subsequently remains in being one would expect it to move (following Sidgwick) in considerable degree toward a more unitary form. This effect has been more recently achieved in Nigeria through the extremely sanguinary means of civil war.

However, it is not possible to argue that federation, as such, is merely one stage in the *growth* of a unitary state. As Professor Greaves points out,[16] this argument could easily be reversed, given that almost all federal states devolved from unitary states, i.e. acquired independence from an imperial power. In the circumstances, federation could equally easily be read as one stage in the *demise* of a unitary state. In such a case, however, the new federation becomes part and parcel of the transfer of control from an external to an internal locus. The new federal system provides a distinct legal structure for the new state, not a mere amendment to the old. Thus this form of devolution of power is distinct in kind and not only in degree

169

from that which obtains when the centre transfers power but still retains sovereignty—or the right of ultimate control. The new federal state can disintegrate or stagnate or grow more firm. Although it is not possible to say that, once established, federations *must* grow more firm, they have almost always done so—except in rare cases of disintegration (like that of the defunct Central African Federation). Federations have in fact tended to grow more centralized. This, in itself, is neither good nor bad. Even the American 'liberal' has always tended to be centralist and not an advocate of states' rights. He has been interested in the protection of civil liberties. The greatest danger to these in America has as much stemmed from local particularism as from a rapacious extension of central control.

Federalism is often viewed as an instance of one particular liberal solution, or attempt at solution, of the political problem of securing protection against the abuse of governmental power. In the degree that it is so understood, it must be evaluated on the basis of that understanding. Following such an evaluation it will often be found that the complications and legalism of federal constitutions do as much as not to abort effective protection against governmental abuse. Federal legalism may prove to be as nugatory to civil liberties as not; and its geographical pluralism is sometimes extraordinarily inappropriate. The important thing is not to view federation as an end or as equipped with an essence. It must be seen as a technique which is only sometimes appropriate and never identical to previous experiments when invoked.

It is only in regard to the *original* American model that any federation even seems to be distinctly characterized by the 'co-ordinate spheres of government' principle, each government being putatively supreme in its own sphere. And this could only seem so in America to the extent that the question, whether the state units had (or would be recognized to have) a right of succession, remained ambiguous. So long as the answer to this question might be said to remain ambiguous, for so long could it be said that the central and local governments were equal, separate, and supreme in their respective spheres. One factor that would and did promote this ambiguity was the failure on the part of many to recognize that there can be no watertight, once-for-all demarcation of authority between these distinct centres, which means that disputes will inevitably ensue, usually based on the text of the Constitution as the ultimate source of reference, regarding which authority belongs to whom. Once it is accepted that an organ of the central government should decide this, and that the central executive should be empowered to enforce its decisions, the issue must be regarded as closed. Thus, the idea of co-ordinate spheres of authority will only appear to be true of a federal system for so long as the issue regarding the presence or absence of a right of secession is unsettled. Although the notion of co-ordinate spheres of authority may occasionally seem accurate (i.e. when the union more nearly approximates to confederation: which is to say, when it still seems open to constituent state units to secede) it would obviously prove misleading to view this descriptive notion as a doctrine or prescription about the universally appropriate relationship between central and local governments within any federation.

One basic situation in which the utilization of a federal technique will appear appropriate—ideological cant about freedom, balance, pluralism, etc. apart—is when what is desired is the ultimate accommodation of diverse peoples over wide areas to a single government. When that accommodation has gone reasonably far, the legal structure, too, will subtly change, in response to quite new demands and problems. What is to be avoided at all costs is the conversion of the technique into an end, description into norm, an occasionally appropriate principle into a generalized ideology. Such conversion obtains, however, when one opposes the alteration of a federal structure because its present or prior form, abstractly considered, appears to reify an ideal, as when one opposes or favours the establishment of a federal government because, abstractly considered (which is to say, apart from the conditions governing the choice), it either seems too 'weak' a government or (on the other hand) to promote 'freedom'. The danger that derives from viewing federation as doctrinal is that it may be opposed in principle because it appears to represent little more than a complicated legal structure expressly intended to promote procedural liberty at the expense of any substantive unity. If we remove federalism from federation, we may at once lay aside both the ideal of 'Liberty' and that of 'Unity'. Neither Liberty nor Unity can be absolute; federation should not be seen as a legal-political doctrine which promotes the one and opposes the other; it may properly be viewed as merely one variable means of reconciling specific sorts of unity with specific areas of relative independence.

Federal government does not *in itself* necessarily fulfil the 'liberal' intentions with which it is often identified by its admirers. This is no reason, however, for such persons (or for any persons) to reject it in governments new or old. Federal structures, like everything else in a Heraclitian world of flux, have evolved and been altered in ways that make then quite distinct from what they originally were. They have adopted new responsibilities and purposes in response to new circumstances and conditions. It is these which must be examined in any situation where it is proposed that a federal system be installed or changed. It is essential that such proposals should not be accepted or rejected on the basis of ideological (i.e. *a priori*) considerations of balance, separation of powers, pluralism and so on.

CONCLUSIONS

Federation is a form of government which serves as a series of responses to specific problems. As 'federalism', however, it may come to be viewed as a doctrine growing out of a more general liberal tradition, and responding to the *a priori* imperatives of decentralization, general diffusion of power, local autonomy, and so on. 'Federalism' and federation are significantly different phenomena.

Liberalism, considered in terms of its aversion to governmental abuse of power, and in terms of the theories of contract which served generally to formulate this aversion, was originally a revolutionary doctrine. It sought to protect the citizenry against the abusive use of governmental power and authority. But liberal concerns tended to degenerate, in their institutional form, into an *a priori* interest in the reduction, spread, balance, or even elimination of a central governing power. Pluralism, in its various aspects, was frequently intended, or usually intended, as an updating gesture towards traditional, individualistic, Benthamite individualism. In the case of writers like J. N. Figgis and Ernest Barker, the opposition of the group to the state was

seen as the most appropriate replacement of that of the individual to the state. Liberalism tended to lose its relevance and its
appeal because it settled into an habitual and out-dated response
to what were new circumstances, and new problems arising
within these circumstances. Thus we have reached a point where
the liberalism of the early nineteenth century has become the
tedious conservatism of the mid-twentieth century.

Liberalism became a conservatism in the nineteenth century
when its universal and *a priori* desire for individual freedom
(autonomy) forced it into a defence of the *status quo*: its demands
for autonomy ruled out the theoretical justice of governmental
intervention (in whatever manner or degree) to prevent or
adulterate the exploitation of certain individuals, or classes of
individuals, by others. It was primarily in spite of liberal
doctrine that demands were made to halt the oppressive
exploitation of working people by businessmen, by the wealthy,
by capitalists. And these demands were most urgently and insis-
tently advanced by socialists (who, naturally, developed and
perpetuated their own dogmas).

The important point here is that federal systems have been
altered out of all recognition by virtue of compromises with
legitimate socialist and centralist demands. These changes, however, cannot be readily accommodated for so long as federal
systems are seen more as the embodiment of 'federalism', rather
than merely as different federations attempting to establish
coherent systems of government (which must differ significantly
pari passu with the different circumstances in which they have
been established).

The *de facto* triumph of socialist programmes—whatever they
may now be called—need not impose upon the tradition of
liberalism complete contemporary irrelevance. This is true to
the extent that a quest for 'freedom' may be supposed to
imply respect for human personality and a present willingness
to preserve it from the barbarities which extreme material
deprivation will force upon it, and true to the extent that a
more centralized organization of society need not necessarily
prove prejudicial to civil liberties.

Liberalism, as its best self, may perhaps be reduced to a habit
of reasonableness, tolerance and compromise. The disposition
to interpret problems from different standpoints, to take account

of opposing arguments, to tolerate, in short, and to debate, simply cannot be memorized. To the extent that such a disposition is ritualistically inculcated, it simply becomes a dogma. In politics, reasonableness and tolerance are to be cherished in the degree that they facilitate the appreciation of truth or the execution of justice. But, in this respect, they constitute means, not ends. Ends or principles, understood as injunctions covering what we ought to do under any and all circumstances, are absurd. Anyone who accepts tolerance (similarly with federalism, balance of power, etc.) as an exclusive end, has simply got himself up in the broad, dark cloth of a dogma. Tolerance is an excellent habit, but is ultimately right or wrong, depending on the end to which it is directed. For there are some things which we simply ought not to tolerate.[17]

In conclusion, federation is a political phenomenon fully worthy of study. But it should not be seen, or favoured, merely as the reification of federalism, which we may conceive to embody a universal, *a priori*, indeed even ideological demand for 'balance', for 'decentralism', for a proliferation of powers. These things, in some sense, always exist in all governments (the order within a government can always be read as a balance; and the delegation of authority—which is inescapable—can always be read as decentralism). But where we accept, in some sense, that they do not exist (one central government, for example, controls local education, another does not) it is impossible to say that, in all circumstances, it is only the central or the local authority that is the most appropriate agent of control.

Thus, tolerance, federalism, pluralism, etc. are not universally valid. This is to say that, treated as universal recommendations, they must fail, since each of them will in some circumstances prove inappropriate and inapplicable. But a study of the sub-structure and operative character of tolerance in a society, of the functional structure of federations, of subordinate corporate groups within the state, of the formal (legal) and informal (political, psychological, etc.) flow of influence and control exercised by government, of the highest (formal) decision-making body in the state—all of this must prove highly useful. This does not reduce to behaviouralism or to the elimination of norms and a rational recommendatory process—nor to the suggestions that these concerns should be relegated to an intellectual limbo. The point, rather is to recognize, as Kant remarked in a footnote to his *Critique of Pure Reason*, the independent importance of judgement, the mastery of which no abstract, procedural norm (put to memory) can provide.

NOTES AND REFERENCES

1. M. P. Follet, *The New State* (London, 1918), p. 267.
2. H. R. G. Greaves, *Federal Union in Practice* (London, Allen & Unwin, 1940), p. 10.
3. Henry Sidgwick, *Elements of Politics* (London, 1st edn. 1891; 4th edn. 1919), p. 544. Sidgwick believes, partly for the same reason, that 'a confederation of states, if it holds together, has a tendency to pass into a federal state'. But this movement from confederation to federation has actually happened only in a few cases, such as in Switzerland and in the United States. Minimally a confederation is a formal treaty arrangement for common defence and assistance; such arrangements may, of course, grow firm, but they are just as likely to lapse, once the pressures which occasioned them dissolve.
4. Ernest Barker, *Essays on Government*, 2nd edn. (Oxford University Press, 1951), p. 87. This is rather a dramatic formulation, although conventional support for this view is also found in J. Gough, *The Social Contract* (Oxford University Press, 1957).
5. Notably his *Economic Interpretation of the Constitution of the United States* (New York, Macmillan, 1913) and *Economic Origins of Jeffersonian Democracy* (New York, Macmillan, 1915).
6. *The Federalist* was a collection of essays originally published during 1787-8 as a series of articles to influence voters favourably towards the new U.S. Constitution which had just been agreed upon at the Philadelphia Constitutional Convention.
7. Geoffrey Sawer, *Federalism: An Australian Jubilee Study* (Melbourne, 1952), p. 222.
8. Cf. Rudolf Schlesinger, *Federalism in Eastern and Central Europe* (London, Routledge, 1945). Article 13 of the 1936 Constitution of the USSR describes it as a voluntary union (in fact as a 'federal state') of the Socialist Soviet Republic (p. 402). It provides for a second (territorial) chamber and for the reservation of non-specified powers to the member states (p. 403). Schlesinger finds no grounds on which the USSR can be denied the character of a federal state. He believes 'it would be completely wrong to assume that the enormous power of the Communist Party will ever be exercised so as to destroy national variety and autonomy' (p. 409). In general terms, he believes: 'Soviet federalism does not mean so little as it may seem to do when looked at from outside' (p. 410).
9. K. C. Wheare, *Federal Government*, 3rd edn. (Oxford University Press, 1953), p. 5.
10. Ibid., p. 2.
11. Jay, Madison, Hamilton, *The Federalist* (Oxford, Blackwell, 1948) Max Beloff (ed.), p. 3.
12. James Madison, *Debates in the Federal Convention of 1787*, Gaillard Hunt and James Brown Scott (eds.) (New York, Oxford University Press, 1920), p. 115.
13. Ibid., p. 129.
14. Ibid., p. 130.

KNOWLEDGE AND BELIEF IN POLITICS

15. Claude Bower's *Hamilton and Jefferson* (London, Constable, 1925) provides an excellent comparative analysis of Hamilton and Jefferson (conceived respectively as aristocrat and democrat) and covers the founding of the union, and the subsequent collapse of the Federalist Party.

16. Greaves, op. cit.

17. Cf. my more elaborate discussion of 'The Problem of Tolerance' in *Government and Opposition*, 6 (2) (spring, 1971), pp. 172-207.

The Character of
Modern British Conservatism

W. H. GREENLEAF

I

Consider Beethoven. First, the Symphony No. 3 in E Flat Major,
the '*Eroïca*'. This has often been supposed to be programmatically concerned with the character of the hero, a sort of
Carlylean meditation in music (if the anachronism may be
forgiven). Whether or not this is really what it is all about may
perhaps be doubtful. But one thing is quite clear: the motif deals
in contrasts. A European critic, Paul Bekker, analysing the first
few bars of the opening movement in the Napoleonic terms,
said that in these initial passages Beethoven has succinctly
depicted 'the two cardinal antitheses of his hero's character,
his "forward-pressing energy" and his "mournful reflective
resignation"'. But, secondly, take the impact of another work,
and exegesis in an alternative mode. There is the story that, on
hearing the great C Major entry of the finale of Beethoven's
Fifth Symphony, a veteran of the Old Guard (how one loves
to think it might have been Papa Barlasch!) sprang to his
feet exclaiming '*C'est l'Empereur!*' Here we have the character
reflected differently in one magnificent and unified anthem.

And so, in this musicological context, are exemplified two
different styles of representation. On the one hand, the matter
rests on a single theme, recognized at once as a blend of all that
is fundamental and necessary. On the other, there is ambivalence, more complex, and encompassing a contrast of distinctive features.

Now, these are also the possibilities before us in the attempt
to describe a political institution, in the present case, the

ideology of modern British conservatism. (And I use the term 'ideology' not at all in any sophisticated way but to refer simply to the ideas deployed by some of those who have been called 'conservatives'.) Are we to elicit a single set of key concepts that must be called the core of this doctrine and on the recognition of which we spring up saying '*C'est le conservatisme!*'? Or should we take the other path and look instead for a range of lineaments linked in more diverse resemblance and presenting therefore a perhaps more confusing appearance? If we pursue the former task and concentrate on distilling the essence of conservatism, a group of fundamental notions necessarily unchanging (or altering very little), the great difficulty is that by no means all the writers or politicians whom in this country we describe as conservatives will be likely to reflect these basic ideas in the same way or combination or to the same extent. The subjects that we discern as vital to the thought of W. H. Mallock or the practice of Austen Chamberlain may not be deemed in the same way essential to the consideration of Coleridge or Enoch Powell. It is rather too simple and artificial to say (in the usual sort of listing) that conservatism above all can be reduced to a set of basic ideas because it is essentially static; that all conservatives in some mysterious way share, for instance, a sense of religion and divine order, a veneration of Christian virtues; a particular and rather pessimistic view of human nature with an emphasis on unreason; an organic and hierarchical conception of society; a belief in the family as the basic social unit; the importance of private property; an acceptance of political and spiritual authority; a stress on tradition and prescriptive experience; a sense of empire; the understanding that the realm of politics is essentially limited; or whatever. Statements of this kind are frequently found invariably coupled with the suggestion that a 'history of conservative thinkers . . . necessarily involves over and over again the same ideas'.[1] An abstraction of this fixed sort can be constructed and called conservatism. But, in the first place, its generalities might often be accepted by people who do not regard themselves as conservatives at all. And, secondly, it is not easy satisfactorily to reduce to such a denominator the rich variety of personalities and ideas we all know: too much refuses to fit in. Of course, we could reject the title of conservative for those who fail to conform to this stereotype. But a procedure of this sort, which so violates common political usage, could hardly commend itself. And this is true, of course, of similar attempts to do the same kind of thing with liberalism, socialism or any other ideology. So, let us not look for a crucial nucleus of doctrine.

What we must rather do is avoid designation of this sort and try instead to define in the sense of delimitation. We must accept and somehow embody in our characterization the fact of diversity and contrast, the recognition that an ideology is not a single thing at all but a range of ideas and reactions. And this scope can only be identified by indicating the extremes of which it is capable, by describing the 'cardinal antitheses' of this political disposition as revealed in modern Britain.

Nor is such an enterprise without incidental difficulties. There is, for instance, the problem of relating different levels of political expression. A conservative philosopher such as Oakeshott or a historian such as Keith Feiling or Robert Blake may be expected to achieve a degree of coherence in expression and argument rather more effective (in academic terms) than even a conceptually minded man of affairs like Eustace Percy or the Third Marquess of Salisbury; while the latter type of person may attain an intellectually more satisfactory statement of ideas and policies than a simple politician or publicist however eminent who has no pretension to theoretical competence. In this last respect, think (for instance) of someone like Baldwin or Bonar Law or the authors of a run-of-the-mill piece of party propaganda such as a popular policy statement. Yet somehow or other it has, nevertheless, all to be linked together whatever the level of articulation involved.

There is, too, another related aspect to this problem, the question of sincerity or obliquity of speech. I do not use these words in a pejorative sense for I would expect no other situation to obtain in this context. Politics is, in good part at least, a matter of persuading people to act or to refrain from doing something. A participant in this process, while (like anyone else) priding himself on his consistency and straightforwardness, is nevertheless likely to use arguments and ideas which, consciously or otherwise, he feels his audience will deem convincing, and he may not always hold them really strongly himself. When Joseph Chamberlain, in expounding his Dartford

Programme, speaks of the necessity of pursuing the greatest happiness of the greatest number, we ask: is it, to him, simply a persuasive phrase deployed as a rhetorical device merely; or are we entitled to suppose at least some subscription to the utilitarian paraphernalia associated with it even if this is not formally expounded? Of little significance, perhaps, in studying the thought of the consciously intellectual political writer who will invariably try to explore his presuppositions, this difficulty arises progressively as we consider the active participant in political life. And, of course, the study of a party ideology such as conservatism is intolerably incomplete unless this practical dimension of its expression is examined. Studies of ideologies of this kind that deal only with their consciously intellectual expression are sadly limited and of little use.

Necessary stress on this point leads also to another factor of discussion. Just as it is no good analysing only the overtly theoretical expositions of a political doctrine, so it is not very helpful if this doctrine is not seen concretely in its relation to a developing historical context. I do not, by this remark, mean to imply wholehearted acceptance of those theories of interpretation associated with the 'sociology of knowledge' which, on the whole, I find somewhat deficient. But it is obvious that a political creed, especially as embodied in the writings and speeches of active politicians and propagandists, is supremely a matter of reacting to contemporary problems and issues as seen through the distorting spectacles of prejudice, ambition, tactics, interest and doctrine.

And here—in order to give the matter specific reference—I have to establish, though I hope not too foolishly, some historical framework or perspective. And for this purpose, I will suppose that conservatism, like any contemporary political ideology in this country, is a reaction—though not always the same reaction —to that crucial aspect of the modern British scene that may be called (for want of any more neutral term) the development of 'collectivism'.

II

What I mean by this can be indicated by a piece of historical abridgement, a summary view which I have not invented but which owes much to such writers as St.-Simon, Dicey, Halévy and many others without (I think) having ever been fully worked out.

British political life in recent times may be seen (in this perspective) as a tension or interplay between two opposing tendencies, libertarianism and collectivism. Each institutional cluster of political events, every focus of ideas, is a phase—these terms are in fact Herbert Spencer's[2]—in a continuous metamorphosis of these conflicting elements in varying proportion. What do they imply?

By libertarianism I mean several things. First, the thought and activity that stresses the fundamental importance of individuality, that is to say, the rights and freedom from interference of the person, freedom from both social and political control and arbitrary treatment of any kind. These are the traditional inherent claims protected by the common law and stated in the great charters of the realm. It followed from such presuppositions—and this is the second feature of libertarianism—that the role of government must in an important way be limited: it could not legitimately interfere in (or at least permanently eliminate) the basic sphere of individuality. Its function is not to tell individuals how to run their lives but to maintain the framework of public order within which individuals may pursue their own ends and interests. This does not necessarily (though it may) imply *laissez-faire*. Government might properly be required to remedy a manifest evil in society—the exploitation of child labour, for example; but such regulation would always be specific and limited by what might be called the libertarian ground rules. It would in principle always be distinct from continuous intervention as a means consciously and deliberately of imposing a substantive and uniform order of things on civil society. Thirdly, and clearly involved in this pattern, is a diffusion of power and a decentralization of decision-making. The logic of this is simply that, in Ortega's phrase, 'Liberty and Plurality are Reciprocal'.[3] Libertarianism therefore supposes that the power of government must not be overwhelmingly great and must be jealously watched; that a devolution of authority is desirable, say to local and regional agencies; and that the existence of extra-governmental foci of influence and power—churches, trade unions and associations, voluntary bodies of various kinds—is proper and desirable as a counter-poise to government's own activities and demands. Finally, there is the great constitutional doctrine of the rule of law, classically formulated by Dicey and which, with its rejection of wide arbitrary and discretionary power, and its stress on the formal equality of all citizens before the law, is hostile to the growth of privileged and extensive governmental initiative.

Now libertarianism (seen in some such way as this) is, I suggest, a major strand in the traditional ethos of our political life. It is reflected in theoretical statements at least from Locke's *Second Treatise* on; in the Whig doctrine of the ancient constitution, limited government and the separation of powers; it is assumed in aspects of utilitarianism. And it was implicit in many long-standing constitutional arrangements and conventions: the government of the country through local bodies, specifically the Quarter Sessions and the County Meeting; the old preference for a local militia rather than a standing army as the 'constitutional force' for the defence of the realm; the deliberate acceptance of a multiplicity of offices and the consequent administrative confusion; the acknowledged role of autonomous 'corporations'; the hostility to centralization; the supremacy of Parliament; jealousy of the Crown and independent executive discretion; the concept of rights inherent in the individual; the stress on the vital political importance of private property.

Collectivism is, definitionally, simply the antithesis of all this. It brings to the fore not so much personal rights but the good of the public. It is the idea that the community itself has a purpose and interest superior to that of the individual. It is a notion of social justice, taken to mean the deliberate imposition of conditions of equality and security for all. And, for this end, government is the natural instrument. Collectivism implies, therefore, a system of society in which public authority does more and more for the individual given that he seems unable by his own efforts to secure his interest or to aid the general welfare. There is necessarily a growing concentration of power in government which is to be used for and justified by the achievement, maybe the consciously planned achievement, of the public good.

Now, the perspective I have to suggest is an obvious one. It is that over the past century and a half there has been an at first sporadic and then a deliberate growth of collectivism, and that British political activity, its institutions and ideas, reflect this increasing emphasis.

The reasons for this development are numerous but clear though this is not the place to explore them at length. But above all there is the impact of modern war which was, as Halévy saw it, the grim harbinger of collectivism;[4] next there are the effects of industrial change and population growth such as the problems raised for government by intensive urban concentration; the difficulties of periodical mass unemployment and other waste of resources; the results for the domestic economy of growing foreign competition; the impact of an extended franchise and the social demands of mass democracy; the cumulative process of administrative momentum itself. These and many other factors have helped the collectivist tendency to get under way and accelerate rapidly.

There is no doubt about this at all. Geoffrey Elton said recently, it will come as no surprise to anyone that during the nineteenth century there was a great upsurge in the activity of government.[5] The fact of the matter can be established indubitably by examining—as a sort of index—the evidence of the increasing scope and scale of government activity in this country over the period in question. For instance, total central and local government expenditure as a proportion of National Income has increased from roughly 10 per cent in the last part of the nineteenth century to something like 40 per cent in recent years. Similarly, the element of the total working population in government employ has increased in the same period from under 4 to over 25 per cent (substantially more than this if the nationalized industries are included).

This kind of change has radically affected our political institutions and may be discerned, too, at work in our political ideologies.[6]

It has taken some time to come to the point of this paper (or at least the end of its beginning). The suggestion is that our political doctrines may best be regarded as illustrating or embodying this tension or interplay between libertarianism and collectivism. Each is not so much a core of unchanging themes as a dialectic between these opposing tendencies. Liberals do not share the same basic ideas simply. They range from Cobden and Herbert Spencer on the one side to Lloyd George and the exponents of the 'Yellow Book' on the other. And for all the apparent common ground and the identical nomenclature there is a world of difference between these wings, a hiatus discerned and described at the crucial point in its emergence by L. T. Hobhouse. Likewise there is the ambivalence of modern British socialism. This comprises not only an indivi-dualist protest by pluralists such as the guildsmen and christian moralists like R. H. Tawney, and reflected too in the strong free-trade influence, but embraces as well something rather different: the call of technocratic efficiency achieved by exten-sive public direction as in the arguments of the Webbs and the so-called state socialists. This ambivalence, the uneasy alliance of freedom and control, is reflected broadcast in the socialist tradition and exemplified most nicely in the many works of Harold Laski. And conservatism—this is the point—is not otherwise. It too has a dual inheritance of the same sort,[7] which will now be described, but all too brusquely for obviously space permits only the broadest outline. First, its collectivist aspect will be reviewed and exemplified and then its more libertarian strand.

III

In a famous essay Herbert Spencer described the liberalism of his day (he was writing in the 1880s) as 'The New Toryism'.[8] His intention was, of course, to stress the increasingly collectivist tendency of liberal ideas and policies and to highlight the system of compulsory cooperation they involved. But it is significant (in the present context) that he does this by pointing to an important aspect of conservatism which, if it had also empha-sized the responsibilities of power, had (in his view) traditionally stressed the role of established authority. As a result—and this is, of course, Spencer's meaning—the Tory doctrine has never, in principle, been uncongenial to state intervention. And in fact not a few conservatives have prided themselves on this pater-nalistic heritage. Sixty years ago, one of them (who did not in fact find it entirely congenial) put it in this way: 'Less averse than the earlier Liberals from invoking the hand of authority, Conservatives outstripped their opponents in the endeavour to remedy the distresses of the poorer classes by legislation.' Or, in much more recent expression, it is said, 'A good Tory has never been in history afraid of the use of the State'; and, again, 'Toryism has always been a form of paternal socialism'. Certainly the amount of social and economic regulation that conservatives have sponsored for one reason or another since 1800 is not inconsiderable.

Yet it is not altogether easy to bring together and express both the scope and the chronology of this Tory interventionism and the range of motives and reasons involved. Yet while I am sure it is not an exclusive categorization, I would refer to the following aspects or factors: humanitarianism; *noblesse oblige*; piecemeal concession; radicalism; and the reaction to economic crisis.

It is hardly necessary to labour the first. A good many Tories are as sensitive to social evil and human suffering as any one else. At the very outset of the period with which we are concerned, the reforming energies of Lord Shaftesbury, Richard Oastler and others like them are sufficient indication of this. And there is no reason at all to suppose that this simple, paternalistic humanitarianism has ever ceased to exert some moral influence in conservative ranks and to find its outlet in personal charity and remedial legislation.

Noblesse oblige refers, of course, to the duties of class leadership. This is exemplified in classic form by the social and political theory of Disraeli who invariably expressed in such terms a consistent view of the English polity and its leaders' duty of social amelioration. The constant premise of his ideas in respect of domestic policy was a stress on the preponderance, in what he called the 'Territorial Constitution of England', of the landed and agricultural interest (which, incidentally, he did not define at all narrowly but considered to embrace 'the vast majority of the English nation'). It was the feudal and local values of this predial tradition by which he set so much store. The responsibility of the realm rested on the shoulders of the social leaders in each county and parish. These were the sentiments at the core of Young England, and these were the romanticist ideals expressed in the trilogy of political novels which Disraeli wrote in the 1840s, of course to make money, but nevertheless also as a sort of manifestos to influence opinion. For instance, at one of the climaxes in the plot of *Coningsby*, when the hero of the story defies his grandfather and tells that formidable and rather unpleasant old man that he cannot agree to stand for Parliament on this patriarch's terms, he justifies himself by reference to the ideas mentioned: 'What we want, sir', he says, is 'to establish great principles which may maintain the realm and secure the happiness of the people. Let me see authority once more honoured; a solemn reverence again the habit of our lives; let me see property acknowledging, as in the old days of faith, that labour is his twin brother, and that the essence of all tenure is the performance of duty. . . .'[10] What was then lacking in Britain—this is the lesson—was a sense of community. There was only association or gregariousness: two nations instead of one; and this because the propertied class was not meeting its obligations.

This was the theoretical rationale of Disraeli's opposition to Peel over the abolition of the Corn Laws: their repeal was a step that would strike at the heart of the landed interest and therefore at the ancient constitution of the kingdom itself. This was why (after the deed was accomplished in 1846) Disraeli continually supported policies designed to protect the land and the people dependent on it. This explains as well his diagnosis of major contemporary social and political problems. Not only were some of the traditional landed classes (like Lord Marney in *Sybil*) not fulfilling the duties of their position but, further, a new group of wealthy men was emerging, in commerce and manufacture, many of whom likewise showed no sense of the responsibilities of their position and privileges. Labour, he said, in a speech at Shrewsbury in 1843,

also has its rights as well as its duties; and when I see masses of property raised in this country which do not recognise that principle; when I find men making fortunes by a method which permits them (very often in a very few years) to purchase the lands of the old territorial aristocracy of the country, I cannot help remembering that those millions are accumulated by a mode which does not recognize it as a duty 'to endow the Church, to feed the poor, to guard the land, and to execute justice for nothing'. And I cannot help asking myself, when I hear of all this misery, and of all this suffering; when I know that evidence exists . . . of a state of demoralisation in the once happy population of this land, which is not equalled in the most barbarous countries . . .—I cannot help suspecting that this has arisen because property has been . . . created and held without the performance of its duties.[11]

However, if the country was to be 'turned into a spinning jenny machine kind of nation', Disraeli's ideal was embodied, for instance, in the figure of Mr Millbank, the capitalist who (in *Coningsby*—his counterpart in *Sybil* is Mr Trafford, the mill owner) is described not only as an extremely efficient entrepreneur but also as one who cares for the good reputation of his order and for the health and welfare of his work people. And the factory town over which Mr Millbank paternalistically presides is in the sharpest possible contrast to the dirt and misery prevailing in Wodgate that the spuriously ennobled Mowbrays have negligently allowed to grow up and fester under their aegis. It contrasts, too, with the misery of the decayed rural town of Marney.[12]

It is, then, in this context of an almost feudal sense of *noblesse oblige*, of the social responsibilities of property (which Disraeli believed was the ethos of traditional England) that he sees the condition of the people question. He had taken some trouble to familiarize himself with the facts about urban and rural poverty: Lord Morley, who was no disciple, acknowledged Disraeli's grasp of the real nature and magnitude of the social crisis brought about by rapid industrialization.[13] And he always expressed the keenest interest in eliminating what was 'rotten in the core of our social system', that amid prosperity and a superabundance of wealth, 'the working classes, the creators of wealth, were steeped in the most abject poverty and . . . the deepest degradation'.[14] This was a theme publicized most elaborately and effectively perhaps in his famous speeches at Manchester and at the Crystal Palace towards the end of his long political career in 1872 in which, as leader of the party, he committed Toryism to a policy of sanitary and other social reform. Of course, there was always the hostility to centralization—England, as he once put it, should be governed by England, and not by London—nevertheless action by the imperial Parliament could be crucial to the process of change.

Now, in the hagiography of this kind of conservatism Disraeli takes pride of place. His doctrine (as just described) has undoubtedly been a potent influence of almost mythical impact on the later development of the conservative mind. Moreover, it has usually been supposed that when, from 1874 to 1880, Disraeli finally achieved supreme office with effective parliamentary power, what he did was, quite simply, to act on and carry through the programmatic implications of the ideology he had long expounded. But it is now clear that considerable care may be necessary in the assessment of this traditional picture. And what recent historical inquiry has revealed about the genesis and working out of the policies of this administration indicates, too, what is meant by the third factor mentioned, piecemeal concession: political recognition of practical or administrative necessity. In mind here, of course, is the corrective to the conventional view provided by Dr Paul Smith in his most impressive study *Disraelian Conservatism and Social Reform*.[15] It is not denied that, considered as a whole, the measures implemented during Disraeli's premiership constituted the biggest instalment of constructive legislation passed by any one government in the nineteenth century.[16] Yet, it is also urged, these measures were often inadequate or ill-conceived, promulgated (it would seem) reluctantly, more a series of concessions made necessary by the pressing demand of circumstances than the required practical outcome of the ideological predisposition. Indeed, the attitude of Disraeli's ministers (as now revealed by the archives) was, far from being congenial to paternalistic regulation, rather conditioned by the predominant anti-interventionism of the day. They dealt as they did with slum clearance, the over-insurance of merchant shipping, and so on because of *ad hoc* political necessity arising out of particular pressures, a specific investigation, the interest of a minister and the like, and not because they saw themselves as implementing a philosophy.

Perhaps, persuasive as it is, this new view of things does go rather too far. There is some contrary evidence—Disraeli's personal persistence in the matter of the labour laws, for instance; and the legislative programme could have been otherwise. That it was not is, to put it at the lowest level possible, an indication that, when circumstances pressed, there was nothing in the conservative ideology to make legislative intervention of this sort utterly impossible. Spencer at least would not have been surprised at what Disraeli and his colleagues did; it was characteristic of Toryism as he understood it.[17] Nor—and perhaps this is more important than (so to say) what actually happened—has Disraeli's subsequent reputation and influence been otherwise: it is the myth of the Disraelian heritage rather than the reality (whatever that may have been) that has counted. And this is why not a little space has been devoted to the doctrine here.

In a famous letter to *The Times* in 1907, Sir John Gorst described what he took to be involved in the domestic policy of Disraeli, his 'ancient master' as he called him. And its nub was the principle that governmental power must be used to achieve, and is justified only to the extent that it does promote, the happiness and welfare of the common people.[18]

Certainly—and here the next factor emerges—this supposed Disraelian interventionism was easily married to the various forms of political radicalism that appeared among some leading Conservatives in the last years of the nineteenth century. I have in mind, of course, the Tory Democracy of Lord Randolph Churchill and the sometimes indistinguishable views associated with Joseph Chamberlain, the ethos of which he took over to the Conservative benches when he broke with Gladstone over Home Rule.

Tory Democracy was a set of ideas about the role, structure and policies of the Conservative Party in an age of increasing popular tendency. Its themes were consciously formulated on the supposed Disraelian model—as Churchill's famous article 'Elijah's Mantle' makes clear[19]—but it was hardly coherently thought out. What it came to was a Tory version of the old Liberal cry for peace, retrenchment and reform with the difference that the last item meant not constitutional change but dealing with social issues, in connection with which Churchill was prepared to advocate government action to deal with a large number of contemporary problems ranging from control of railway rates and conditions of labour to the drink question and the provision of free elementary education.[20] If in many respects vague and unformed, the general attitude involved was not unfavourable to the extension of state activity.

Lord Rosebery, in his short and perceptive (though sometimes misleading) study of Churchill, observed correctly that 'Randolph found himself on the verge of collectivism'.[21]

It was this aspect of late nineteenth-century conservatism that—ideologically—made it not too difficult for the party to absorb Joseph Chamberlain and his 'unauthorized programme'. His notions were, of course, formed in the mould of political nonconformity and local politics. But Chamberlain might, alternatively, be seen (in Disraelian terms) as the new man of commerce fulfilling the duty his wealth and position imposed on him. The flavour of the policies he came to espouse, as a pioneer of municipal socialism and later as a leading member of the radical wing of the Liberal Party, is reflected in the preface he wrote to that little red book of the day, *The Radical Programme*, which he had inspired and which reflected his views. These proposals, he said,

> sound the death-knell of the *laissez-faire* system; . . . The goal towards which the advance will probably be made at an accelerated pace is that in the direction of which the legislation of the last quarter of a century has been tending—the inter-vention . . . of the State on behalf of the weak against the strong, in the interests of labour against capital, of want and suffering against luxury and ease.[22]

He saw clearly that the centre of political power had shifted to the working classes and that inevitably political policy would be concerned with 'social subjects'. 'How to promote the greater happiness of the masses of the people, how to increase their enjoyment of life, that is the problem of the future.'[23] And he was blunt about what was involved: the reforms he had in mind would have to be financed through progressive taxation of income and property. 'What ransome', he asked, 'will property pay for the security it enjoys!'[24] Not long after he was writing of the 'Favourable Aspects of State Socialism'.[25] This was the sort of attitude that Chamberlain grafted on to the Conservative party of Lord Salisbury, stressing as he did so the interventionist side of Toryism.[26]

Nor was this the only effect Chamberlain had on the develop-ment of this aspect of conservatism: I will return to this further point in a moment. But, at this stage, it is appropriate to note that his commitment to social reform through state action was fully shared by his son, Neville.

The great Tory defeat of 1906 led in some quarters of the party to what would nowadays probably be called a period of rethinking. For the following decade or so there is ample evidence of discussion of reform policies and of the need for government aid and action in respect of town planning, housing, wage boards, co-partnership in industry (even workers' control) and the like.[27] The Great War itself was of considerable impact to this end as well. Neville Chamberlain shared these interventionist views. Like his father, he served his political apprenticeship as Mayor of Birmingham where he was associated in particular with the problems of health, housing and town planning which he insisted should be seen in an overall, related way. And, at the end of the war, he was quite prepared to support extensive public action at central and local level to deal on a planned national basis with key problems such as these as well as in respect of the stimulation of industrial activity. For much of the 1920s he was a most active Minister of Health. When he assumed office he submitted to the Cabinet twenty-five measures he wanted to pass. All but five were on the statute book when he left the department (and these others were embodied in later legislation). The presuppositions on which these policies were formed had long been held by him and have become (in Sir Keith Feiling's phrase) among 'the strongest determinants of our modern life': a radical readiness to employ the power of the 'supervisory State', using regulation to aid voluntary effort, social insurance, replacing small by large areas of administration in the major services, and block grants to stimulate activity.[28] And this all constituted a wide-ranging coherent strategy of change that made for one of the outstanding legislative achievements of the century in the field of social reform.

Finally, there is the vital series of conservative reactions to Britain's economic crisis brought about by increasing foreign competition and the gradual passing of this country's commercial hegemony, by technological change, and by the impact of depression and mass unemployment. In the minds of many conservatives these problems implied an extension of state activity of an important kind. Social legislation was one thing;

and *ad hoc* treatment of specific industrial problems was another. But the deliberate and considerable use of the authority of government to regulate the general pattern of the country's economic life was an altogether different proposition.

Here again Joseph Chamberlain was an important figure in the development of this new economic ethos, the first stage of which is closely associated with the policy of protection. Chamberlain held that a tariff would fulfil three purposes. It would help hold the Empire together through a system of trade preferences; provide revenue for social reforms such as an old age pensions scheme; and enable government to safeguard industry (for instance, by relieving unemployment and depression) as well as to improve our bargaining position in trade negotiation. His tariff reform programme reflected, therefore, an important collectivist tendency for it was an invitation to the government, not to stand aside as free-trade doctrine demanded, but continuously to intervene for political and economic purpose. Beatrice Webb saw this at once and noted in her diary of 1903 that Chamberlain's raising the protection issue would advertise enormously 'the need for investigation and the desirability of deliberate collective regulation'.[29]

After the Great War this kind of thinking was reinforced. The General Strike of 1926 showed something basically wrong with industry. Rising unemployment and the long slump, the seemingly ineradicable problem of the depressed areas, argued that the economy was fundamentally ill. Neville Chamberlain, as Chancellor from 1931 to 1937, had a great responsibility. His main remedy was a full policy of protection and a limited programme of public works and investment particularly in the special areas; though he refused to unbalance the budget and use a deficit to stimulate trade. Given the still strong orthodox finance and economic sentiments of the time (for instance, the ardent commitment to free trade of labour leaders such as Snowden, and the need for the famous agreement to differ and subsequent resignations in 1932), he went perhaps quite a long way.

Yet there were those in the Tory ranks who would have gone farther and faster, as Harold Macmillan and his ideology of the 'Middle Way' indicate. For, in the 1920s and 1930s, Macmillan was in the vanguard of Tory statism. A recent comment shows that his hero was Disraeli, and he revealed the pedigree of his opinions when he noted (of an early speech) that it said nothing remarkable: 'It was a mixture of . . . "Young England", Shaftesbury, Joe Chamberlain, and all the rest'.[30]

It began with the so-called 'Y.M.C.A.' in the 1920s: a group of young Tory MPs with a conscience. Its members included (as well as Macmillan) Oliver Stanley, R. S. Hudson, Robert Boothby, Anthony Eden, Duff Cooper and a few others. Its foremost figure and intellectual leader was Noel Skelton. His pamphlet of 1924, *Constructive Conservatism*, had a great effect on them all. A number of them represented industrial constituencies and were anxious about the problems of these areas; but what they had in common, too, was war-time experience in the trenches that gave them a sense of responsibility towards their soldiers: a good officer looks after his men. Their attitude seems really to have been as simple as that. It was this rather undesigning and eager sense of responsibility which, shocked as they were by the conditions in the country and especially the problems of housing and unemployment, led them to demand state help to deal with these difficulties. Their first collective manifesto was a volume on *Industry and the State* which appeared in 1927. It was one of several books and statements by conservatives which came out at this time and which looked to a more extensive government control of the broad lines of industrial policy than it had been usual to envisage in peace-time. In a series of volumes, speeches and articles appearing over the next ten years, Macmillan elaborated what in his view this policy meant. He called his approach the 'Middle Way' because, without lapsing into state socialism it envisaged going substantially beyond the free market economy of *laissez-faire* theory. He put forward, for instance, the idea of a national plan and detailed schemes of public investment and industrial reorganization. His propensities in this direction were reinforced by wartime experience at the Ministry of Supply and subsequently emerged strongly, too, in the manner of his organization of the house building programme of the early 1950s. Also, after the traumatic electoral defeat in 1945, he was able to affect the reformulation of party policy that ensued, being a significant influence, for example, on the drafting of the *Industrial Charter* (1946) which one commentator referred to, indeed, as a second edition of *The Middle Way*. And, of course, these ideas came firmly into their own during Macmillan's premiership.[31]

The so-called 'new conservatism' of the period after 1945 reflects in a great degree the collectivist tendencies so far described. Although Churchill was much preoccupied with external affairs, his long record as a liberal leader and social reformer meant that he never wholly lost interest in these domestic matters. It was under his aegis, for instance, that Butler was allowed to go forward with the 1944 Education Act and that the Conservative Party was committed to a policy of maintaining full employment. The general style of the refurbished Conservative image was reflected in a speech made at the party conference in 1947 by Anthony Eden (who had, in the 1920s, adhered to the group of young radical Tories). We are not, he said, a party of unbridled brutal capitalism and never have been: conservatives had a long record of opposition to state inaction and were never averse to the use of legislation to deal with industrial and social problems.[32] These are the genuine accents of orthodox Tory collectivism.

These diverse strands, then, have gone to make up one brand of conservatism. In these different ways and for these various motives conservatives have often—and increasingly—been prepared for the power of the state to be used to intervene in social and economic life. Of course, they have always repudiated anything like complete government control and the deliberate abolition of private property and free enterprise. But the trammels they have been prepared to place on the competitive system have been considerable.

Yet there has always been another and sometimes very different aspect of conservative ideology, to a review of which it is now necessary to turn.

IV

This libertarian strand in conservatism deploys a varied range of arguments and is premeditated on rather different sets of premises, sometimes social and economic, sometimes religious and philosophical, depending of course on the interests and disposition of the exponent. But broadly its disciples fall into two groups: the adherents of a more or less orthodox *laissez-faire*

and free-trade doctrine; and the supporters of a modified
position which draws a firm distinction between social and
economic intervention, the former being permissible and the
latter, generally, not.

Burke laid down the law in 1795 in his *Thoughts on Scarcity*
when he asserted the state should confine itself to what was truly
public and not meddle in what properly belongs to (what he
called) 'manners'.[33] This was the orthodoxy supposed to be
supported by the classical economists. It meant non-intervention
at home and free trade abroad. During the nineteenth century
a good many conservatives, like everyone else, accepted this.
For instance, speaking at Liverpool in 1872, Lord Derby said:
'For those social improvements which we all desire and which
are in everybody's mouth, we must look to the community
acting for itself in the first instance, and to Governments and
legislators only in rare and exceptional cases.'[34] He and others
warned strongly against entering the regions of paternal government. Various reasons were urged in addition to the orthodox
economic theories. The doctrine of self-help and the moral
significance of voluntary action were invoked, as were the
dangers of centralization: the campaign of the Tory publicist
and barrister, Joshua Toulmin Smith, is evidence here. There
was the feeling, too, that any social evil or discomfort was
divinely ordained and so had to be accepted. The realm of
political action was transcended as well in the perspective which
saw government intervention as tampering dangerously with a
natural process of organic evolution in society. There was also
the fear that Parliament, dominated by representatives of a
majority mandated to carry out the popular will, would constitute the basis of a new tyranny more effective and extensive
than that of royalist absolutism: it could only end in redistributive taxation, the insecurity of property and otherwise in a
threat to the social order itself. Dr Smith's summary of the
position of the Conservative Party in the 1860s and 1870s is that
it 'was, in fact, predisposed against rather than towards governmental intervention in social questions'.[35]

Northcote reflected the libertarian conservatism of the time.
He had always been a free-trader and supported repeal of the
Corn Laws even before Peel's conversion. He was prepared for
legislative control of the labour of children and women who

could not properly fend for themselves. But the adult male was a free agent who should largely look after his own interests. In a letter he wrote in 1875 to G. J. Holyoake, Northcote said the working classes must be got to work out their own improvement for themselves.[36] He believed the conditions of economic life were largely beyond control and was, therefore, sceptical about attempts at state regulation.

Another typical manifestation of these sentiments was the Liberty and Property Defence League, a body with a largely conservative membership formed to resist 'overlegislation', to maintain freedom of contract and to advocate individualism. One speaker, at a League conference, reflected its main themes in his address:

> Freedom is the true solution for many of our troubles—the utmost freedom that can be given to industry—the utmost freedom for a man to contract, or to bestow his labour on any subject he chooses, without State interference, while the only protection which the Government has a right and duty to extend over its subjects is the protection of life, liberty, limb and property, from injury by others. . . .[37]

Not surprisingly, there was strong opposition within the League to the schemes of radical and Tory democrats and the hope was expressed that conservatives would disengage themselves from this disastrous tendency.[38]

At the end of the nineteenth century, the libertarian wing of conservatism was of some significance: it had leaders of note and could draw on considerable electoral and other support.[39] There was an accession of strength at this period, too, because some of the unionists who split from the Liberals over home rule were free traders and (like Chamberlain on the other side of the doctrinal fence) carried their ideas with them over to the Conservative side. And, being opposed to state intervention to protect home industry, they were logically bound to reject proposals to extend public control in other ways.

Goschen is a good example here. Having long supported the Liberal cause, he aligned himself with the Conservatives in 1886 and joined the party in 1893. He was a lifelong libertarian and throughout his career his political opinions were (as he himself said) coloured by 'objection to the encroachment of Government interference on the freedom of individual action'.[40] Although he had supported electoral reform in 1867 he was always concerned about the possible collectivist impact of the change and in fact opposed further legislation in this respect. And he was a fervent enemy of compulsory equality because it would annihilate freedom.[41] He opposed Chamberlain's tariff reform campaign on the ground that protection would increase government power and further pave the way to state socialism.[42]

Other members of this conservative free-trade group were Hicks Beach, C. T. Ritchie, Lord Hugh Cecil and his brother Robert, Elliott (editor of the *Edinburgh Review*) and John St. Loe Strachey of *The Spectator*.[43] Strachey reflects the familiar syndrome of actions and attitudes. He ceased supporting the Liberals over home rule and differed with many unionists over tariff reform. Under his aegis *The Spectator*, though strongly unionist and imperialist, favoured non-intervention in domestic affairs and was firmly, even vituperatively, opposed to the kind of social policy espoused by Chamberlain (or Lloyd George).[44]

Many of these strands of anti-statist sentiment were brought together after 1905 in the British Constitution Association, founded to resist the rethinking tendencies in the Conservative Party and specifically to oppose everything that Joseph Chamberlain stood for in respect of economic and social reform. Its doctrine was indebted to Mill and the 'older economists' but was largely (so to say) by Samuel Smiles out of Herbert Spencer, the last-named being clearly the main intellectual influence at work.[45] The argument was that legislative supervision and control insulated people from the consequences, advantageous or otherwise, of their actions, tended to decrease a sense of personal responsibility and so to diminish initiative. It therefore inhibited the full development of character, retarded individual and social development, and lowered the quality of the people and the strength of the nation. 'The spread of Collectivist ideas . . . threatens to destroy the moral fibre of the British people by encouraging all classes to rely for their well-being upon Parliament or Municipalities rather than upon their own efforts.'[46] The essentially limited (if vital) function of the state is put, in effect, in terms of Spencer's law of equal freedom: it is 'to maintain the freedom of the individual, limited only by the like freedom of other individuals'. In the same style, it is asserted to be crucial that the earnings of each individual should be sacred to him and not taken from him to subsidize the inefficient. Collectivism is thus seen as a force contrary to the path of natural evolution.[47] On this kind of basis the association opposed, for example, schemes for a universal system of old-age pensions, the provision from public funds of meals for school-children, unemployment relief, limitation of the working day, municipal trading, compulsory education, and the like. And, of course, government was warned off the economic sphere which properly belonged to private enterprise.[48] A. V. Dicey was a supporter of the Association and, speaking at its conference in 1908, heavily stressed the importance of resisting class legislation because such collectivist intervention and reform limited the freedom of the individual through mistaken motives of benevolence and electoral popularity.[49]

Lord Hugh Cecil was a member of this Association and, in the interesting and quite extensive corpus of his theoretical writings and speeches, developed at some length a rationale for the view of conservatism involved. There were the usual reminders in this exposition of Spencer's doctrines but the greatest weight of Cecil's argument about the nature and role of government is thrown on his interpretation of Christianity and the ethical tenets it implies. These provide the normative standard by which political policy is to be judged and are, in his view, to be found in the New Testament. He admits that there is little direct discussion of politics in that source except an invocation to obey the state in its own sphere, that of maintaining order and repressing crime. But he thinks that this omission is itself significant and implies that the main message of Christianity does not therefore attribute major importance to political actions and institutions at all. The emphasis is other-worldly and spiritual and concerned primarily with the individual conscience and character. It discusses the value of concern for one's fellows as opposed to self-love, the importance of charity, the spiritual danger of riches and the like. 'If', he says, 'Christianity is to reform the social system'—and he admits the inferior ethical calibre of a society based on competition—'it can only effectually do it by inducing people to substitute love for self-interest. Nothing is more certain than that the mechanism of society will only express human character; it will not regenerate it. Character will transform the social system, but it takes something more vivifying that a social system to transform character.'[50] He therefore denies the usual principle of the reformer that a change of the institutions of society will produce an improvement in the character of the individuals composing it. In his view the matter is the other way round. For instance, because it stresses institutional change, socialism would simply transform the mode of self-interest and competition and not eliminate them.[51] Moreover, the methods of reform envisaged serve no ethical purpose: unselfishness enforced by law is a contradiction in terms for virtue consists not merely in doing right but in voluntarily choosing to do so. The good Samaritan aided the distressed man at his own cost; he did not run after the priest and the Levite and force them to minister to the poor man's sufferings; and *a fortiori* the Gospel story does not justify the wounded traveller himself compelling those who would pass him by to give him relief, for he would thus be little better than the footpads who had despoiled him. Yet this is, thinks Cecil, 'a fair parallel for a majority of voters' who exert their political power to confiscate wealth by law and distribute it among themselves. From the moral point of view, the mere transfer of material wealth from one pocket to another is indifferent if done by just means and dishonest if otherwise achieved.[52]

How, then, does Cecil view the specific role and duty of the state? As already indicated, his concern is with the moral framework of political action and he puts this in terms of a discussion of 'Justice'. The state must always act justly even when it is acting on behalf of the public as a whole. This means it must not inflict undeserved injury or withhold a benefit rightfully belonging to someone (except as punishment for a crime). So far as the institution of property is concerned, Cecil holds simply—though the argument is developed in some detail and sophistication—that where a system of private property happens to exist the principle that it is wrong to inflict an injury suffices to sustain this system.[53] And, in general, the duty of public authority is limited to activity necessary to the welfare of the whole community. On this his view is less restricted than Spencer's and he is prepared to concede that such activity covers the vital functions of maintaining security of life and property, public health, transport, lighting, and similar amenities.[54] Yet because of the restrictions he persists in envisaging, his view is clearly a libertarian one.

He asserts the necessity of sustaining a large sphere of individuality on which the community may not entrench because the widest possible opportunity of choice is essential for the development of the individual and of the race. Only the most exceptional circumstances could warrant putting aside this principle in favour of the 'costly palliative' and 'enervating hand' of government interference.[55]

Cecil rejects therefore the authoritarian pursuit of equality as both unreal and incompatible with genuine liberty. He looks forward instead (in terms of what might be called a christianized Spencerism) to a gradual evolution towards a sort of libertarian anarchy in which men live together in a 'spontaneous cohesion of virtuous wills'.[56]

Cecil also holds that the role of the state in economic life is of the second order. It cannot itself do more than clear the way for the optimum operation of primary economic forces. He cannot accept therefore the statist implications of tariff reform in respect of the regulation of trade and industry. Similarly, he is loath to accept any public responsibility for the general relief of suffering or for a programme designed to eliminate inequalities of wealth. This could only be achieved by an attack on property: and no one may rob to give alms.

Cecil is concerned, therefore, to show that (as he sees it) Christianity does not imply extensive social reform and economic control by the state. Increments of either may be necessary but they are to be kept to a minimum because they involve compulsion and perhaps injustice. The stress is rather upon individual or group action and the moral regeneration of character through this voluntary process. Yet a similar libertarian conservatism could be established on more secular grounds as the writings of Sir Ernest Benn showed.

Benn's point of view is, in fact, mannered in presentation, never systematic, and peculiarly his own. It was, however, broadly representative of a notable range of conservative opinion in the decades after the end of the Great War and indeed of recent years. Looking back a little while ago to the 1930s, Harold Macmillan said there were many in the Conservative

Party 'who believed that private enterprise, left alone and allowed to operate untrammelled, would . . . produce wealth on a greater scale than any other system'. The pure doctrine of *laissez-faire* might have been modified in the practice by the long growth of government intervention (as prompted, for instance, by the development of trade unionism) and by the reintroduction of protectionist policies. But a good number of Conservatives had originally been Whigs or Liberals and still cherished the general view that the less interference there was with private enterprise the better.[57] This was, in fact, a not uncommon theme in the party literature of the twenties and thirties. To take one instance only, a propaganda leaflet issued in 1925 urged the voter to support the Conservatives because they opposed 'excessive state control' and bureaucratic interference. The state, it said, 'cannot successfully direct industrial operations . . . and take the risks which individuals do': economic progress depends on 'individual enterprise'.[58] But Benn's was perhaps the most sustained defence of the libertarian position by a conservative publicist during the period concerned. He was (so to say) the Samuel Smiles of his day, the doctrine being also firmly rooted as usual in the ideas of the classical economists and the political evolutionism of Herbert Spencer.

Benn's family was active in liberal and radical politics and he was himself thus involved at one time and affected by the twin forces of evangelicalism and utilitarianism that moulded this background. He was, too, impressed by the possibilities of state action as a result of his experience as a temporary civil servant during the Great War. But he then quickly changed his mind and repudiated these 'economic wild oats'. Probably this was the result of the influence on him of Sir Hugh Bell, the individualist and free trader, and of a visit to the United States in 1921 during which Benn was greatly impressed with what he saw as the energy, efficiency and freedom of economic life there. He thus became the exponent of an unbending individualism, the flavour of which is indicated by the titles of a couple of his books: *The Return to Laisser-Faire* (1928) and *The State the Enemy* (1953). He formally and firmly broke with the Liberal Party in 1929 because he objected to the 'socialistic' doctrines of Lloyd George and the Yellow Book. He described the attitude he held thereafter as 'a full-blooded, die-hard Tory point of view'.[59]

In the thirty or more books and pamphlets Benn wrote (not to mention innumerable articles and speeches), he expounded his view of essential human freedom and defended the economic system based on private enterprise. Government intervention was always the foe to be attacked.

The basic doctrine has two aspects: a traditional constitutional libertarianism, and the economic belief in free enterprise and profit-making.

Liberty first and foremost is the supreme value as only through free choice can the moral qualities of the individual develop. State interference with the freedom of the subject must be reduced to a minimum; the executive must be once again subordinated to the legislature and judiciary; the rule of law must be fully asserted; administrative decentralization should be encouraged; the tendency for people to depend less on self-help and more on a paternalistic government is to be deplored.

So far as the economic field is concerned, the state must stay out as much as possible. Trade must be freed from restrictions; and profit (which is a premium on economy and efficiency) regarded as the proper motive of commerce. The price mechanism should be allowed to work freely as the only effective practical measure of exchange possibilities and the satisfaction of demand. The free enterprise, competitive system was indeed the analogue of political democracy: each was the most effective machinery to reflect and meet popular wants.

Benn was thus the opponent of the 'new despotism', 'bureaucracy triumphant',[60] the welfare state, confiscatory taxation, high public expenditure, the pursuit of social equality by legal compulsion, and all the rest. He fought a continual, and continually unsuccessful, rearguard action against state intervention. He never seems to have become discouraged, however; and was not without considerable support at times, for instance, from the Society of Individualists which he founded in 1942.[61] Of course, Benn reflected a point of view that has come to seem increasingly outmoded, and he never presented it in a complete and coherent fashion. He was a pamphleteer, not a political theorist. Yet it is clear he reflected and was an able exponent of the libertarian strand of conservatism under review.[62]

Nor has this doctrine been unreflected in the party itself in the period since 1945. There were, for instance, the reservations

about the kind of policy embodied in the Industrial Charter of
1947 expressed by such conservatives as Heathcoat Amory and
Waldron Smithers.[63] There was also the sentiment embodied in
such Tory slogans as 'Set the people free' and in the 1955
election cry, 'Conservative freedom works'.

Signs of this tendency were visible, too, in some important
aspects of the publications and speeches of the so-called 'One
Nation Group' of Conservative MPs.[64] The title of the first,
eponymous pamphlet (1950) clearly revealed the Disraelian
heritage; but there was more than one strand in the ideas of the
group and the libertarian element was indicated by the heading
of a major section in a later booklet, *Change is Our Ally* (1954),
which discussed 'The Return to a Free Economy'. John
Strachey in *The New Statesman* was in no doubt that what was
being preached was 'the pure milk of the gospel of classical
liberalism'.[65]

These expressions of opinion in fact owed a good deal to the
influence in the group of Enoch Powell whose speeches and
writings over the last two decades have constituted what is
arguably the most extensive and coherent recent statement of
conservative libertarianism. Something must be said about this
if only because the range and pattern of Powell's themes on
matters other than immigration have tended latterly to be
forgotten. Like most politicians he could be accused of inconsistency, of changing his stance. In fact, Powell freely admits this
is true of his attitude to the Empire and Commonwealth, and
to the Common Market issue. In each such case, no doubt
genuine changes of sentiment become indistinguishably mingled
with questions of political tactics. But the concern here is
primarily with the domestic role and duty of government, and
on this it is clear that Powell has not changed much at all since
he entered politics after the last war, though he has become
more uncompromising.

Basically he makes a distinction between two areas of the life
of a society, and he holds that the duties of a government dedi-
cated to freedom are different in each.

First, it is necessary to provide the nation with 'a secure and
civilised framework of living'. This covers, of course, defence,
maintenance of law and prevention of crime. But there is a
further aspect of this provision of common services which may

or may not involve the state. He thinks that what is done in this respect in any particular country will depend upon its history and circumstances. A motorway might be built and run as a public highway or a toll road; and hospitals might be the responsibility of central government, the municipalities or voluntary bodies. It depends. And so far as Britain is concerned Powell thinks that, while it might have been otherwise, we have, in these respects, become used to a good deal of public control and operation and have achieved high standards. This he is prepared to accept.[66] So it is quite clear he is not an exponent of extreme *laissez-faire* views in the style of Herbert Spencer or even Ernest Benn. When founding a university, establishing medical benefits, a social security scheme, a system of general education, the great urban services, a government is acting on other than economic criteria. There are dangers in so doing, to spontaneous development and change, but the alternative may be, too, a pitiful narrowing of human possibilities. If profit will not get the thing done, then government is necessarily drawn in.

Yet, secondly, in the economic sphere things are quite otherwise. For Powell is an unrepentant critic of the 'superstition' that government can and should try to control economic affairs. And his commitment to the free market economy arises in good part because he sees it as the 'unique key' with which 'to unlock imprisoned energies'.[67] And the role of government is primarily to see that this economic process goes on as undisturbed as possible. This means that very often its duty is 'to do nothing and let things happen', something that may require a great deal of political courage.[68] On the other hand, it may be that positive action is needed to remove obstacles or stop interference with the free flow of economic forces as when a system of controls is dismantled or a subsidy scheme abolished.[69] Further it may be appropriate for government to adjust to this same end the framework of law within which industry and commerce operate, for instance, by the prevention of restrictive practices, the revision of trade union law, or the treatment of monopoly.[70] Not surprisingly, therefore, Powell is largely opposed to a wide range of state ownership and would like to see this public sector resume its place in a free economy. And, of course, government attempts to direct the course of industry and commerce by planning or similar means are quite anathema to him. In his view, a national economic plan is an illusion and will not work. The complexities involved are too great; the information available for decision-making on this scale is woefully inadequate in both quantity and 'promptitude'; too much power comes to rest in the hands of a small group of politicians and civil servants; given the scope of things involved any mistake made will have enormous consequences; it is too rigid and slow to adapt (especially as it may be politically difficult to admit an error) and this can freeze a given distribution of labour and resources and so prevent development; it can also cause hardship by creating shortages as with the housing problem (which is the direct result of government attempts to peg rents, subsidize building and allocate output); it inhibits energy and enterprise and thus helps to reduce the reservoir of wealth on which the adequate provision of common services depends. But, above all, a national plan is the enemy of free choice; it means control: 'I happen to believe that when a society's economic life ceases to be shaped by the interaction of the free decisions of individuals, freedom is in a fair way to disappear from other sides of its existence as well. The terms "free economy" and "free society" are to me interchangeable.'[71] He also believes that the evils of inflation—surely the major economic issue of the day?—are the direct consequence of excessive government expenditure and the way in which this is financed; just as the recurrent balance of payments crises are attributed to control of exchange rates. Nor does Powell find any more congenial the collectivism by stealth that is involved in the procedure whereby, without invoking the law, government requests or intimidates persons and organizations to assist in its policies of control, as with schemes of 'voluntary' price or wage restraint. Reality—which is simply another name for freedom—will always force itself through illusions about the controlled economy though not, perhaps, before these illusions have wrought all sorts of untoward consequences. Given all this, Powell holds that the Conservative Party should stand clearly for capitalist free enterprise and against all forms of economic *dirigisme*. He recognizes, too, that this would require the repudiation of certain paternalistic or collectivist tendencies in the party's own tradition and record.

It is wrong, therefore, to see Powell simply as an old-fashioned classical liberal. He is prepared to have government play a significant role in the affairs of the community, especially in matters which concern the quality of its life. But he is undoubtedly very dubious indeed about the contemporary tendency to extend state control over the details of economic activity whether this be reflected in the conscious pursuit of state socialism or in the perhaps less committed but nevertheless ominous march towards the mixed economy or the middle way which has found substantial support in the leadership and body of both major parties at least for the last thirty or forty years. To this degree he certainly wants to turn the clock back; or leap forward: it depends how you see it.

Among conservatives Enoch Powell has thus put forward an extensive and considered case for a libertarian point of view. It is not the most profound exposition: this has, in recent years, been presented in the writings of Michael Oakeshott whose attack on collectivism and 'telocratic' government and whose defence of 'the political economy of freedom' and of a society infused with a sense of individuality and the rule of law are, in an important way, related to his idealist philosophy. He therefore gives these political and social views and the conservative attitude he associates with them an intellectual dimension and profundity they may often seem to lack. So in this context (as well as some others) he is a figure of very considerable significance. But I do no more than mention his work here because I have (as they say) written about it elsewhere.[72] Nor does Powell's exposition stand alone for a number of other conservative publicists have recently urged various aspects of a similar attitude. David Howell, for instance, has argued that 'a sharp and tough competitive climate' needed to be developed in economic life; Timothy Raison has adopted the same view and recognized the role of government in these matters can only be secondary; and Peregrine Worsthorne has written of the urgent need for conservatives to forsake the collectivist path and to defend the capitalist free economy.[73] Nigel Lawson, in stating a broadly similar case, has interestingly cast the discussion in terms of precisely the kind of ambivalence in conservative doctrine here being reviewed.[74] And, of course, the declared strategy of the present Conservative Government was precisely to change the collectivist direction of all post-war administra-

tions, Conservative or Labour, and thus to initiate an indivi-
dualist tendency in our affairs.[75] Certainly 'less government'
was the goal in respect to which a specific commitment was
made in the 1970 White Paper on *The Reorganization of Central
Government*.[76] And (to take one instance among many possible
examples), the Chancellor of the Exchequer, in a speech
delivered a few months after the last election, pledged the
government to 'the cutting of public expenditure' and 'the
reining back of state intervention and control in industry'.[77]
The intention was thus clearly expressed: it is not for me to
defend the subsequent record in this light.

V

Here, then, on this central issue is the range of ideas that
constitutes the ideology of modern British conservatism and
that indicates its character. No conservative accepts complete
state control of economic life: this is held to be socialism.[78] But
some, perhaps most, conservatives will welcome a varying
degree of state provision in the social field. Others, nowadays a
few, may repudiate even this. From minimal government the
doctrine extends to embrace a considerable interventionism. A
range of contrasting positions is therefore possible, each of them
equally at home in the conservative tradition. As to the motives
involved, they extend (as has been indicated) from humanita-
rian sentiment to administrative necessity, from the desire for
radical political reform to the need to grapple with economic
crisis. Similarly, the arguments and idioms used to sustain this
variety of viewpoint are also diverse and embrace the languages
of social evolutionism, Christian theology, constitutional history,
economic theory, and so on. And, of course, what bulks largest
is discussion of specific economic developments and social and
political problems. There is not, if the truth be told, a great
deal of conscious theoretical elaboration and (except in the
case of Oakeshott whom I have only briefly mentioned)[79]
nothing that deserves the name political philosophy.

There is one obvious point of criticism that might be levelled
at this characterization of conservatism. It is that while the
ideological ambivalence suggested above may be real, it *must*
nevertheless be true that conservatism essentially differs in

crucial respects from other doctrines such as socialism and liberalism.[80] In meeting this point, I would be right to concede two things.

First, that however much a collectivist conservative might be prepared, for instance, to admit or encourage state intervention, he would always do so with certain important reservations in mind, the most important of which would be that, in principle, the rights of property must be respected. Yet this point alone might not distinguish him from liberals or even a good many socialists. Further, the extent to which many conservatives have been prepared to entrench on private rights in the general interest (through redistributive taxation, for instance) has in practice been considerable. So much so that on a wide range of issues the views of many conservatives are well nigh indistinguishable from those of their opponents.[81] Then again, libertarian conservatives share many theories and ideas with their counterparts elsewhere. There is, for example, a great deal of common ground in the Christian moralism deployed before the Great War by Lord Hugh Cecil and the kind of sentiment set down in Tawney's *Commonplace Book*; and many free-trade liberals have easily found a home in the conservative ranks.

Then, secondly, there is the point that the conservative case (whether collectivist or libertarian) is usually expressed in its own special idiom. Conservatives traditionally speak the language of authority, continuity, appeal to the nation (rather than to the people), hierarchy and the like. Yet these concepts are abstract and not a little vague, and are thus capable of widely differing use or interpretation. So that when their emptiness is filled out concretely, when they are programmatically cashed, the basic antinomy easily re-enters.

There remains the continuing assertion that there *must* be common characteristics in conservative ideology of a meaningful and distinguishing kind. Nevertheless, and whatever its superficial appeal, this must be denied, and the counter-question asked: What *are* the goals, methods, and assumptions that are shared by Stafford Northcote and R. A. Butler, Joseph Chamberlain and Enoch Powell, Mallock and Macmillan? They do not even oppose the same things. The conclusion must be the rather Namierite one that a party's unity has to be found elsewhere than in its doctrines. Moreover, given the range of oppugnant attitudes of which conservatism consists and also given the cognate variety of posture to be found embraced by other political creeds as well, it is not surprising that genuine ideological opposition between parties is often no stronger—or less harsh—than it is within them.

NOTES AND REFERENCES

1. S. P. Huntington, 'Conservatism as an Ideology', *American Political Science Review* LI (1957), pp. 465, 469. Cf. R. A. Butler's remark, 'Conservatism . . . is no mere collection of catchpenny slogans and ephemeral theories; it is an abiding attitude of mind, a code of values, a way of life,' in *The New Conservatism* (London, Conservative Political Centre, 1955), p. [8]. Also R. T. McKenzie and A. Silver, *Angels in Marble* (London, Heinemann Educational, 1968), p. 21, on the 'shared understandings' of conservatism.

2. H. Spencer, *The Study of Sociology* (1873; repr. University of Michigan Press, 1961), p. 163.

3. J. Ortega y Gasset, *History as a System and Other Essays* (1941; New York, Norton, 1961), p. 58.

4. Elie Halévy, *The Era of Tyrannies* (1938; London, 1967), pp. xix, 205.

5. G. R. Elton, *Modern Historians on British History 1485-1945* (London, Methuen, 1970), p. 120.

6. I am at present engaged on a general survey of the 'British Political Tradition' on these lines and the present paper is an abridgement or summary of some part of this.

7. The existence of this contrast is not hypothetical but recognized by conservatives, e.g. N. Lawson in R. Blake and others, *Conservatism Today* (London, Conservative Political Centre, 1966), p. 57. A very similar range of conservative attitudes is also the basis of analysis in Nigel Harris, *Competition and the Corporate Society: British Conservatives, the State and Industry, 1945-1964* (London, Methuen, 1972). Unfortunately the present paper was already in final form when this most interesting and carefully researched study came to hand so I was unable here to take advantage of the many insights it contains.

8. H. Spencer, *The Man* Versus *the State* (1884; repr. Harmondsworth, Penguin, 1969), pp. 63 ff.

9. Lord Hugh Cecil, *Conservatism* (London, 1912), p. 72; R. A. Butler and H. Macmillan cited in H. Glickman, 'The Toryness of English Conservatism', *The Journal of British Studies*, I (1961), pp. 127, 134.

10. Benjamin Disraeli, *Coningsby*, Book VIII, Ch. iii.

11. T. E. Kebbel (ed.), *Selected Speeches of . . . the Earl of Beaconsfield* (London, 1882), I, p. 52.

12. *Coningsby*, Book IV, Chs iii-iv; *Sybil*, Book II, Ch. iii, Book III, Chs iv, viii.

13. John Morley, *The Life of Richard Cobden* (London, 1881), I, p. 297.

14. Cited W. F. Monypenny and G. E. Buckle, *The Life of Benjamin Disraeli* (rev. ed.) 2 vols. (London, 1929), I, p. 629.

15. Paul Smith, *Disraelian Conservatism and Social Reform* (London, Routledge, 1967). This scholarly work raises very interesting questions about the relation of ideology to policy and action, issues which parallel in the Disraelian sphere the

recent controversy over the role of Benthamism in the process of nineteenth-century change.

16. Ibid., pp. 2-3, 202, 322. Cf. R. Blake, *Disraeli* (London, Eyre & Spottiswoode, 1966), p. 553.

17. H. Spencer, *The Man* Versus *the State*, ed. cit., p. 80.

18. *The Times* (6 Feb. 1907) cited Monypenny and Buckle, op. cit., II, p. 709. Gorst's radicalism is reflected in some of his articles, e.g. 'Social Reform: the Obligation of the Tory Party', *Nineteenth Century*, LIII (1903), pp. 519-33.

19. *Fortnightly Review*, n.s. (1883), pp. 612-21.

20. See, for example, L. J. Jennings (ed.), *Speeches of . . . Lord Randolph Churchill . . . 1880-1888* (London, 1889), II, pp. 370-3.

21. Lord Rosebery, *Lord Randolph Churchill* (London, 1906), p. 154.

22. *The Radical Programme* (London, 1885), pp. 13, 17.

23. C. W. Boyd (ed.), *Mr. Chamberlain's Speeches* (London, 1914), I, p. 137.

24. Ibid.

25. In the *North American Review*, CLII (1891), pp. 534-48.

26. For example, *Speeches*, ed. cit., I, pp. 76-7; II, pp. 259-60. See also J. L. Garvin and J. Amery, *The Life of Joseph Chamberlain*, 6 vols. (London, 1932-69), II, pp. 423, 608, 615-16.

27. See the review of these matters in W. J. Wilkinson, *Tory Democracy* (New York, Octagon, 1925), pp. 260, 266-7, 270-3.

28. K. Feiling, *The Life of Neville Chamberlain* (London, 1946), p. 130.

29. Cited in B. Webb, *Our Partnership* (London, 1948), p. 267.

30. *Winds of Change: 1914-1939* (London, Macmillan, 1966), p. 210. It would be proper to add Keynes to this list.

31. For instance, with the stress on national and regional economic planning, planning of incomes ('incomes policy'), rationalization of industry by state intervention, more subsidized housing, help for depressed areas, N.E.D.C. etc.; and higher public expenditure generally.

32. Cited in *The New Conservatism*, ed. cit., pp. 11-12.

33. Edmund Burke, *Works* (World's Classics ed., London, 1907), VI, pp. 30-2.

34. Report in *The Times*, 10 January 1872 cited Smith, op. cit., p. 161.

35. Smith, op. cit., p. 34.

36. Letter cited in Smith, op. cit., p. 205.

37. E. Pleydell-Bouverie, *The Province of Government* (London, 1884), p. 15. Bouverie had been a Liberal M.P. but had become disenchanted with the direction that the party, under Gladstone's leadership, was taking.

38. Liberty and Property Defence League, *Annual Report (1893-4)*, pp. 6-7.

39. Cf. R. B. McDowell, *British Conservatism, 1832-1914* (London, 1959), p. 168.

40. A. R. D. Elliot, *The Life of George Joachim Goschen* (London, 1911), I, p. 60.

41. Goschen's *Addresses* (Edinburgh, 1885), p. 12 and other references cited by, T. J. Spinner, Jr. 'G. J. Goschen: the Man Lord Randolph Churchill "Forgot" ' *Journal of Modern History*, XXXIX (1967), pp. 415-16.

42. Ibid., p. 424.

43. McDowell, op. cit., p. 168.

44. Ibid., pp. 169-70. Cf. Strachey's *The Adventure of Living* (London, 1922), Chs xxvi-xxviii and his *The Problems and Perils of Socialism* (London, 1908).

45. See, for example, M. H. Judge (ed.), *Political Socialism* (Westminster, 1908), pp. 87ff., 161-8; also C. W. Saleeby, *Individualism and Collectivism* (Westminster, 1906), *passim*.

46. Judge, op. cit., p. 179.

47. Ibid., pp. 5, 87, 90, 174-5, 181.

48. Saleeby, op. cit., p. 16; B.C.A. leaflet, *The Education Act of 1906; Constitution Papers* No. 3 (Aug. 1906), p. 10, No. 5 (Apr. 1908), pp. 57-9, and those for 1909, *passim.*

49. *Constitution Papers*, No. 14 (Sept. 1908), pp. 117-18.

50. Lord Hugh Cecil, *Conservatism* (London, 1912), p. 91.

51. Ibid., pp. 91-5. Fabianism is Cecil's target here of course.

52. Ibid., pp. 96-9 and *Liberty and Authority* (London, 1910), pp. 16-18, 24. Of course, Cecil distinguishes between this sort of compulsory redistribution of wealth to relieve the wants of whole classes of citizens from legitimate taxation necessary to defray essential community services: see *Conservatism*, pp. 152-8.

53. Cecil, *Conservatism*, pp. 120 ff., 165-8.

54. Ibid., pp. 139-40.

55. Cecil, *Liberty and Authority*, pp. 16-18, 24, 36-7, 46, 67.

56. Ibid., pp. 68-9.

57. Macmillan, *Winds of Change*, p. 501; cf. ibid., p. 510.

58. *Why You Should be Conservative and Unionist* (1925; No. 2078) in British Museum 'NUCA Tracts and Leaflets' (2035-2206), [press mark: 8139 dd.]. For another, rather different, contemporary reflection of these ideas see F. J. C. Hearnshaw, *Conservatism in England* (London, 1933), pp. 285-6, 291-5, 303-7.

59. Ernest Benn, *Happier Days* (London, 1945), pp. 160-1.

60. Sir Carleton Allen wrote a book with this title (London, 1931). He was a long time associate of Benn and shared his views. The libertarian opinions of Lord Hewart, author of *The New Despotism* (London, 1929) are well known.

61. This body followed a number of earlier organizations of a similar kind. Still in existence, its membership has invariably included a number of Conservative MPs and it had some influence recently in the campaign to establish the office of Parliamentary Commissioner for Administration: see F. A. Stacey, *The British Ombudsman* (Oxford, Clarendon Press, 1972), pp. 28-32, 37, 67-8, 340.

62. The activities of Aims of Industry and the Institute of Economic Affairs (founded in 1942 and 1957 respectively) have in fact latterly been directed broadly to sustaining in the public view the kind of economic and political attitudes represented by Sir Ernest Benn.

63. Lord Butler, *The Art of the Possible* (London, Hamish Hamilton, 1971), pp. 143-4; *Keesing's Contemporary Archives* (1946-8) col. 8945, (1948-50) col. 10286; H. Macmillan, *Tides of Fortune, 1945-1955* (London, Macmillan, 1969), pp. 303-4.

64. This group, all of whom were elected for the first time in 1950, initially consisted of C. J. M. Alport, R. Carr, R. Fort, E. Heath, G. Longden, I. Macleod, A. Maude, J. E. Powell and J. Rodgers.

65. Cited A. Roth, *Enoch Powell: Tory Tribune* (London, Macdonald, 1970), p. 111. See especially E. Powell and A. Maude, *Change is Our Ally* (London, 1954), pp. 47, 96-7. Also a later 'Our Nation' pamphlet by Lord Balniel and others, *The Responsible Society* (London, Conservative Political Centre, 1959), pp. 5-8, 11.

66. For example his realization of the problems and defects inherent in a nationally organized and financed health service does not lead him to advocate or anticipate any radically different alternative: see his *A New Look at Medicine and Politics* (London, 1966), *passim.*

67. J. Wood (ed.), *Freedom and Reality* (Kingswood, Surrey, 1969), pp. 26-7.

68. J. Wood (ed.), *A Nation Not Afraid* (London, 1965), p. 33.

69. Ibid., pp. 4, 33-4.

70. Ibid., pp. 14, 119 ff.; *Freedom and Reality*, pp. 193-214.

71. J. E. Powell, *Saving in a Free Society*, 2nd ed. (London, Inst. of Econ. Affairs, 1966), p. 8.

72. See my *Oakeshott's Philosophical Politics* (London, Longman, 1966); also my

'Idealism, Modern Philosophy and Politics' in P. King and B. C. Parekh (eds.), *Politics and Experience* (Cambridge University Press, 1968), Ch. 5 (a volume which also contains, Ch. 14, a bibliography of Oakeshott's writings). Although Professor F. A. Hayek has specifically denied he is a conservative it is rather the collectivist brand of conservatism that he repudiates; and, in general, his political ideas are clearly of this libertarian type: see especially *The Constitution of Liberty* (London, Routledge, 1960), which is, surely, one of the most important statements of this doctrine to appear in many decades?

73. D. Howell in M. Wolff and others, *The Conservative Opportunity* (London, Batsford, 1965), pp. 99-104; T. Raison, *Conflict and Conservatism* (London, 1965), esp. pp. 11-15; P. Worsthorne in R. Blake and others, *Conservatism Today*, ed. cit., pp. 18-24, 28-30.

74. N. Lawson in Blake and others, op. cit., pp. 55-7, 59-60.

75. Cf. P. Cosgrave, 'Edward Heath's Strategy', *The Spectator*, CCXXVII (16 Oct. 1971), pp. 546-7.

76. Cmnd. 4506, p. 3, para. 2.

77. Reported in *The Times* (16 Oct. 1970).

78. Misleadingly held, of course: because there are many anti-statist forms of socialism too.

79. I am conscious, too, that I have also not referred at all to many other conservative writers and publicists of some importance: there is nothing on Mallock, Maine, Salisbury, Balfour, Eustace Percy, Amery and a host of others, all of whom had a great deal to say. But I am persuaded the general framework of analysis would happily accommodate them and that the illustrations I have given are broadly representative.

80. An earlier and shorter version of this paper was read at seminars at a number of universities and this point was invariably made, thus showing the wide, but (in my view) false, appeal of a nuclear definition.

81. Hence the existence of such figures of journalistic fun as 'Butskell' and 'Heathkins'.

The Ideology of Labourism

JOHN SAVILLE

The history of British society in the last century and a half exhibits certain striking political and intellectual contradictions. The virtual elimination of the peasantry from the countryside before industrialization got under way at the end of the eighteenth century meant that the majority of the population in town and country were wage-labourers: a social structure that remained unique in the world during the nineteenth century.[1] The fact of proletarianization had some important consequences. One was that the Chartist demand for universal suffrage, had it been accepted, would have given an automatic majority to those without property. The challenge of Chartism before 1850 turned on this point, since all over Europe in these years political democracy involved economic and social implications.[2] This is what Engels was referring to in *The Condition of the Working Class in England in 1844* when he commented that the Six Points of the Charter 'which are all limited to the reconstitution of the House of Commons, harmless as they seem, are sufficient to overthrow the whole English Constitution, Queen and Lords included. . . . The English Chartist is politically a republican, though he rarely or never mentions the word, while he sympathizes with the republican parties of all countries, and calls himself in preference a democrat. But he is more than a mere republican, his democracy is not simply political.'[3]

Two years before Engels published these words the Liberal

historian, Lord Macaulay, delivered himself of an alarmist speech on the occasion of the debate in the House of Commons on the presentation of the second national Chartist petition. His words summed up the attitudes of the propertied classes:

> But I believe that universal suffrage would be fatal to all purposes for which government exists, and for which aristo-cracies and all other things exist, and that it is utterly incom-patible with the very existence of civilisation. I conceive that civilisation rests on the security of property . . . and if it be the fact, that all classes have the deepest interest in the security of property, I conceive, that this principle follows, that we never can, without absolute danger, entrust the supreme Govern-ment of the country to any class which would, to a moral certainty, be induced to commit great and systematic inroads against the security of property.[4]

The Chartist movement, the first mass movement of working men in the history of industrial capitalism, was destroyed partly by a judicious combination of force and guile on the part of the propertied classes, partly as a result of internal dissension and uncertainties within the movement itself. Thereafter, in the second half of the nineteenth century, the central paradox of domestic politics was the failure to develop an independent working-class party. Chartism had stamped the working class as an essential part of the British political scene, and even with the rapid decline of the Chartist movement in the early years of the 1850s, there was a notable carry-over of certain of its ideas into later decades. Most important, the fact of class conscious-ness was now widely pervasive among working-class groups, although more often than not it was a variant of the 'them against us' syndrome rather than a clear definition of prole-tarian independence; and with the virtual elimination of a socialist ideology class consciousness assumed distinctly muted 'economist' forms rather than clear-cut political attitudes. During the third quarter of the nineteenth century, with the collapse of the Chartist movement, there evolved in the vacuum thus created a labourist ideology among working men sub-ordinate to the dominant ideas of the bourgeoisie, and this ideology thrust increasingly deep roots down into the soil of British society as the decades went by. When socialist ideas and a socialist movement returned to Britain in the last twenty years of the century, the most serious obstacle to the acceptance of a position of intellectual and political independence was the strength and tenacity of this labourist tradition.

The starting point for an analysis of labourism in Britain must be the intellectual and political hegemony achieved by bourgeois thinkers, artists and politicians over their overwhelming proletarian society; and the consequent subordinate position occupied by the working people. Hegemony, in the words of Gwyn Williams, who takes the concept from Antonio Gramsci,

> is an order in which a certain way of life and thought is dominant, in which one concept of reality is diffused throughout society in all its institutional and private manifestations, informing with its spirit all taste, morality, customs, religious and political principles and all social relations, particularly in their intellectual and moral connotations.[5]

In its political aspects hegemony involves the acceptance of leadership by consent rather than by naked coercion. In the British case we must begin with the profound break in ideological trend represented by the disintegration of the Chartist movement. Political independence was subsumed beneath an increasingly firm attachment, on the part of the articulate working class, to the emerging Liberal Party of the late 1860s; intellectual independence was splintered into many separate strands, with no cohesiveness between the various parts or a structured framework of ideas but rather a series of *ad hoc* islands of radical thought with little or no connection between them. At best working-class radicalism was a limited and partial critique, not of society as a whole, but of individual segments of society. Labourism, as it developed through the third quarter of the nineteenth century, was a theory and practice which accepted the possibility of social change within the existing framework of society; which rejected the revolutionary violence and action implicit in Chartist ideas of physical force; and which increasingly recognized the working of political democracy of the parliamentary variety as the practicable means of achieving its own aims and objectives. Labourism was the theory and practice of class collaboration; it was a tradition which in theory (always) and in practice (mostly) emphasized the unity of Capital and Labour, and the importance of conciliation and arbitration in industrial disputes. These social attitudes, which stressed the unity of classes, found an outlet in various aspects of petty-bourgeois ideas and practice, such as the doctrine of self-help, and in support of movements of personal amelioration, such as the temperance movement. A naive expression of the labourist approach was reflected in one of the *Songs for English Workmen to Sing*, first published in 1867:

> Work boys, work and be contented
> So long as you've enough to buy a meal;
> The man you may rely
> Will be wealthy by and by
> If he'll only put his shoulder to the wheel.

Whether many, or any, working men ever sang this kind of song is not altogether certain, but a more sophisticated approach, and one which was widely accepted, was summed up in the slogan, 'A Fair Day's Wage for a Fair Day's Work'.

The pith of the labourist ideology is in this phrase.[6] There was, on the one hand, a recognition that 'fair' dealing was available and obtainable in bourgeois society; on the other, a stubborn insistence upon bargaining rights at the point of production. In the liberal-labour tradition there was always a central emphasis upon certain limited purposes and functions of trade unions. In no other area of life was 'independence' so clearly manifested; and while the ideological framework narrowed significantly the terms of reference within which industrial bargaining took place, there was much to be argued about and struggled for. Any threat to the legal status of trade unions, and what were regarded as its traditional rights, always called forth great reserves of militant intransigence and class consciousness. This was the product of decades of opposition and conflict in the productive process with the employers of labour, who were traditionally much tougher and less compromising than their political representatives and leaders. Trade unionism in the nineteenth century, both after as well as before the Act of 1875, was always confronted with a steady and unrelenting hostility; and it is this which more than anything else shaped and moulded working-class attitudes and sentiment. Whatever trade union leaders were to say in public about the need for the joint partnership of Capital and Labour, the realities of life in the factory, workshop and mine meant a commitment to opposition—which at times involved struggle— very different from the public pronouncements so often quoted.[7]

Therein, however, lay a contradiction which goes far to explain the 'fractured' consciousness of the organized workers in nineteenth-century Britain. On the one hand, an 'economist' class consciousness continuously renewed from within the industrial sector; but on the other, a pervasive sense of colla- boration in political affairs. The contrasts are striking, and they can be seen in every industrial area of the economy, but no group of workers illustrate better this break of consciousness, this fractured comprehension of their contemporary world, than do the miners before 1900.

The industrial history of the mining communities in the nineteenth century is more adequately documented than for any other occupational group, and it needs no summary here. It was not until the 1870s, and for most areas the 1880s, that stable trade unions existed among the miners, but by the last twenty years before 1900 most mining regions had developed a massive sense of class solidarity that found reflection in increas- ingly powerful union organizations. An industrial leadership had emerged which was notable both for its firmness on industrial issues and for its political moderation. The majority of miners' leaders were strongly attached to the Liberal Party, and parliamentary attitudes and practices had no more vigorous advocates among organized working men.

The historical reasons for both the industrial and political attitudes of the miners allow of a reasonably straightforward analysis. On the industrial side the degree of exploitation of the labour force, the monopoly control of the mine-owners in what were nearly always single-occupation regions, the geo- graphical isolation of the miners from other sections of the working class, all contributed to the emergence of a highly developed sense of class solidarity. Not that solidarity was an attribute that developed in any automatic or linear way. For many decades the miners found it impossible to establish viable unions—their bargaining power, against the background of

continuous inwards migration to the coal-fields from the rural
areas, remained weak; and the constant and hostile pressures
of the mine-owners against the militants in terms both of jobs
and houses were major obstacles to that complete unity of the
labour force without which no long-term organization was
possible. Victimization, defeat after defeat in strikes, the
repeated failure of local and regional unions—these were the
common experiences of the mining communities before more
or less stable unions established themselves in most regions in
the closing decades of the nineteenth century. And once
established, there was no diminution in the bitterness with
which industrial disputes were conducted.

The paradox—between the miners' industrial class-conscious-
ness and their political attitudes—was therefore sharply defined.
In the year 1900, which saw the formation of the Labour
Representation Committee, there was no group of organized
workers more totally committed to the Liberal Party than the
miners. Socialist propaganda had made little headway, and
hardly a miners' leader had repudiated the Lib.-Lab. alliance.
For reasons that are well known, the miners for many decades
had looked to Parliament for redress of their grievances. It was,
indeed, their conviction that only through parliamentary action
could they hope to offset the local monopoly of political and
economic power enjoyed by the mine-owners. When political
democracy came to be extended in the last thirty years or so
of the nineteenth century, the miners were in a unique position
to take advantage of the new political opportunities, largely
because they lived in single-occupation villages and small towns
and were thereby numerically preponderant. A majority of
miners in the country as a whole were excluded by the Second
Reform Act of 1867, but they were enfranchized twenty years
later in 1884; and the creation of School Boards (in 1870),
County Councils (in 1888) and Parish Councils (in 1893) all
helped to increase their local political importance. The typical
biography of a miners' leader between 1880 and 1900 would
show election to all, or most of the bodies mentioned above,
and in some cases there would be added a constituency election
for Parliament. Out of eleven working-class MPs in 1885—all
of them accepting the Liberal Whip—six were miners.[8]

There were other factors that worked in the same direction

of political moderation. Religion was one. It is now appreciated that there were large segments of working-class communities in nineteenth-century Britain that remained untouched by religious beliefs; but among those groups in which religion, and particularly the religion of Nonconformity, played an important part, the miners were especially notable. In England and Wales a considerable proportion of miners' leaders—and they were probably a majority—belonged to the chapel; in some areas—Durham, Northumberland, Derbyshire and South Wales—the miners' lodge and the chapel were almost interchangeable in terms of their social composition and particularly of their leadership. The relationships between religion and occupational groups were always complex, but on the whole the chapel tended to discourage violence; and at the same time it encouraged—outside the basic solidarity of the pit—certain individualist values on matters such as temperance which helped to strengthen the ties between the Liberal Party and the mining communities.

Once the values of parliamentarianism had been accepted, and the relations between Liberalism and the miners had come to be established, political and social momentum carried the political attitudes involved well into the twentieth century. It is important to appreciate how tough and tenacious the labourist tradition was among the mining communities. The leaders through whom the labourist tradition found expression had been the pioneers of trade unionism in their own areas. It was they who in their younger days had so often suffered victimization and it was they who had finally built the unions as stable organizations. The miners' leaders in the last decades of the century, always ready to pay fulsome tributes to W. E. Gladstone, the 'People's William', were tough and hard negotiators in industrial issues; their record in rescue work was usually outstanding; their service to their fellow men was for all to see, not only in union affairs, but on the school board, local council or Board of Guardians. It was a vigorous, reforming tradition, with nothing soft or sentimental about it when it was a matter of the interests of their own miners. The intellectual and political horizons of these miners' leaders were sharply limited, but to those who remembered earlier days, the facts of material progress in the present could not be gainsaid.

Writing of the differences between England and France, George Eliot in 1848 offered a despairing but pertinent comment on English politics: 'And there is nothing in our Constitution to obstruct the slow progress of *political* reform. This is all we are fit for at present. The social reform which may prepare us for great changes is more and more the object of effort both in Parliament and out of it. But we English are slow crawlers.'[9] As George Eliot was suggesting, British society, as it evolved during the second half of the nineteenth century, was to a degree an 'open' society in which the opportunities for change were realizable within strictly defined limits. Change was possible, but it was always slow, uneven in its incidence, piecemeal rather than complete, never more than a partial adaptation or re-structuring of existing practices or traditional arrangements. Political philosophers in Britain have often extolled the refusal of politicians to effect a root and branch upheaval, and it is a much commended thesis that the British are an empirically-minded people, given to practice, and slow-changing practice at that, rather than to elaborate theoretical constructs. What has usually been omitted from the argument is the economic and social context in which such political decisions have been taken. In a society in which the absolute majority of a wage-earning proletariat was established so early, the interests of the propertied classes could only be on the side of change, if change there had to be, that was both slow and piecemeal. The history of electoral reform is a central illustration of the point. The working-class majority of the British population were totally excluded from the electoral process at national level until 1867, at which time most working men in the towns obtained the vote. In order to offset this working-class increase to the urban electorate, the vote was not extended to wage-earners living in the rural areas, and this excluded large categories of workers, including agricultural labourers and most miners. Nor was the Reform Act of 1867 followed by a redistribution of seats, and the great urban centres continued to be grossly under-represented while the small country towns, overwhelmingly Conservative in political affiliation, exerted a disproportionate influence. It was not until nearly twenty years later, in 1884, that those living in rural areas were now included in the electorate, and only in the next year was there a redistribution of seats which brought voting patterns more in line with the distribution of population. Until 1911 the House of Lords, dominated by the Conservative Party, had an absolute veto over all legislation except, by tradition, money Bills. Women were wholly excluded from the vote until 1918, and they were not put on an age parity with men until 1929. Moreover, a formal recital of constitutional change conceals as much as it reveals, for at least down to 1914 many obstacles hindered considerable sections of working men from exercising their vote at both parliamentary and local elections. Of these the difficulties of electoral registration were the most effective.[10]

The most illuminating statement of the tactics and strategy demanded by a ruling class within a proletarian society was provided by Walter Bagehot. In the preface to the 1872 edition of *The English Constitution* Bagehot set out his advice, which may be summarized thus: First, there was the supreme danger of a 'permanent combination' of the working people. The extension of the suffrage in 1867 had injected a new factor into the political situation which obviously made the reality of a working men's party much more of a possibility in the future. The ways to avoid this coming about, Bagehot wrote, would require 'the greatest wisdom and the greatest foresight in the higher classes'. They must not only be prepared to remove every actual grievance which the masses of the people experienced, but, if possible, they must try to eliminate every 'supposed' grievance. The ruling classes, Bagehot emphasized, 'must willingly concede every claim which they can safely concede, in order that they may not have to concede unwillingly some claim which would impair the safety of the country'—another way of stating Macaulay's 'security of property' argument. Bagehot noted that this approach would demand both restraint and understanding, and that in particular what must be avoided were those political battles over issues which were not fundamental (i.e. to property relationships) and which the ruling class would lose anyway, but which could easily be prolonged over a long period of time, with the result that the working classes would acquire both cohesion and experience in the struggle.

Bagehot's advice, pertinent and sensible, was not a complete statement of strategy and tactics for the ruling groups in Britain. But in the context of the present discussion of the ideas and practices of labourism, his remarks are especially apposite. It is the real possibilities of piecemeal reform that have provided the underpinning for the acceptance of a modest, evolutionary approach to politics and social change that has found its expression in the labourist ideology. Essentially these were, as they still are, defensive attitudes. E. P. Thompson made a valid point when he commented that after the working class (in the Chartist period) failed to overthrow capitalist society, they then proceeded, in the decades after 1850, 'to warren it from end to end'.[11] A variety of organizations of self-help came into existence and flourished—skilled workers' trade unions, friendly societies, co-operative stores, self-education groups, mutual help societies of one kind or another. All this is indisputable, and so are the densely structured sub-cultures within which these organizations grew up. The historical perspectives involved were, however, basically defensive—these were the ways in which the working class—in its varying occupational and geographical contexts—reacted to, and provided safeguards against, the gross insecurities of industrial society. While what they were doing had many positive aspects—it was within their own cultural groups that working people maintained their sense of class, which on one level is another way of talking about independence and self-respect—in global terms, in the context of society as a whole, it meant that the working class were accepting a subordinate role and had become a corporate class.

While the philosophy and doctrines of labourism are deeply rooted in the historical evolution of industrial society, it does not follow that it was 'inevitable'—to the point that all other possibilities can be excluded—whereby the working class *had* to adopt an intellectually, and therefore politically, subordinate position. There were, as indicated above, many factors encouraging the acceptance of an intellectually subordinate way of looking at the social and political world; but what helped to make it 'inevitable' was the absence of any sustained critique of bourgeois society by its traditional intellectuals. Such a statement immediately raises the crucial question concerning the role of ideas, and their transmission, in industrial societies; and while the matter cannot be argued at any length here the discussion that follows is founded upon Gramsci's ideas which themselves developed out of a thesis put forward by Lenin in the early 1900s. Lenin, it will be recalled, argued in *What is to be Done* (1902) that by themselves the working class were incapable of going beyond 'economist' ideas; and that socialism had to be brought to them from outside their experience by middle-class intellectuals. Gramsci's discussion of the differences between 'organic' and 'traditional' intellectuals emphasized that it was sections of the latter, less closely identified with the dominant class than the 'organic' intellectuals, who could be expected to develop a critique of their society to the point where they identified themselves with the working-class movement.[12] In the case of Britain in the nineteenth century what is striking is not only the vigour of the 'organic' intellectuals in the first half of the century, but more relevant is the relative weakness and lack of major influence of the more critically minded traditional intellectuals. Most of the latter remained in fact uncritical, conformist and complacent, or were involved in less central issues such as that of evolution and Biblical interpretation. Of the critical minority only Carlyle (before 1850) and Ruskin are at all important. The subtle analyses of Coleridge had only a limited influence and the same is true of John Stuart Mill, largely because in the 1860s Mill's radical practice ran ahead of his writing and he never set down at any length the shift in his ideas that can be discerned in the last decade of his life. Neither Carlyle nor Ruskin, moreover, achieved anything approaching a comprehensive critique, although both had a very considerable influence upon working men. Had their arguments gone beyond a critique of industrialism to a consideration of the possibilities of a new social order their contribution to the intellectual enlightenment of working men would have been much more far-reaching. As it was, their analysis was partial and their impact and influence blurred and uncertain. Only William Morris, who acknowledged Ruskin as his master 'before my days of practical socialism' moved beyond the categories of romantic protest against the commercialization of bourgeois society to accept 'that amidst all this filth of civilization the seeds of great change, what we others call Social-Revolution, were beginning to germinate'. Morris, in the same passage, goes on to comment that acceptance of the practical possibilities of a new social order saved him from 'crystallizing into a mere railer against "progress" ' on the one hand, and from middle-class utopianism on the other.[13]

The striking fact about English intellectual life in the nineteenth century is its general mediocrity, its complacent acceptance of the fundamentals of bourgeois society, its failure to probe, dissect and analyse the causes of the spiritual anaemia that afflicted all sections and classes of society. In the only country that had been industrialized since the beginning of the nineteenth century, there was one major intellectual and no more than one—William Morris—who found his way towards a root and branch critique and accepted the practical consequences thereof. Such, however, was the conformity of intellectual life, despite the new winds that were beginning to blow towards the end of the century, that after his death in 1896 Morris's acceptance of a revolutionary socialist position was quickly and easily overlaid with misinterpretation and misunderstandings to the point where its revolutionary content was ignored.[14]

Socialism, as a body of ideas and as a movement, returned to a Britain in the 1880s in which labourism was already strongly rooted. While it is worth noting that socialism in the first decade of its return meant a variety of Marxism, by 1900 the dominant philosophy of the Left was a hybrid of ILP emotionalism and Fabian hardheadedness; and it was the latter who were to provide the basic intellectual ingredients for the labour movement after 1900, and in so doing reinforce the fundamental assumptions of the labourist ideology. In particular the Fabians rejected any theory of the state as a coercive power, and thereby fully accepted all the implications of parliamentarianism. Bernard Shaw's early pamphlet *The Impossibility of Anarchism*, published in 1892, is a key document in this context. The Fabians, secondly, offered a historical perspective within which the existing labourist ideas could find a natural place, and which provided an intellectual rationale for evolutionary and reformist practices. The Fabians, it is often forgotten, were as historically determinist as the most dogmatic and naive Marxist; gradualism, it was argued, was built into the evolution of British parliamentary democracy; it was both necessary, in terms of working-class demands, and inevitable, given the pressures of the working-class majority in a parliamentary system.

The Marxist tradition, re-established in the 1880s, offered a dogmatic theory which inspired an active minority to attempt to radicalize the working-class movement. The same is broadly true of the ILP tradition which was more religious and emotional in its approach. Both, however, though sustaining large numbers of militants, failed to develop any but reformist pressure within British society. What has been remarkable in the twentieth century has been the failure of the socialist movement to develop and maintain a critique of contemporary society that seriously grappled with its dominant ideas. British socialists have shown themselves highly competent at description and factual analysis. R. H. Tawney offered striking insights into the moral values of an unequal society; but with the partial exception of Harold Laski and perhaps of George Orwell, the fundamental problems of a working class in a sophisticated capitalist society eluded the theoreticians of the British labour movement. It is notable, to give one example from the post-World War Two years that the only sustained critique of Oxford philosophy has been by a liberal, Ernest Gellner. There are two areas in particular in which the theoretical weaknesses of British socialism have been especially marked. One is the theory of the state and the second is the still partial attempt at a re-interpretation of British history in Marxist terms.

In part, at any rate, these theoretical weaknesses can be accounted for by the general parochial quality of intellectual life in Britain during the twentieth century. It is reasonable to argue that without Pareto, Mosca, Michels, Sorel and Croce there would have been no Antonio Gramsci; that we can ascribe part of the reasons for the failure to sustain a comprehensive critical analysis of British society to the intellectual 'greyness' of that society. This is, of course, only a partial answer but whatever the reasons, there was certainly no continuous assault upon the theoretical foundations of the labourist position; and in some periods indeed—the decade of the 1950s being one—the further elaboration of the gradualist approach went virtually unchallenged.

H

Labourism, as a theory and a practice, is deeply rooted in the social structures and organizations of the British working class. It has the enormous force of a tradition established and practised over many decades. This side of economic and social catastrophe, it is likely to prove stubbornly resistant to change. Which is not to say that change cannot, or will not, come.

NOTES AND REFERENCES

1. British historians are still somewhat shy about emphasizing this important fact, which explains so much of British politics in the last century and a half. For the historical background, see my 'Primitive Accumulation and Early Industrialisation in Britain', *Socialist Register* (1969), 247-71.

2. E. H. Carr, *The Soviet Impact on the Western World* (London, 1947), p. 8; R. McKeon (ed.), *Democracy in a World of Tensions* (United Nations, Paris, 1951), *passim*.

3. From the chapter headed 'Labour Movements'.

4. *Hansard Parliamentary Debate*, Third Series, Vol. 63 (1842), cols. 44-52.

5. 'Gramsci's Concept of *Egemonia*', *Journal of the History of Ideas*, XXI (4) (Oct.-Dec. 1960), 586-99.

6. At the beginning of the socialist revival of the 1880s, Engels wrote a famous series of articles, in which, *inter alia*, he dissected the 'Fair Day's' slogan. The articles were published in the *Labour Standard* in 1881 and have since been reprinted in a number of places.

7. This is a much discussed matter. For an early statement in the debate, see R. V. Clements, 'British Trade Unions and Popular Political Economy, 1850-75', *Economic History Review* (1961), 93-104.

8. Thomas Burt (Morpeth, Northumberland); Ben Pickard (Normanton, Yorkshire); John Wilson (Houghton-le-Spring, Durham); William Crawford (Mid-Durham); Charles Fenwick (Wansbeck, Northumberland); William Abraham (Rhondda, S. Wales). Biographical entries for all six will be found in J. M. Bellamy and John Saville (ed.), *Dictionary of Labour Biography*, Vol. 1 (1972).

9. Letter to J. Sibree (February 1848) in *George Eliot's Life, as related in her letters and journals*, J. W. Cross (ed.), New York, Harper Bros. 1884, p. 99.

10. Neal Blewett, 'The Franchise in the United Kingdom, 1885-1918', *Past and Present* No. 32 (December 1965), pp. 27-56.

11. E. P. Thompson, 'The Peculiarities of the English', *Socialist Register* (1965).

12. For Gramsci's analysis of the role and place of intellectuals in society see *The Modern Prince and Other Writings* (New York, International Publishing Co., 1957), pp. 118-25; *Selections from Prison Notebooks of Antonio Gramsci* (Quintin Hoare and G. Nowell Smith (ed.) (London, Lawrence & Wishart, 1971), esp. pp. 5-23. For a brief introduction see Louis Marks, 'Antonio Gramsci', *Marxist Quarterly*, III (4) (October 1956).

13. William Morris, *How I Became a Socialist* (many editions).

14. E. P. Thompson, *William Morris: Romantic to Revolutionary* (London, Lawrence & Wishart, 1955), esp. Pt. IV, pp. 735-845.

National Interest *Versus* Ideology in American Diplomacy

STEPHEN KIRBY

In the abstract analysis of foreign policy a distinction has frequently been made between policy that is inspired by an ideology and one that is based upon the pragmatic calculation of national interest,[1] and nowhere in recent years has this distinction been more readily applied than to the foreign policy of the United States.[2] It provides the intellectual foundations of quite different explanations of the major developments of her recent foreign policy, the most important of which has been the acquisition of 'Empire', or that process where America abandoned the reluctant and spasmodic involvement in world events before 1941 for the full participation in, and eventual domination of, events in the post-war world. Although accounts and histories of this transition abound both in number and in nuance, it is possible to see two schools; one that sees American policy propelled by the force of her ideals and the other that sees American expansion as a consequence of the deliberate pursuit of political and economic interests. For both schools America's involvement in Vietnam is regarded as a vindication of their explanation. This paper seeks to examine the meanings of ideology and national interest in conventional foreign policy analysis, and to see to what extent they are appropriate for the explanation of American foreign policy.

The concept of national interest can be used in both political analysis and political action. It can 'describe, explain, or evaluate' a nation's foreign policy and can be used 'as a means of justifying, denouncing, or proposing policies'.[3] That is to say, it is both a practical rule of thumb to guide the statesman in the formulation and execution of foreign policy,[4] and a standard against which the statesman's success or failure may be judged.[5] But neither the rule of thumb nor the standard of judgement are absolute; they are drawn from a tradition of diplomacy and a tradition of scholarship that are firmly rooted in classical notions of realism and of the balance of power. Charles A. Beard in his classic study of the idea of national interest notes the passing of formulas such as dynastic interests, *raison d'état*, and national honour as pivots of diplomacy. From the early nineteenth century the idea of national interest becomes '. . . almost universally employed in international relations' and 'is particularly associated in time with the rise and growth of the national commercial state, and with the evolution of republican control over national affairs.'[6] Indeed, national interest defines not so much a particular set of concrete objectives, for these will change over time,[7] but a style of diplomacy and statesmanship best suited for defining and achieving foreign policy goals in a balance-of-power world.

In such a world there is a plurality of political units, each autonomous and independent, each the locus of power, interest, and values that are peculiar to the nation and that are firmly and finitely identified with the state. Each state is a singular and self-sufficient political and moral entity in that it entertains no international values beyond the prudential injunction to cooperate with the other morally introverted and self-sufficient entities of international society to ensure their mutual survival. The prudential, almost cynical, implication that enjoins states to cooperate with others despite their different internal value systems is clearly expressed in George F. Kennan's realist definition of America's national interest. 'The fundamental interest of our government in international affairs is . . . to assure that we should be permitted, as a people, to continue our Pilgrim's Progress toward a better America under the most favourable possible conditions, with a minimum of foreign interference, and also with a minimum of inconvenience or provocation to the interests of other nations.'[8] The interests of other nations are, presumably, to continue their version of their Pilgrim's Progress to a better future.

In other words the balance of power is concerned with the interaction of a number of sovereign political entities, each of which creates its own political and moral purpose, defines its own national interest, and may choose legitimately to defend them by force. It is to cope with this political pluralism and the frequency of conflict between states that the concept of national interest can be distilled into positive precepts to guide and judge the statesman. In the words of an eminent realist '. . . it is the duty of statesmen to be concerned first of all with the nation whose destiny is entrusted to them. The necessity of national egotism derives logically from what philosophers called the state of nature which rules among states.'[9] But the realist would not regard the national interest as served by a diplomacy of brute force, for although each state may be legitimately preoccupied with its own interests it must 'not be entirely blind to the interests of others,' for to do so would threaten the fabric of international society itself.[10] Instead the statesman is enjoined to abide by the ultimate, if somewhat limited and procedural, value that underlines the concept of national interest—prudence.[11] 'To be prudent', Aron reminds us, 'is to act in accordance with the particular situation and the concrete data, and not in accordance with some system or out of passive obedience to a norm or pseudo-norm; it is to prefer the limitation of violence to the punishment of the presumably guilty party or to a so-called absolute justice; it is to establish concrete accessible objectives conforming to the secular law of international relations and not to the limitless and perhaps meaningless objectives, such as "a world safe for democracy" or "a world from which power politics will have disappeared".'[12] Thus whatever the concrete foreign policy goals a state may set itself they will be in the national interest only if they are sought prudently and if they are based upon a calculation of the state's advantage within the changing circumstances of the existing international order of sovereign independent states.

This is not to imply that prudence is the only value that states will bring to bear upon the formulation and execution of foreign policy, nor that, even in the most *real politik* of states, ideology has no part to play, for all statesmen have an ideology in the parochial sense of a set of national attitudes that will condition and colour their way of perceiving and interpreting international events and of judging values. In this sense F. S. Northedge can say 'Without ideology a nation does not exactly perish, but it can hardly know what to approve and disapprove,'[13] but the implication of what it means to have an ideological foreign policy is something more than this. It is not that states will profess values and ideals and seek no concrete goals, nor that they will be blind to opportunities for self-advancement presented by the changing circumstances of international relations. It is rather that the dominant values and purpose of the state are not egocentric but associated with an entity or an ideal that is greater than the self, and also that the foreign policy interests derived from these values are ultimately disruptive of international society as a community of sovereign independent states. Such a set of values and beliefs may be coherent and well integrated like the 'Marx-Leninism' that many authors and statesmen believed motivated Soviet foreign policy,[14] or a more vague and loosely knit body of general values such as the 'Utopianism' that was popularly supposed to have inspired the foreign policy of America since the Presidency of Woodrow Wilson.[15] In either case the pragmatic and expedient pursuit of advantage with a context of the existing international order is abandoned in favour of moral and ideological crusading to redeem and transform the world.

Thus an ideological foreign policy is one that seeks the transformation of international society, and is marked off from a more traditional diplomacy by the scope and inclusiveness of its values and the goals that reflect them, and also by the zeal and enthusiasm with which they are pursued. But the disruptive force of an ideological foreign policy may be one of two kinds. It may encourage a deliberate rejection of the circumspect, cautious and ultimately accommodatory style of balance-of-power diplomacy, as Kennan believed communist ideology did for Soviet foreign policy. Its effect upon Russian conduct in international society was, he said, that '. . . there can never be on Moscow's side a sincere assumption of a community of aims between the Soviet Union and powers which are regarded as capitalism'.[16] Or alternatively, an ideology, in the looser sense of a body of altruistic values, can disrupt international society unintentionally. This is because the very nature of the values will so cloud the vision of statesmen to the political and moral pluralism of international society that they fail to see the relativity of their own position, and fail to see the violent and disruptive consequences that will invariably follow an enthusiastic pursuit of universalistic moral values in a pluralist political world.[17]

It is this second notion of ideology that has figured as the central theme of the conventional liberal explanation of American twentieth-century foreign policy. It has particularly powerful exponents in the realist school of the 1950s,[18] but the controversy over Vietnam has led to something of a revival.[19] The main focus of this explanation is upon the uniqueness of American ideals and intellectual premises about world politics which are the product of her sheltered and, until recently, isolated international experience. The basis of these ideals is a reverence for abstract and selfless moral principles—democracy and freedom—and a belief that international society can be successfully founded upon moral and legal norms. These ideals are worthy and honourable of themselves, but contain a danger and an irony. First, it is claimed, they are too vague and general to act as a reliable guide to policy in a power political world and must inevitably result in a neglect of national self-interest and a lack of purpose in foreign policy, and second, that they are prone to be '. . . tempted into universalism . . . and even messianism',[20] whenever America becomes deeply involved in international affairs, because she interprets the innate conflict of political interest in the real world as a moral competition between the forces of good and evil. It is the failure to understand the nature of international society that explains for the liberal America's alternation between globalism, which is the desire to eradicate the scourge of war and oppression once and for all, and isolationism, which is a rejection of the world's complexity and hypocrisy.[21]

In the post-war world America no longer had the option of isolation or withdrawal because the power vacuums that were left in the wake of the Second World War and the weakness of her allies, Britain and France, meant that America was 'thrust into the role of great power and world leadership in a time of historic change'.[22] This unpreparedness, even reluctance and distaste, for a world role combined with her excessive idealism to produce a capacity for self-deception and a proneness to illusion about the causes and consequences of international events. Indeed, for the liberal, the crisis of American diplomacy is not the magnitude of the problems it faces in reality, but the fact that America's own '. . . policy is mired with illusion,'[23] and produces not calculated and deliberate policies, but moral impulses that reflect little of the reality of international life.[24] This inability to understand reality might have resulted in nothing more than an inflated sense of concern for the moral welfare of other states were it not for the perceived global threat from a monolithic communism to all the ideals that America held most dear. With the onset of the Cold War America became an unwilling but inevitable contestant in an ideological struggle,[25] and lost completely the ability, essential to a balance-of-power state, to define and redefine interests and to differentiate between them. America began to view the world as '. . . polarised into good and evil, free and slave' and no longer made 'fine distinctions between . . . the Soviet Union, China, Korea and Indochina'.[26] Foreign policy was based upon an obsessive anti-communism expressed by the universalism of the Domino Theory which assumed that the defence of peace and freedom was an indivisible whole and that a threat from communism to one part of the free world was a threat to the entire free world. In this way America, convinced of the validity of her ideals and the benevolence of her purpose, began to assume responsibility for the security and freedom of an ever-increasing number of the world's states and embarked upon a road of expansion that was ultimately to embrace Vietnam.

The intellectual failure of American statesmen to understand international reality was compounded by the ineptitude and failure of its diplomatic and military institutions. The liberal explanation draws attention to the structural weakness and dislocation of the foreign policy-making bureaucracy which was unable to coordinate national policy or make a systematic survey of the national position;[27] to the style of 'closed politics' where senior policy-makers narrow the circle of those consulted and therefore reduce the availability of specialist knowledge whenever issues become critical;[28] and to the careerism that infests the diplomatic service and leads to each agency over-emphasizing the importance and success of their assignments, thereby reducing even further the capacity to make balanced judgements.[29] On the other hand America's enormous military establishment became so influential and so entrenched during and after the Second World War that it became 'the agency for both the militarization and the enlargement of our inter-ventionist policies'.[30] Indeed, it was the professional demands of the military that were among the factors that 'brought American universalism in time into a messianic phase'.[31] It was the military, according to the conventional explanation, who promoted direct intervention into crises, illusory or real, where diplomacy and tact may have sufficed. It was the military that persuaded America to adopt global strategies and who gave successive administrations an exaggerated notion of their ability to intervene successfully and almost painlessly anywhere in the world. The strength and influence of the military and the weakness of the diplomatic institutions meant that America became progressively less able to make balanced judgements or to adjust to new circumstances, and that policies and commitments generated a momentum and rationale of their own.

For the liberal, America's idealism, anti-communism, the failure of its diplomacy, and the momentum of old policies and attitudes was bound to culminate in a tragedy. Arthur Schlesinger explains how the United States was 'beguiled' into an imperialist foreign policy and an expansionist cause' . . . which reached its disastrous climax in Vietnam'.[32] Others have seen Vietnam as 'the most complete triumph of specious abstractions' in American foreign policy and have likened President Johnson to 'a heroic figure in a Greek tragedy'.[33] While Paul M. Kattenburg, a member of the Johnson adminis-tration, explains America's deepening involvement between 1965 and 1968 as a dynamic in which 'an uncontrolled (and probably uncontrollable) civilian bureaucracy interacted with an equally self-propelled military establishment, ever more over-estimating its needs, to accomplish vague and diffuse ends'. America had become an 'out-of-control monster' and a 'military-bureaucratic juggernaut'.[34]

Most of the implications of the liberal explanation of American post-war history are highlighted by their interpretation of the Vietnam war. The first is that America's globalism is the product of good intentions and grand ideals that have become corrupted in their application because they are divorced from political realities. This is compounded by the gross incompetence of American diplomatic and military institutions and gives rise to the second contention that there has been a complete lack of selfish national interest in her foreign policy. Schlesinger says that 'The wreckage we wrought in Vietnam had no rational relationship to a serious assessment of our national interest or to the demonstrated involvement of our national security'.[35] And many liberal scholars are prepared to accept the frequently repeated assertion that successive administrations have sought no advantage, no territory, no bases, no clients from the war.[36] The evident lack of national interest is amply demonstrated, they claim, by the clear disparity between the cost of the war to America and any possible potential gain.[37] The conclusion most frequently drawn is that America's post-war expansion in general, and the Vietnam tragedy in particular, must be seen as a result of the strength and the primacy of her ideological commitment.[38]

It is reasonable that the liberals should argue that the Domino Theory and its associated anti-communist ideology played a central and dominating role in foreign policy in the 1950s for at the very least contemporary international events could plausibly be made to correspond to them. But the suggestion that the Domino Theory, in the sense of a physical threat from monolithic communism, still existed in the 1960s[39] is to substitute for plausibility a wilful ignorance and stupidity, or a mutilation of international facts that ignored the poly-centric forces in world communism and the forces of national-ism in the Third World. To hold this view is surely to grossly underrate the political intelligence of the United States and to run down the quality of its area specialists in an exaggerated way.[40] It is also to ignore the fact that after the McNamara strategic revolution when the security of America came to depend more and more upon sophisticated strategic hardware, the Third World states assumed a smaller and smaller signifi-cance in the defence of America's physical security.

A more plausible explanation is that the United States had

swopped the political ideology of the 1950s that lost sight of the particularities of challenges and substituted in its place a military ideology that lost sight of the particularities of responses. By the 1960s the United States no longer suffered from an ideology that generated fear about a universal and monolithic challenge; it had an ideology that generated confidence about a universal and monolithic solution—a solution that had been devised in the formative years of the Kennedy-McNamara era under the twin headings of Graduated Response and Nation-Building and which included crisis management, counter-insurgency warfare, controlled escalation, economic development and pacification. It was an amalgam of techniques that produced an everwhelming belief that if United States power is applied to a crisis and is managed correctly it must always prevail. It was no longer the case that America remained unable to define the particularities of crises or their relative importance to America. It was the case, however, that the strategy of graduated response did not require them to be considered for its basic assumption was that America, as the world's most powerful state, could take any state with which it was in conflict up a ladder of escalating costs and risks to a point at which the adversary must rationally decide to pull out because of its inferior strength; the more inferior the state the lower down the escalation ladder it could be induced to settle. It was therefore assumed that settlements would always be within the bounds of cost acceptable to the United States and in this way the traditional diplomatic requirement of assessing potential cost against potential gain was shrugged off. Although one could no longer say that the challenge in Cuba and the challenge in Vietnam were part of the same monolithic threat, one could say that the technique used to solve Cuba was also appropriate to Vietnam—if Moscow backed down in Cuba when faced with the threat of graduated escalation then there was no reason to believe, at least until 1968, that Hanoi should not do the same in Vietnam. This latent confidence about the power reality behind the retained slogans of the 1950s was noted by the editors of the Pentagon Papers who say '. . . . behind the foreign-policy axioms about domino effect, wars of liberation and the containment of China, the study reveals a deeper perception among the President and his aides that the United

States was now the most powerful nation in the world and that the outcome in South Vietnam would demonstrate the will and ability of the United States to have its way in world affairs.'[41] The fact that America's confidence was misplaced in the case of Vietnam certainly helps explain the acknowledged current crisis of United States diplomacy and the frustration of its policy in Vietnam, and to some extent it supports the contention that America became more deeply involved in the war than she had originally intended. But at the same time it removes the quality of innocence and generosity of purpose that is usually imputed to America's role in the world.

This leads directly to another of the deficiences of the liberal explanation for it implies that the United States has been unable to define its national interest and has lacked purpose in its foreign policy. This contention neglects the fact that since 1941 the United States, with the exception of a few minor reverses, has been highly successful in its international affairs and that its record of direct military interventions, until Vietnam, has been successful. This record of success is amply demonstrated by the fact that both Richard Nixon and Lyndon Johnson feared becoming the first President to lose a war; that is to say they feared the consequences of leading the nation into its first significant foreign policy failure. For a state apparently so prone to illusion and misjudgement, and so handicapped by the ineptitude of its diplomacy, this consistent record of success and America's rise to dominance is hard to explain.

The conventional explanation also neglects to show that since 1945 United States military expansion and intervention has invariably had an economic dimension. In Europe, in the decade after the war, Marshall Aid was designed to restore the war-shattered capitalist economies of Europe[42] and in such a way as to aid them in their defence against the Soviet Union. W. M. Scammell explains how the attempts that followed the Bretton Woods conference to build a stable international economic system were affected by the Cold War. 'As the rift between the democracies and the communist countries widened the international relations of the Western powers changed imperceptibly in emphasis from economic reconstruction to defence. The mask was dropped and loans and accommodating finance were given by the United States to promote defence production or to cement alliances, while ends desirable in themselves . . . were harnessed to the build-up of forces against a feared communist aggression.'[43] The same point can be made about the military expansion of the United States in the Third World where an essential part of the American effort was to give economic aid to promote economic development and 'nation-building' on liberal free-enterprise lines. In other words America not only has a record of successful military expansion but also a successful record of restoring liberal-capitalist systems in the developed world and creating them in the developing world.

It must also be noted that through the dynamics of inter-national trade, international loans and foreign investment, the economies of developed nations have become integrated into a world system that has come to involve and enmesh the economies of the Third World. It is a system that has produced a complex web of economic relations that, although unequal, are nevertheless interdependent. The prosperity of the developed nations depends to a very great extent on the stability of a global economic system, including its ties with the Third World, in something like its present form.[44] Scammell has also pointed out that at Bretton Woods the states of the world, not least amongst them the United States, recognized that their own welfare depended upon international economic stability which required 'the views of new countries, old countries, self-supporting and importing countries, great powers and tiny states (to) be fused'.[45] In a post-Keynsian, post-Bretton Woods world the control and manipulation of an international economic system has become a possibility and a constant activity of the developed nations. They recognize that the stability and health of that system depends upon constant cooperation or, failing that, regulation of the partici-pants in it. It would seem that America, as the state that has risen to a position of economic preponderance within this system, would be amongst those most concerned to apply the necessary regulations to states, or events that threaten the stability upon which her strength was founded. In this context the close parallel between American military and economic expansion and her promotion of non-communist political regimes would appear to be more than a coincidence, and the liberal thesis of an expansion prompted by an ideological drive that ignored the interests of the United States seems untenable.

One of the most sophisticated attempts to accommodate the impact of idealist and anti-communist ideology on the United States since 1945, and to reconcile this with America's evident success as a promoter and guarantor of a system of political and economic regimes that have developed in close parallel with her military expansion, has been made by Robert W. Tucker, and it is an explanation that arrives at a classical realist conclusion that America has not been driven by an obsessive anti-communism to acquire an unwanted empire divorced from her self-interest, but that she has become a classical exponent of power political diplomacy with a strong conception of self-interest.

Robert Tucker in his book *Nation and Empire* acknowledges that 'it is not enough to attack the pernicious myths of American policy whilst leaving aside the essential interests of policy',[46] and he sets out to define them. At the core of American interests is an extended notion of security in which 'the safety of the nation's institutions and, more generally, the quality of its domestic life are made dependent on the preservation and the eventual realization of these institutions elsewhere in the world', moreover the 'preservation and the eventual realization of these institutions may be found to require a congenial world order'.[47] Tucker advances the familiar hypothesis that America's political and economic institutions will wither away if similar institutions disappear abroad.[48] The clear and substantial threat to American interests emanated principally from communist states, for the rise and growth of communism would signal the end of capitalism and America as a model upon which a future world civilization would be mainly based, and this 'prospect of the irrelevance of the American purpose must raise, in turn, the issue of American security'.[49] In a later book Tucker goes on to argue that it was inevitable that America should become involved in a cold war with communism because it challenged her notion of security in the greater-than-physical dimension and threatened 'a world in which American economic and political frontiers might become increasingly co-extensive with its territorial frontiers, and thus a world in which prosperity and democracy in America might itself be imperilled'.[50] In this light containment in Europe and its application to other parts of the world was a calculated, deliberate and realistic defence of a genuine threat to America's security, and was not the consequence of illusion or a crude and obsessive ideology of anti-communism. It is in the necessity and the success of the containment of communism that Tucker sees the roots of American expansion, for it sets in motion a dialectic 'as old as statecraft itself' where 'To contain the expansion of others, or what was perceived as such, it becomes necessary to expand ourselves. In this manner a course of containment becomes a course of empire.'[51]

America's unusual notion of security is not solely ideological for it is 'solidly rooted in the will to exercise domination over others'.[52] Tucker emphasizes that both liberal and radical critics of American foreign policy 'persistently ignore the deeper sense of collective self-aggrandisement' and the 'identification of the collective self with something greater than the self', which he regards as so endemic a trait of great and powerful states 'that it may be considered to form part of their natural history'. He also points out that it is power itself rather than a particular form of power which prompts expansion, and that 'dominion is its own reward and that men may sacrifice material interests in order to rule'.[53] The conclusion that Tucker comes to is 'that America has behaved very much as other great nations have behaved and if there is a quality unique to American diplomacy it consists in the greater than usual disparity between ideals professed and behaviour'.[54]

Yet even this greater than usual disparity cannot explain some of the anomalies in Tucker's insistence that America has acted in a power political way as other great states have in the past. He propounds a thesis that suggests it is the disparity of power and the urge for domination, glory and aggrandisement that is an important part of America's expansionism and interventionism, but aggrandisement is precisely that goal which the United States has so frequently and fastidiously foresworn, particularly in Vietnam. This is most odd, since an urge for domination and aggrandisement is fulfilled only by its proclamation and not by its denial, and one would have expected from successive administrations enthusiasm rather than the disquiet and embarrassment that has greeted the recent 'discovery' of an American Empire. American statesmen must be rare indeed if they can indulge their impulse for aggrandisement in private. Even if one were to argue that America sees the mere proliferation of her example as a form of self-aggrandisement, it is hard to see any reflected credit in the political regimes of some of her allies (although their economic structures are invariably impeccable!).

But it is the notion of security in the greater-than-physical sense, and the need to see defence in a correspondingly expansive way that marks off American expansion from the way great powers acted in the past. A congenial world order in the nineteenth century implied a willingness to recognize a plurality of states and a plurality of domestic value systems; it did not imply a willingness to share political and economic institutions. A congenial world order in the past was one in which caution, circumspection and prudence prevailed between the states of international society and not the enthusiasm and positive involvement in an interconnected web of military, political and economic arrangements implied and demanded by American foreign policy. The traditional notion of security implied only that the state should have assurances that the pursuit of its interests and the defence of its values should be free from excessive foreign interference if it, in turn, refrained from excessive interference in the interests of others. Those assurances the nation provided for itself by the creation of a national army or at most by participating in a temporary alliance with others. Indeed, because in traditional diplomacy the foundation of strength and the ability to defend oneself were located in national economies, national armies and national institutions, there was a positive disincentive to see their strengths exported overseas. Britain must have feared the spread of her industrial revolution, and therefore her industrial advantage, to France, Germany and America in the last quarter of the nineteenth century, just as post-revolutionary France rued the adoption by Prussia of the Napoleonic national conscript army. In both cases the dissemination of essential national economic and military institutions served to undermine national security and advantage rather than to enhance it. America is understandably less reluctant to export liberal-capitalism and military techniques in an age when economic and strategic systems are interdependent and no longer exclusively national.

The conclusion that may be most readily drawn is that post-war American foreign policy can be explained adequately neither by the benevolent, but ultimately corrupted, utopianism aimed at creating and defending an international order of free and independent states against communist aggression, nor that she has become a traditional imperialist bent upon the suppression of the legal sovereignty and independence of other states to create a *Pax Americana*. The feature of America's post-war expansion has been the retention by her allies of the formal trappings of legal independence and sovereign statehood, but the severe restraint of the economic and political freedom of action that may be exercised by them. Two factors help explain this apparent anomaly. The first is that states can no longer hope to be economically self-sufficient or isolationist, because they are integrated into a unified system in which the instability or weakness of one state can threaten the prosperity of all, and where the removal of one element of the intricate web of economic relations can fundamentally alter, and possibly throw into chaos, the rest of the system. The second is that challenges to that economic stability have been coloured by the presence of not just a substantial number of communist states that remain outside the mechanisms that regulate and control it, but that these states also profess a political creed that encourages others to follow their example. In this sense the willingness of the United States to identify the economic deviations of new states with a leaning towards communism becomes more understandable, for political creed is an essential part of the willingness to remain within the economic arrangements upon which the security and welfare of a large part of the Western world depends. The main point is that in an interdependent world national interest can no longer carry the implications it did in the classical period of balance-of-power politics. Political and economic pluralism is no longer tolerable, least of all to the United States who has become the main guarantor and the main beneficiary of the integrated world system. Nor can caution and circumspection be a feature of its foreign policy in a situation where confidence and vigour play so important a part in the validity and vitality of the order it seeks to defend against the encroachments of a rival system. America is aware that in the eyes of her allies, particularly those in the Third World, the prudence that marked the old diplomacy could easily give the appearance of uncertainty and backsliding. For America in the post-war world, globalism is the national interest.

NOTES AND REFERENCES

1. See Joseph Frankel, *National Interest* (London, Macmillan, 1970), p. 116. A similar but more general distinction between politics based upon value and ideals and politics of a pragmatic kind has been made by Giovanni Sartori in 'Politics, Ideology and Belief Systems', *American Political Science Review*, Vol. 63, No. 2 (June 1969), pp. 398-411.

2. For a review of the realist/idealist debate on American foreign policy see R. C. Good, 'The National Interest and Political Realism: Niebuhr's "Debate" with Morgenthau and Kennan', *Journal of Politics*, Vol. 22, No. 4 (Nov. 1960), pp. 597-619; Grayson L. Kirk, 'In Search of the National Interest', *World Politics*, Vol. 5, No. 1 (Oct. 1952), pp. 110-15; and Quincy Wright, 'Realism and Idealism in International Politics', *World Politics*, Vol. 5, No. 1 (Oct. 1952), pp. 116-28.

3. James N. Rosenau, 'National Interest', *International Encyclopedia of the Social Sciences*, Vol. 11 (New York, 1968), p. 34.

4. This is R. C. Good's use of the term when he says national interest 'defines the outermost limits of choice, beyond which responsible statesmanship may not trespass . . .', op. cit., p. 597.

5. It is against the criterion of the national interest that the realists denigrate U.S. foreign policy of the 1900-50 period. See Kirk and Wright, op. cit., and also Warner R. Schilling, 'The Clarification of Ends or, Which Interest is the National', *World Politics*, Vol. 8, No. 4 (July 1956), pp. 566-78.

6. Charles A. Beard, *The Idea of National Interest: An Analytical Study in American Foreign Policy* (Chicago, Quadrangle, 1966), p. 22.

7. See Raymond Aron, *Peace and War: A Theory of International Relations* (London, Weidenfeld, 1966), p. 91; and Vernon Van Dyke, 'Values and Interests', *American Political Science Review*, Vol. 56, No. 3 (Sept. 1962), pp. 569-70, for arguments that foreign policy goals cannot be permanent or objectively defined.

8. Quoted in Kirk, op. cit., p. 112. From George F. Kennan, 'Lectures on Foreign Policy', *Illinois Law Review*, Vol. XLV (1951), pp. 718-42.

9. Aron, op. cit., p. 580.

10. R. C. Good emphasizes this point with a quotation from Reinhold Niebuhr, see Good, op. cit., p. 600.

11. Prudence is the value defined by Aron, but the moral underpinnings of national interest for realists like Kennan, Niebuhr and Hans J. Morgenthau are different, but they all enjoin the statesman to act cautiously and to recognize the interests of other states and their shared interest in the continuity of international society.

12. Aron, op. cit., p. 585.

13. F. S. Northedge in F. S. Northedge (ed.), *The Foreign Policies of the Powers* (London, Faber, 1968), p. 13.

14. The most famous example is George F. Kennan's 'The Sources of Soviet Conduct', reprinted in his *American Diplomacy 1900-51* (University of Chicago Press, 1970), pp. 107-24.

15. See Note 2.

16. Kennan, op. cit., p. 113.

17. See particularly E. H. Carr, *The Twenty Years' Crisis 1919-1939*, 2nd ed. (London, Macmillan, 1962), for his comments on Utopianism.

18. See earlier notes on the realists.

19. See particularly Edmund Stillman and William Pfaff, *Power and Impotence: The Failure of America's Foreign Policy* (New York, Random House, 1966); and Arthur M. Schlesinger Jr., *The Bitter Heritage: Vietnam and American Democracy 1941-1966* (Harmondsworth, Penguin, 1967).

20. Arthur Schlesinger, Jr., 'Vietnam and the End of The Age of Superpowers', *Harper's Magazine* (March 1969), p. 41.

21. A good example of the Globalism/Isolationism syndrome can be found in Stillman and Pfaff, op. cit., p. 15.

22. Andrew M. Scott and Raymond H. Dawson (ed.), *Readings in the Making of American Foreign Policy* (New York, Macmillan, 1965), introduction p. 8; see also Stanley H. Hoffman's explanation on pp. 25-26.

23. Stillman and Pfaff, op. cit., p. 15.

24. Ibid., p. 74; see also Howard Trivers, 'Myths, Slogans and Vietnam', *Virginia Quarterly Review*, Vol. 48, No. 1 (winter 1972), pp. 1-23.

25. See Hoffman in Scott and Dawson, op. cit., p. 28.

26. The Committee of Concerned Asian Scholars, *The Indochina Story: A Fully Documented Account* (New York, Pantheon, 1970), p. 228.

27. See particularly Townsend Hoopes, *The Limits of Intervention* (New York, McKay, 1969), pp. 1-8; and W. W. Rostow in Scott and Dawson, op. cit., pp. 16-18.

28. The Committee of Concerned Asian Scholars, op. cit., pp. 157-63; and Paul M. Kattenburg, 'Vietnam and U.S. Diplomacy, 1940-1970', *Orbis*, Vol. XV, No. 3 (Fall 1971), p. 839.

29. The Committee of Concerned Asian Scholars, ibid., p. 160; 248-49; 250-51; and Kattenburg, ibid., pp. 838-39.

30. Schlesinger, op. cit., p. 43.

31. Ibid.

32. Ibid., p. 41.

33. Trivers, op. cit., p. 9 and p. 14.

34. Kattenburg, op. cit., p. 832.

35. Schlesinger, op. cit., p. 44.

36. Stillman and Pfaff, op. cit., p. 173.

37. See, for example, Hoopes, op. cit., p. 58; Trivers, op. cit., p. 19.

38. See, for example, Stillman and Pfaff, op. cit., pp. 171, 177; and Noam Chomsky, *At War With Asia* (Harmondsworth, Penguin, 1971), pp. 27, 63; Schlesinger, *The Bitter Heritage*, p. 72; and Conor C. O'Brien in K. T. Fann and D. C. Hodges (eds), *Readings in U.S. Imperialism* (New York, Sargent, 1971), p. 11.

39. This suggestion has been made, for example, by Kattenburg, op. cit., p. 827, but the frequency of its articulation by Administration policy-makers is best seen in Neil Sheehan (ed.), *The Pentagon Papers* (London, Routledge; Bantam, 1971). See, for example, p. 87 for Johnson's version; p. 150 for Rusk's version; pp. 274-5 for Maxwell Taylor's version; and p. 154 for the view of the Joint-Chiefs-of-Staff.

40. A good many authors have suggested that America's professional diplomats were too shrewd to take the Domino Theory in its literal sense; see, for example, Noam Chomsky, *American Power and the New Mandarins* (Harmondsworth, Penguin, 1969), p. 207; and Kattenburg, op. cit., p. 829.

41. Sheehan, op. cit., 255.

42. See Gabriel Kolko, *The Politics of War-Allied Diplomacy and the World Crisis of 1943-1945* (London, 1969), for an extensive and radical analysis of United States economic war aims.

43. W. M. Scammell, *International Monetary Policy*, 2nd ed. (London, Macmillan, 1965), p. 13.

44. See, for example, Gabriel Kolko, *The Roots of American Foreign Policy: An Analysis of Power and Purpose* (Boston, Beacon Press, 1969), esp. p. 55.

45. Scammell, op. cit., p. 9.

46. Robert W. Tucker, *Nation or Empire? The Debate Over American Foreign Policy* (Baltimore, Johns Hopkins Press, 1968), p. 156.

47. Ibid., pp. 36-7.

48. This thesis was powerfully expounded by Thomas I. Cook and Malcolm Moos, *Power Through Purpose: The Realism of Idealism as a Basis for Foreign Policy* (Baltimore, Johns Hopkins Press, 1954).

49. Tucker, op. cit., p. 119.

50. R. W. Tucker, *The Radical Left and American Foreign Policy* (Baltimore, Johns Hopkins Press, 1971), p. 105.

51. Ibid., p. 109.

52. Ibid., p. 111.

53. Ibid., p. 151.

54. Ibid., p. 148.

Ideology and Political Development

C. H. DODD

INTRODUCTION

The object of this paper is to discuss in relation to ideology some of the principal features of the theories of political modernization or political development that have appeared (or reappeared) in political science during the past decade. The theories in question are for the most part those developed by American political scientists of sociological bent—like G. A. Almond, J. S. Coleman, R. Braibanti, L. Page and D. E. Apter, to mention some of the best-known names. Their theories are largely unacceptable to Marxists who have their own version, with variations, of the economic, social and political destiny of man. They are regarded with some scepticism by many historians and political anthropologists, for whom their generalizations must often seem ill-founded and tendentious.[1] That there is some truth in this general line of criticism we shall see later.

IDEOLOGY

Before proceeding to discuss political development it is necessary first to state briefly what is here meant by ideology. Ideology is a more or less integrated set of ideas—in which the integration may be more or less explicit or implicit. Besides being much else Marxism is a highly integrated, explicit ideology. Liberal democracy is neither so integrated nor so explicit a set of ideas. The ideologies we encounter in primitive

245

and traditional societies would often best be described as implicitly integrated sets of beliefs and attitudes rather than ideas, since they lack the degree of conceptualization needed to lift them to this level. They are not, however, excluded from the definition of ideology used in this paper. Finally, a theory of political development may be said to constitute an ideology in so far as it fails to provide general satisfaction as a theory of explanation, for we think of ideology not just as an integrated set of ideas and beliefs, but also to some degree persuasive. An ideology seeks to persuade and guide in an area where truth is difficult to establish. To try to determine whether theories of political development constitute ideologies is a major task. In the scope of this paper it is not possible to do more than reveal the contours of this and associated problems.

POLITICAL DEVELOPMENT

To turn now to 'political development' the first difficulty is to disentangle this term from 'political modernization', which is also much in vogue. This is not easy because the volume of literature on these themes is great, the writers are prolix, and their language often obscure. They nearly all employ the opaque vocabulary of modern sociology, justifying its use on the grounds of its purity—of its lack of contamination by ordinary and everyday usage.

There are three strands in the emergence of the concept of political development. To follow J. S. Coleman,[2] these strands or 'perspectives' are the historical, the typological, and the evolutionary. 'From the historical perspective', he writes, 'political development refers to the totality of changes in political culture and structure associated with the major transformative processes of social and economic modernization first unleashed in Europe in the sixteenth century, and which have subsequently spread, unevenly and incompletely, throughout the world.'[3] This process of change, which is usually called political modernization by other writers, is analysed differently by different writers, but could generally be said to constitute a political modernization syndrome comprising the following:

(a) the expansion and centralization of governmental power accompanied by the differentiation, specialization and subsequent integration, of political functions and the structures which perform them;

(b) increased egalitarianism, especially in matters of political participation and the distribution of economic and other perquisites;[4]

(c) greater popular identification with the political system;

(d) increasing secularization of politics, meaning by this that with enhanced knowledge of himself, his world, and his own use, man becomes more rational, less motivated by religion or ideology.

The second strand in the theory is the 'typological'. 'The typological perspective envisages the "historical" process in a movement from a postulated pre-modern "traditional" polity to a post-traditional, modern (or developed) polity . . .'[5] Coleman here refers to a long tradition of writing in this school stretching back beyond modern times, but of which Sir Henry Maine, Tönnies, Durkheim and Weber in the nineteenth and early twentieth centuries, and F. X. Sutton and F. W. Riggs, more recently, provide examples. Sutton and Riggs[6] highlight the differences between the traditional and the modern by using the pattern-variables developed by Talcott Parsons. These refer to styles of behaviour. Modern man is achievement-oriented, whereas traditional man is primarily attuned to matters of status or ascription. Modern man is universalistic—inclined to seek general and impartial solutions to problems (e.g. recruitment by merit to a public bureaucracy), whereas traditional man is particularistic. (Not appreciating the need for an impartial and efficient bureaucracy, he would recruit relatives and friends to bureaucratic positions.) This 'typological' approach is close to the 'historical', but refuses to be limited by the shortcomings of history—by the inadequacy, often, of the record or the lack of insight by historians.

The third strand or 'perspective' in political development theory is the evolutionary—'that open-ended increase in the capacity of modern man to initiate and institutionalize new structures, and supporting cultures, to cope with, or resolve, problems, to absorb and adapt to continuous change, and to strive purposively and creatively for the attainment of new society goals'.[7]

A word of elucidation seems necessary here. The basic idea is that man evolves by a process of differentiation in order to cope with environmental problems. As Herbert Spencer put it, 'any existing species—animal or vegetable—when placed under conditions different from its previous ones, immediately begins to undergo certain changes fitting it to its new conditions'.[8] Spencer accepted the Lamarckian (and later Darwinian) view that the species is enabled to change through the inheritance of acquired capacities, though how these arise is a matter of some difficulty.[9] The evolutionary component of political development theory postulates that man has the capacity to adapt to his environment, though it is usually asserted, as by Coleman in the quotation above, that the capacity itself increases. How does this come about? The answer seems to be that, following Lamarck and Herbert Spencer, development theorists accept that as an organism's activities change in response to the environment, so too do its structures—new patterns of coordination of brain and muscle are created. So in society man sets up new and almost invariably more complex patterns of economic, social and political activity for the solution of his problems. This inter-relationship of function and structure was quite evident—self-evident it seems—to Herbert Spencer.[10] Structural functionalism, as it has become, was for him and is still for many development theorists the obvious means of reconciling the dynamic of evolutionism with what might appear to be the purely static conditions of social structure. Evolution injects change, but the process of change works out through the, often slow, adaptation of structure to function.

The evolutionary perspective of modern political development theory provides an explanation of gradual and orderly political change that is neat and seductive. It is replete, however, with the difficulties and ambiguities inseparable from the transference of specifically biological theories to broader and more complex domains. Not least is the problem of whether political man is evolving by adapting himself to the environment or the environment to himself. Are the new political structures and functions in the quotation from Coleman part of political man, or of the political system, or of the environment? The contention is presumably that they are a response by political man to change, but is this his striving 'purposively and creatively for the attainment of new society goals'? This would appear to be the introduction of an extraneous ideological factor into the evolutionary 'perspective'.

These three strands in political development theory that we have now considered are interwoven most completely, if not always consciously, by Almond and G. B. Powell in a well-known book.[11] The 'perspectives' are combined, we might say, to make up a total picture, though the typological viewpoint is not incorporated at all well.

To start with the historical 'perspective', on this view certain historical trends are observable in the history of the developed world, trends which it would seem reasonable to suggest will in some measure be repeated in Third World states as they develop economically. As we have noted earlier, this broad process of change is often referred to as political modernization.

Now these historical trends are usually seen to give rise to developmental 'crises' or problems, by Almond and Powell as well as by other writers in the field.[12] For instance, a general historical trend towards greater equality in a state with a monarch ruling by divine right is likely to create a problem about authority. Or again, the growth of central power is likely to create the need to provide a differentiated but yet coordinated central administration—this would be part of the 'crisis' or problem of 'state-building'. Where the church supports the state increasing secularization may well create the problem of 'nation-building' on a new basis. There is a certain air of artificiality about the scheme if only because to separate the elements of the modernization syndrome from the problems to which they may give rise is not an unambiguous exercise. A historical trend featuring as an element in one writer's modernization syndrome may appear as a problem arising from the syndrome in another's scheme.

But the usual assumption, as in Almond and Powell's work, is that there are problems of national identity, legitimacy, distribution, participation and the like to be solved by the political system. It is then claimed that political development ensues if the problems are solved. 'The significance of such development is in general to increase the effectiveness and efficiency of the performance of the political system, to increase its capabilities.'[13] 'But a system must have adequate resources of extraction and regulation before it can begin to distribute resources',[14] i.e. before it can begin to solve the developmental problems which a political system faces, its structures must be differentiated and specialized. In other words, problem-solving induces differentiation and specialization (which enhances capabilities), which in turn eases further problem-solving, which then produces more political development (more differentiation and specialization).

In this rather involved way the evolutionary is worked in with the historical strand. There is a concern for typology in this scheme. But the classification of political systems presented tries rather studiously to avoid contrasting the ancient and the modern and building up a classification composed of different mixes. Instead, a classification system is built around the concepts which make up the definition of political development. These are 'increased differentiation and specialization of political structures' and 'increased secularization of the political culture'.[15] To exhibit these features to a greater degree is to be more developed.

To sustain analysis in terms of these criteria is in practice difficult, so that when particular political systems are analysed other, particularly 'typological', criteria sometimes enter. For instance, the Inca schools, we are informed, represented a mixture of ascriptive and achievement criteria with a heavy emphasis on the latter.[16] However, these 'typological' criteria do not seriously impede classification in developmental terms, so that it is intriguing, if alarming, to discover that the Inca Empire is classified along with Tudor England.[17]

IDEOLOGICAL ELEMENTS

We now need to ask whether the theory of political develop-ment, in the form outlined, constitutes a number of ideas, beliefs and attitudes about political change which are not demonstrably true and seek to persuade in the light of a particu-lar vision. It is also pertinent to ask whether the political modernization strand in the theory is not influenced by ideo-logical factors. And we might inquire whether the apparent applicability of the modernization syndrome to political change in the Third World means no less than that a Western political ideology has been, and is being, transmitted to Third World states.

To take the more general question first, it is quite evident that in employing evolutionary theory, political development theory accepts from biological theory rather uncritically a dynamic for society. This is not in itself ideological, but translated into social terms it has the implication that man, in this case political man, has the innate capacity to solve new problems as they arise and set new aims for himself—and, moreover, it is assumed that a political system can also do this. This is an optimistic view of the nature of man, with which many would disagree. It was a view which found favour with nineteenth-century liberals.

Then, secondly, this social evolutionism is linked in political development theory with structural/functionalism, and is open to the criticism directed at structural/functionalism generally. It is not, as is often asserted, that structural/functionalists can only be concerned with static political systems. Rather, the opposite is the case. They tackle the problem of conflict by constructing a view of the political system which allows for orderly change. On a structural/functionalist view, it is possible to tolerate change when it allows for other parts of the system to adjust to the change. The persuasive element seems to be this, that a political system will survive and innovate so long as there exists a generally secular (non-religious or ideological) political culture, open means of communication, and the possibility of creating new political structures in response to demands and opportunities.

There is nothing *specifically* ideological in this scheme. Indeed, Almond and Powell are at pains to point out that 'when we talk about different kinds of political systems, we are not arguing that one class of political system is "better" than another. We are simply arguing that one political system differs from another in certain specific ways and that these differences are subject to measurement in the empirical sense of the term.'[18] But it turns out that the most developed political systems by their criteria are the modern liberal-democratic. And who wishes to remain politically under-developed? The ideological overtones are thus fairly well pronounced.

For political development theory a great deal must depend on the acceptability of the modernization syndrome. In the history of the developed world there are difficulties for the uncritical acceptance of the components of the modernization syndrome. For instance, given the oligarchic tendencies of political parties and trade unions, has there been a great gain for political participation? And the national scale of politics seems to make each individual's contribution so ineffectual as to raise similar doubts. Then, it might be asked, how the alleged growth of central power is to be reconciled with the greater degree of participation that has seemingly occurred.

These sorts of questions arise with greater urgency in the states of the underdeveloped world where, on first inspection, the principles of the political modernization syndrome seem to hold sway. Everywhere the power of revealed religion has declined. Even in the Middle East where Islam had so great a share in the formation of the socio-political community, it only remains now for the masses to be secularized. The Holy Law has largely disappeared and has been replaced by systems of law constructed on Western, secular principles. Then again, strong central governmental power is everywhere in evidence; whilst the emphasis on the creation of national unity, of a sense of national identity, is apparent both in political thought and political action. As to the egalitarian trend, there is ample evidence of the socialist inclinations of many Third World intellectuals, though the political participation of the masses seems to be lagging behind. Certainly there is not much support for parliamentary institutions. For the most part they are regarded as sham and suffered, when they existed, from being the creations of Western colonial rulers. In short, with industrialization and economic development the preoccupations of the Third World, it is claimed, are simply becoming those of the West, whether in liberal-democratic or socialist-authoritarian form. On the one hand there is the need for unity and stability for the sake of economic progress: on the other there is the increasing importance of the masses as they become involved in large labour organizations. As society develops so it will be difficult to prevent an increase in political participation.

The case is plausible, but there are a few indications that

the future may be different. A suggestion that affairs might not turn out so lies partly in elements of the ideologies of Third World political ideologists, supported by features of the history of political modernization in the Third World so far.

Nationalism is perhaps the main preoccupation of political thinkers in the Third World. The attention it has attracted suggests that national entities along European lines will grow even stronger. It could, however, be argued that nationalism is a passing phase in the Third World.[19] A consideration of the origins and characteristics of this nationalism suggests why. In the first place, nationalism is not indigenous to Third World states, whereas Europe has possessed states, large and small, for a long period of time. Moreover, Europe has not only had a long history of states; she has also had a long history of uniformity of belief in states—*cuius regio, eius religio*. The rest of the world has not. The Ottoman Empire was a loosely ordered conglomeration of various peoples, languages and religions.

Secondly, the doctrine of nationalism, European in origin, was given particular force in the minds of Third World intellectuals by the nationalist arrogance exhibited by some of the nationals of the colonial powers. Asserting their superiority on grounds of national culture (and sometimes, race), European colonial rulers forced the local intelligentsia to defend themselves by developing their own nationalism along Western lines. The results were often pathetic, or laughable, but the situation was unavoidable. How could the intelligentsia of a colony hold up its head save by pointing to its *own* culture? A national self-consciousness was forced upon the Third World. And one must remember that the intellectuals who developed local nationalisms were dislocated persons. They had lost their moorings in a traditional society, against which they now had to define themselves. They had also to try to define their relationship with the West, whose restless spirit they were now beginning to absorb in a society not conditioned to its exercise.

The situation is now very different. Neo-colonialism is often blown up to extravagant proportions, but essentially the competition of the nationalisms of Third World states is with those of other Third World states. Less anxious to demonstrate this nationalism against his local neighbour than against a colonial power, the intellectual could well be tempted to turn his hate for the foreigner into love for his brother. Since this could lead to millenial preoccupations and the force and violence usually necessary to make everyone live in brotherly love—nationalism could turn into a divisive rather than a unifying force. The unity and stability necessary for economic development may not owe so much to national identity as to the maintenance of traditional patterns of authority. Japanese economic development has owed a great deal, it seems, to the preservation of traditional social forms. And David Apter has argued for the relative ease with which some forms of traditional society have been modernized— the 'instrumental' rather than the 'consummatory'.[20] Finally, the other dominant political ideology of the Third World is socialism—which is one way of giving effect to the increased egalitarianism of the modernization syndrome. Greater egalitarianism is at the root of socialist doctrines in the Third World, but the context is different from that of Europe and so is the flavour. To take socialism in the Middle East, it cannot, save in Turkey, Iran and the Lebanon, seek to destroy the economic and political domination of the capitalists, since they hardly exist. As any large privately-owned concerns are usually foreign, socialism easily slides into nationalism. Moreover, there are relatively few truly urban workers in many Third World states. Socialism tends then to be led by the intellectual middle-class with some support from peasants and workers. The emphasis is on class solidarity, not on class conflicts, and participation is now much stressed. The official adoption of socialism in some Middle Eastern states has had the effect of removing the very rich from the social scene (but not the very poor), and it has removed the obvious (e.g. sartorial) symbols of social difference. Yet its importance may lie more in the future when Third World states are richer than now.

CONCLUSION

We have seen that modern political development theory, as developed chiefly by American political scientists and political sociologists, asserts a view of the nature of political man and the mode of political change which cannot be satisfactorily demonstrated. It is not without significance that the criteria used to determine the degree of political development are most fully satisfied in the case of Western liberal democracies.

If this is one area of doubt about the theory, another is its reliance on a political modernization syndrome which encapsulates a rather simplistic view of the major developments in the history of the Western industrialized world. This Western experience is probably more peculiar to the West than is allowed for in development theory. The West has been able to forge a certain stable relationship between elements of the modernization syndrome—like increased participation and the expansion of governmental power—as a result of hard-won experience not readily repeatable.

Finally, not only the relationship between elements of the syndrome but the elements themselves may not appear in the Third World. Increasing secularization is in evidence, but participation is more doubtful. Moreover, the problems or 'crises' may not arise; as we have seen national unity may not need solving in the same way everywhere, and in some areas of the world could not appear as a 'crisis' to be solved.

Political development theory hardly constitutes an ideology; it is, rather, an illuminating approach to the problems posed by political change, which carries the implicit message that the most developed (not necessarily the best) political system is the modern liberal democratic.

NOTES AND REFERENCES

1. See H. Butterfield, *The Whig Interpretation of History* (London, Bell, 1931); reprinted 1950 and G. Balandier, *Political Anthropology* (London, Allen Lane, The Penguin Press, 1970).

2. J. S. Coleman, 'The Development Syndrome: Differentiation—Equality—Capacity' in L. Binder *et al.*, *Crises and Sequences in Political Development* (Princeton University Press, 1971), pp. 73-100.

3. Ibid., p. 73.

4. One suspects that the assumption here is that the masses improve their lot, though whether mass participation in, say, warfare has been a boon can be given only one common-sense answer.

5. Ibid.

6. See F. X. Sutton, 'Social Theory and Comparative Politics' in H. Eckstein and D. E. Apter (eds), *Comparative Politics: A Reader* (New York, Free Press, 1963),

pp. 67-81, and F. W. Riggs, 'Agraria and Industria: Towards a Typology of Comparative Administration' in W. J. Siffin (ed.), *Toward a Comparative Study of Public Administration* (Bloomington, Indiana University Press, 1957), pp. 23-116.

7. Coleman, 'Development Syndrome', op. cit., p. 73.

8. Herbert Spencer, 'The Development Hypothesis' in *Essays: Scientific, Political and Speculative* (London, Williams & Norgate, 1891), p. 3, quoted in L. Sklair, *The Sociology of Progress* (London, Routledge, 1970), p. 64.

9. See Sklair, *Sociology of Progress*, pp. 56-71 for an account of the problems involved. Early Darwinism would deny that the giraffe species had inherited certain capacities to lengthen its neck, when food was only available higher up. The strict Darwinian view is that, of a miscellany of creatures, only the long-necked ones would survive in these conditions.

10. For an interesting discussion of Herbert Spencer and structural/functionalism see J. W. Burrow, *Evolution and Society* (Cambridge University Press, 1970), pp. 193-196.

11. G. A. Almond and G. B. Powell, *Comparative Politics: A Developmental Approach* (Boston and Toronto, Little Brown, 1966).

12. For the clearest exposition see L. W. Pye, *Aspects of Political Development* (Boston and Toronto, Little, Brown, 1966).

13. Almond and Powell, op. cit., p. 105.

14. Ibid., p. 208.

15. Ibid., p. 105.

16. Ibid., p. 239.

17. The classification is puzzling on the basis of the criteria employed, as well as on more general common-sense grounds. Tudor England was, on the evidence presented, surely more secularized than the Inca Empire. The relative weighting of the two components of Almond and Powell's definition of political development for classification purposes is not clear.

18. Almond and Powell, p. 215.

19. For an illuminating discussion see E. Kedourie (ed.), *Nationalism in Asia and Africa* (London, Weidenfeld & Nicholson, 1970), pp. 1-147.

20. D. E. Apter, *The Politics of Modernization* (Phoenix Books, Chicago University Press, 1967), pp. 85-6.

Industrialism and Ideology:
The Ghanaian Experience

ROBERT E. DOWSE

SOME THEMES OF INDUSTRIAL IDEOLOGY

This essay will be devoted principally to two themes. Firstly, I intend briefly to survey the literature devoted to the problem of the relationship between ideology and industrialization and, secondly, to attempt to relate themes which emerge from the survey to the developmental experience of Ghana. By way of fiat, I do not intend asking whether or not industrialization is a cause or a consequence of the emergence of particular ideological themes.

Ideology can be distinguished from culture or mere propaganda or party platforms by its greater internal coherence and consistency. Furthermore, the ideologue is presumably constrained in his behaviour by the simple fact that he holds and, one assumes, believes in the ideology. For him not all roads are open. As an ideologue he discriminates the good and bad, the useful and the useless, the correct path and the deviation along a dimension which differs from that of the non-ideologue. If his empirical behaviour does not vary systematically from that of the non-ideologue then it is hard to know what it is that sets the ideologue off from the rest.

In order to discuss the relationship between ideology and the process of industrialization it is necessary to outline the general discussion concerning ideology in society. Perhaps the most all-embracing concept is that which relates the emergence of an ideology with the emergence or claim to political power of a social class or group. Benthamite liberalism, Listian economic

I

nationalism, Saint Simonian socialism, colonial nationalism and Marxism have all at one time or another been claimed as underpinning the political pretensions of respectively the English, German and French industrialists and bankers, the unemployed intellectuals of the Third World and, with Marxism, the hegemony of the proletariat or the leading role of the Communist Party.[1] The essential point here is that the ideology identifies the particular and concrete interest of one social group with the wider interest of the total community. Ideology therefore serves in this particular mode of explanation, both as a plea for a place in the sun by a disadvantaged segment of the population *and* as a smokescreen behind which the real interests of that segment are concealed. An alternative explanation usually, but not necessarily, couched in individual psychological terms is that ideologies are simply the rationalizations that men adopt when they pursue public good, political office, economic or military power, etc.—the need for which lies in their individual psychological development. Thus Lasswell following Freud, argues that many people who actively pursue power do so 'as a means of compensation against deprivation'. Such deprivation leads to a low sense of personal esteem or worth and the active public engagement is 'rationalized in the name of the public good'.[2] Private worries are transmuted into public matters and rationalized in ideological form as a common good.

An additional element in this way of looking at ideology is that it can lend a grandeur and cachet to otherwise somewhat dull but necessary everyday political activity. As Apter puts it, ideology 'links particular actions and mundane practices with a wider set of meanings, giving social conduct a more honourable and dignified complexion. . . . From another viewpoint, ideology is a cloak for shabby motives and appearances.[3]

Ideologies, shifting the focus slightly, in this tradition of analysis also imply not merely a claim to a place in the sun but also help to generate the moral idealism or courage or circumstances necessary to realize the end-state which is usually explicit in the ideology. Thus Bell, in now very familiar phrases, refers to 'ideology as a way of translating ideas into action' and claims that 'Ideology is the conversion of ideas into social levers'.[4] Again, Hoffer has stressed the part that 'men of words' can play in 'undermining existing institutions, of familiarizing the masses with the idea of change, and of creating receptivity to a new faith'.[5] Here ideology is not so much a derivation of economic and social juxtapositions but is rather a creative element.

Finally, ideology has been thought of as a consequence of man's need to understand his environment. When the environment is reasonably stable, prosperous and calm, men tend to stick to their lasts and accept the myths, religions or ideologies of the governors without bothering too much about alternative explanations. What is, is unproblematic. When, for whatever reason, the certainties and predictabilities of the society are shaken then men feel insecure and worried since the old explanations no longer embrace the new facts: 'It is a loss of orientation that most directly gives rise to ideological activity, an activity, for lack of usable models, to comprehend the universe of civic rights and responsibilities.'[6] Men need to know and will reward those who can reassure them. And the reassurers are generally the intellectuals. Hence, the analysis of ideology as a product of the need to know and ideology as a cloak for special interest may coalesce. Indeed, the three strands I have isolated are very frequently associated as, for example, in the case of colonial nationalism which is generally advanced by social groups who stand to gain from independence, whose special pleading has a resonance amongst colonized 'masses' and who may use the concept 'nation' to evoke the moral fervour necessary for struggle against a colonial power.

The relationship between ideology and industrialization is simply a special case of the wider outline just presented. Generally the discussion of the relationship takes place on two or three levels:

A. The ideological process underlying the formation of an entrepreneurial or potential managerial class.
B. The ideological process underlying the formation of a class of committed industrial workers.

A and B are, of course, the processes associated with the work of Max Weber, especially in *The Protestant Ethic and the Spirit of Capitalism*. Although it is true that elsewhere Weber rounded out his argument to include other political and economic factors, it is nevertheless the case that he is probably the name most associated with the relationship between attitudinal dispositions and industrialization.[7] Weber's analysis runs as follows. Historically the growth and gradual victory of 'natural sciences based on mathematics and exact and rational experiment' underpin modern capitalism's essential attribute of calculability.[8] Alongside calculability, however, it was necessary that entrepreneurs could believe that in systematically pursuing pecuniary profit over the long term they were not in danger of hell fire in the even longer term. As is well known the trick was worked because Calvinism especially, but also other Protestant sectarian doctrines, led men to believe that 'the pursuit of wealth [was] not merely an advantage, but a duty'.[9] Thus the pursuit of wealth could be conceived of as at least one form of religious devotion. Why not then a more passive form of religious activity? Here Weber brings in a concept that in various forms currently enjoys considerable academic cachet. Worldly activity, he claimed, is a product of 'feelings of religious anxiety' and unworthiness induced in its adherents by the Calvinist doctrine of predestination.[10] And in order to alleviate the tension engendered by the hopelessness of life, men simply indulged in ceaseless activity. Weber also included a sociological dimension to the argument when he, in the words of R. H. Tawney, claimed that 'The pioneers of the modern economic order were . . . *parvenus*, who elbowed their way to success in the teeth of an established aristocracy of land and commerce'.[11]

The final step in the argument concerning the relationship between industrialism and the growth of a capitalist entrepreneurial class concerns saving and investment. Since the unfortunate Calvinist could never be sure he was saved it follows that he would be unlikely to be a sporadic or episodic entrepreneur but rather a continually engaged and full-time businessman. Hence, the spiritual motor for ceaseless investment and work is supplied by religion. Additionally, the Calvinist entrepreneur does not spread his resources around: 'He avoids ostentation and unnecessary expenditure, as well as conscious enjoyment of his power, and is embarrassed by the outward signs of the social recognition which he receives.

His manner of life . . . is distinguished by a certain ascetic tendency.'[12] Thus the rational businessman, who is the essence of capitalism, and of industrialism in Weber's day, is the by-product of a theology which causes him to displace a sense of personal anxiety into ceaseless economic activity. And such activity produces things and constant change so that the only appropriate measure of a man is not his [parvenu] social origin but rather 'those talents, skills, and energies of individuals that contributed to their own individual accomplishments and achievements'.[13]

As is well known the Weber thesis has been attacked on various grounds: that his actual empirical evidence is mostly drawn from a later period and from non-Calvinist sources; that he mistook a particular event for a general category; that it is less a matter of religion than of the local origins of entrepreneurs in semi-hostile environments; that the crucial distinction between the seventeenth century and the Middle Ages was not attitudes but rather an increase in the scope and structure of opportunity for entrepreneurs in the later period.[14] I am not equipped to do more than mention these objections, but the major point is not to isolate a casual sequence, it is rather to suggest a relationship and here the evidence is quite clear: 'There was no inherent theological reason for the Protestant emphasis on frugality, hard work, accumulation; but that emphasis was a natural consequence of the religion of the heart in a society where capitalist industry was developing. It was, if we like, a rationalization.'[15]

On the labour side Weber also offers a number of crucial and interesting observations concerning the development of a fully committed industrial proletariat. 'Capitalism cannot make use of the labour of those who practise the doctrine of undisciplined *liberum arbitrium*.'[16] In the literature on the formation of an industrial proletariat two propositions seem very widely accepted:

A. That the new class has to accept a discipline at least different, and often more onerous, than that of the rural labourer.
B. That the period when this class of people is produced is one of enormous social strain.

The new discipline is that of the factory and the need to adjust work patterns to the demands of mechanized plant, 'the conflict is between two cultural modes or ways of life . . . even before the advent of power the woollen weavers disliked the hand-loom factories. They resented, first, the discipline; the factory bell or hooter; the time-keeping which overrode ill-health, domestic arrangements, or the choice of more varied occupations.'[17] Although not immediately, the working class also cuts, or has cut, its personal kin ties with rural life and gives up an economic connection with the land.[18] As might be expected this process is a painful one for the newly developing working class which, in Marxist terms, is in process of becoming simply a commodity on the market. It is quite probable that for many years—certainly between 1790 and 1840—real wages in the UK did not increase and productivity certainly did. During this 'crucial period when expansion [of consumption] would have run counter to the crucial needs of an industrial economy' the working class in Britain played a central part in developing necessary resources and underwent 'a consciously premeditated and vigorously instilled' process of ideological revamping.[19] In school, working-class children were taught the 'essential virtues of submission and obedience' together with 'a willingness and capacity to work hard for long hours'.[20]

This matter of a willingness or, indeed, an inner need to work long hours is important. As Weber stresses if left to themselves and without any inner compulsion, most people will *not* work beyond enough to keep themselves comfortable. But, for capitalism, 'Labour must, on the contrary, be performed as if it were an absolute end in itself.'[21] Converting workers from a satisfaction with traditional standards was accomplished, Weber argued, by Calvinism which, as in the case of the capitalist, caused labourers to be active in order to overcome feelings of doubt and powerlessness. Work became an inner compulsion. Eventually the urge to work is cut loose from its theological anchoring and becomes a generalized aspect of industrial culture: 'The industrial economy of the present day is an immense cosmos into which the individual is born . . . it forces the individual . . . to conform to capitalist rules of action.'[22]

However, the incipient working class is not simply acted upon ideologically but also responds to the situation as it develops by producing its own ideologies or by producing variants of the dominant ideologies or religions. In Britain, for example, various schools of radicalism and socialism developed themes initially advanced by middle-class apologists whilst institutions like socialist Sunday Schools and Primitive Methodist Chapels were variants of the 'official' versions.[23] But the most obvious general direction in this respect is that in the UK by the 1860s there was no serious working-class ideology that betrayed arcadian yearnings. Socialism and the various schools of trade unionism together with the Co-ops all, in one form or another, accepted the *fact* of a dominantly urban factory civilization and sought amelioration or redistribution within the framework of industrialization. In short, all imply a high degree of commitment to industrial discipline.

Relating these discussions to the preceding general discussion of ideology in society the following points—in no order of importance—seem relevant:

1. Whether or not it *caused* the sort of behaviour that Weber thought Calvinism did it is quite possible that for capitalists it could reinforce and supply necessary justification for behaviours not yet culturally widely accepted. It fulfilled the role mentioned above of giving mundane activities a wider significance: 'The interest of God and of the employer are curiously harmonious.'[24]

2. *Vis à vis* the emergent working class the work ethic in Calvinism acted to help produce attitudes consonant with the interests of employers of labour. It fulfilled the role of interest smokescreen. But the process was a protracted one and certainly not completed even in England by the middle of the nineteenth century.[25]

3. As the religion of 'the rising strata of the lower industrial middle class', although placing no special value on worldly activity, Calvinism nevertheless produced such activity. Groups do not rise without activity.

Perhaps the overall and most significant point to be stressed is that there is a school of thought which claims economic

development to be crucially dependent upon the ideas, ideologies, attitudes, states of mind—or whatever—of either masses
or elites. Thus Rogers gives one a list of ten peasant attitudes
which he thinks of as being 'typical' and argues that economic
development is only possible when these are changed.[26] The
changes are changes of attitude, *not* of the structure of opportunities, reward, or social power. Similarly, Spengler argues
that 'the state of a people's politico-economic development,
together with its rate and direction, depends largely upon
what is in the minds of its members, and above all upon the
content of the minds of its elites.'[27] It is not my intention to
debate this proposition but a number of observations are
relevant. Firstly, if no serious structural changes are necessary
in order to bring about economic development one cannot but
surmise that such a doctrine must offer not inconsiderable
comfort to the incumbent elite, ruling class or wealthy. In
the absence of such a belief it is possible that the analyst might
conclude that a major impediment to economic development is
precisely the structure of the society and the existence of the
elite.[28] Secondly, there is a good deal of empirical evidence
that change, by bettering the structure of economic opportunities in developing countries, is not infrequently met with
by economically rational responses, i.e. peasants and rural
workers are sunk in lassitude, traditional postures, *etc.*, because
they see they cannot better themselves in existing circumstances.[29] Finally, in the absence of extremely complex and
costly field-work, it is almost impossible to know what is
actually in people's heads so that the assumption of attitudinal
determination of behaviour is very problematic indeed.

THE DEVELOPMENTAL EXPERIENCE OF GHANA

The Convention Peoples Party in Ghana came to power after
stressing two issues, those of national independence and
economic development. Since the concept of national independence is discussed elsewhere in this volume I will concentrate
on the theme of the economic development in Ghana. This
division is not really justified for a number of reasons:

1. Nkrumah always stressed that political freedom, the

ability to manoeuvre in the world, was essentially a product of economic independence.[30]

2. A crucial condition of economic development is the presence of a relatively strong and stable political authority.[31]

3. The political behaviour of Ghanaians is not such as to suggest a culture where the distinction is acceptable.[32]

4. The concept of rapid economic development is essentially a politically imposed one: 'It is well to recollect that there is no evidence that the mass of the population anywhere wanted an industrial society. . . . At bottom all forms of industrialization so far have been revolutions from above, the work of a ruthless minority.'[33]

As is well known Ghana at independence was, by black African standards, quite well developed. The CPP, whilst by no means a socialist party in 1954-60 was nevertheless strongly committed to a *dirigiste* and expanding economy, and in this respect was absolutely typical of nationalist parties in office in the developing world.[34] CPP or, better, Nkrumah's thinking on the problem of developing the Ghanaian economy was populist in the sense that the whole country was to pull together in the interests of economic development. The 'entire people' of Ghana, 'farmers, fishermen, masons, lawyers, doctors, the labourers, businessmen, engineers, architects, traders, teachers and students' should devote themselves to Ghana.[35] Additionally, the state would concentrate on building up an economic infra-structure of wider educational facilities, a better public health system, improvement in public communications, and public incursion into banking facilities generally. To the private sector would be left the core of the economy: agriculture, trading, and the development of an import-substitution industry, e.g. soft drinks, tobacco processing, beer and spirits, light plastics, food processing and so on. Broadly, the private sector was self- and bank-financed whilst, of course, the state sector was financed *via* taxes, duties and running down the government's sterling balances in London.

Politically the period was one of consolidation of the CPP as the sole ruling party in Ghana with opposition banished, bought or banned. This period was in many ways the halcyon period of CPP rule since the combination of running down the

London reserves (approx. £200m) together with the rise in world cocoa prices and the increase in Ghana's own crops enabled the government to satisfy most people without demanding much in return.[36] Private consumption increased between 1955 and 1961 (at 1960 prices) from £G278 million to £G364 million and during the same period government expenditure more than doubled from £G47·7 million to £G113·7 million a year.[37] The strategy, in short, was one well calculated to meet the interests of the fairly wide sector of the population supporting the CPP and accorded well with the basic nationalist populist ideology. A little more specifically, however, the achievement of national independence with its rapid replacement of whites by blacks, the expansion of job opportunities, and the better credit facilities for traders was used to favour CPP supporters. In an exceptionally favourable economic situation—for Africa—the CPP and Nkrumah really had no ideology about economic development other than the measures outlined above. Unfortunately the ability or, rather, the means to satisfy most sectors of a population in a developing country is short-lived. Although he stresses that the earlier period was one in which the CPP was fully occupied in destroying the opposition, Genoud concurs in this judgement: 'The effectiveness of such a style of government depended in a large measure on the possibility of investing large sums in development programmes without having to reduce private consumption.'[38] The price of cocoa turned down, the sterling reserves ran out, imports were high and the easier import substitute plants had been set up.

By 1961 the Ghana economy was in a serious situation. It was at this juncture that Nkrumah turned the economy and the ideology of the CPP to something called socialism. Effectively, socialism meant:

(i) A tighter control over the economy through various import/export controls and also through the banking system.

(ii) An increased rate of public expenditure, especially on setting up new industrial projects.

(iii) Increases in the general level of direct and indirect taxation which, in effect, meant a systematic lowering of living standards.

(iv) The incorporation of hitherto independent agencies into the structure of the CPP.

(v) Wide and incessant propaganda that the above measures meant that Ghana was on the road to socialism.

Socialism, in short, was about the deliberate *construction* of a new industrial society where previously there had been none. It was, thus, economically the counterpart of nationalism which involved building a state where previously none had existed.[39] Looked at from this perspective, therefore, socialism was the ideology of political creativity which stressed the fundamental importance of the organised *will* (the CPP) in producing economic change. Involved also was a measure of attitudinal reconstruction amongst the population which may legitimately be understood to be an attempt to introduce a work ethic into Ghana. Thus Nkrumah condemned the extended family, religious holidays and festivals, nepotism, absence of thrift and commented approvingly upon 'Puritanism which encouraged frugality and frowned upon wastefulness and ostentatious expenditure.'[40] Opening a soap factory in 1963 President Nkrumah animadverted upon the theme of work and patriotism. 'The ability of the Ghanaian citizen must reveal itself in work. Love and respect for work and concern for state and co-operative property must be the corner-stone and backbone of our Ghanaian society . . . work must not only be an obligation, it must be also a civic duty.'[41]

The local 'middle class' was held incapable of industrializing Ghana and, anyway, their role in a socialist society was to be a restricted one so it followed that taxes etc. would increase. This would benefit everyone 'in the interest of that socialist objective it will be necessary for all of us to forego some immediate personal desire for a greater benefit a bit later on'.[42] This was to be a dominant theme of the Nkrumah socialist regime: work hard, more efficiently, for longer hours and smaller rewards in order to build the new Socialist Ghana.[43] As with all other ideologies of forced industrialization the present individual was to be sacrificed for the good of the future collectivity. Under the leadership of a modernizing elite—the CPP—Ghana would be pulled into industrialization, not because the 'masses' wanted to be sacrificed, but because industrialism was a good thing. 'The intellectual knows that a government which really *represents* the thinking of the uneducated masses will not attack those problems boldly and comprehensively.'[44]

Socialism was, therefore, about creating an industrial society in an under-developed area. Hard work, labour discipline and self-sacrifice were to be the result of commitment to Ghana as a nation and socialism as an ideal rather than as an externalization of an inner tension. Creation of the industrial society was a function of state bureaucrats, albeit guided and enthused by the CPP under the leadership of Nkrumah. Hence, the role in industrialization that entrepreneurs played in Europe was to be played in Ghana by managers with the private industrialist or innovator having a subsidiary part.[45] Almost certainly it is the case that Nkrumah had little choice but to allot such a decisive role in industrialization to the state bureaucracy since *innovation and risk-taking* seems to be a very low priority amongst Ghanaian businessmen whose major 'long-run objective was to escape the uncertainties of commerce and be able to live off the yield of secure assets . . . the entrepreneurial flame (in Schumpeter's sense) burned low in Ghanaian traders'.[46] Additionally, as is well known, economic success in Ghana almost inevitably brings with it a host of expenses and responsibilities that are difficult to escape but that bring the successful man prestige, status and place him at the centre of a network of obligation, i.e. that are hopefully a source of long-term security.[47] If Ghana was to industrialize it is arguably the case that Nkrumah's choice of doing so by the state owed very little to the ideology of socialism but rather that the overall economic situation compelled him to take a course of action that he then described as socialism.[48] In this he was by no means unusual. Ideology made palatable the nasty inevitable and put the mundane reality of everyday sacrifice into a more glorious setting.

By the 1960s the CPP was politically quite firmly entrenched in Ghana and those sectors of the population who had opposed it had become 'reconciled to the position of a junior partner . . . The higher civil service, the professionals, the businessmen, the judiciary, with few exceptions, gradually . . . fully accommodated themselves to receiving high rewards for their skills and services.'[49] An active state deeply and constantly engaged in economic enterprise was obviously not, to say the least, incompatible with the interests of this group. Looked at from this point of view, socialism as a developmental ideology obviously universalizes the particular interests of the bureaucratic or publicly salaried elite: 'an ideology which rationalizes and legitimates a central role for the state in the economy is as much a reflection of class interest as was the nineteenth-century *laissez-faire* capitalism for the Western middle-class'.[50] And if one considers Nkrumah's consistent denial of the meaningfulness of class analysis and his equation of Ghana and the CPP then it is difficult not to find in this at least an element of ideological special pleading.[51]

As a matter of fact the rate of public investment in Ghana during the period 1961-6 did accelerate quite rapidly and a large number of industrial and agricultural projects were initiated and it is certain that living standards were squeezed to pay for this process.[52] Yet Nkrumah did not succeed in industrializing Ghana in at least the sense that cocoa exports were as large a percentage of the value of exports in 1966 as they had been in 1955. Further, the inter-sectoral linkage of the economy was still by 1966 very restricted indeed whilst nearly all the public enterprises established in the 1960s both lost money and, more important, were extremely inefficient. During this period Ghanaians were positively deluged with propaganda about socialism, about Ghana's increasing stature in the world, about the need for constant vigilance against external enemies. They were invited to work hard, to spend less, save more and in general to 'pull in their belts' and look joyfully forward to a socialist future. Attempts were specially made to ideologize the civil service, the armed forces and the universities.[53] Newspapers, the radio and much of the media in Ghana concentrated on re-aligning attitudes so that they were consonant with the ideology. Yet it is perfectly clear that the attempt was a waste of time—people did not change their economic behaviour in any obvious way. In the remainder of this essay I will discuss this failure.

THE FAILURE OF IDEOLOGY IN GHANA

If we confine the definition of ideologists to those articulating and behaving as though they believed in a well-integrated system of thinking in which one proposition is related to and constrains all others then there is no problem. Ghana, like everywhere else, is at most likely to have a very small body of such people and towards the end of the Nkrumah period they were fully occupied in writing articles for *Spark*.[54] Certainly there is no reason at all to believe that anybody in the leading echelons of the CPP was *behaviourally* committed to socialism and very little to suggest that, for example, Regional and District Commissioners behaved better than the leadership. Adopting a weaker definition of ideology so that it becomes a matter of loosely integrated congeries of attitudes, ideals, slogans and beliefs leads to the difficulty that in practice it is impossible to know when behaviour is modified or determined by such beliefs and when by the hard realities.[55] For example, was socialism—state *dirigisme*—much more than a recognition of necessity in Ghana? Thus, there is an immediate empirical problem to verifying the connection between the ideology of African socialism and the behaviour of actual people.[56]

Ignoring these difficulties and assuming socialism in Ghana was an integrated and potentially constraining ideology we come to a series of practical difficulties that prevented it becoming a serious candidate for internalization by any major segment of the population. These difficulties include the following: the nature of the CPP, the economic behaviour of Ghanaians, and the social structure of Ghana.

Although in pretension a disciplined and centrally articulated mass party the CPP in fact from the very beginning was 'an open-ended omnibus, and many jumped aboard, to further nationalism, social mobility and change'.[57] The very vagueness of the ideology may be seen as a consequence or as a response to the initial need of a nationalist party to appeal to as wide and disparate an audience as possible. By the time Nkrumah attempted to redirect the first generation who were willing enough to mouth slogans and even make speeches with an ideological spicing, but not to change behaviour, the mere presence and importance of men such as Edusei, Adamafio, Coffie, Crabbe and so on was a guarantee that as a serious ideology socialism would be confined to other people's sacrifices and other people's hard work.[58] For such people ideology was a psychic good with a very low cost of production and the masses were given more than their fair share of it—and less than their share of more corporeal goods.[59]

An instrument so seriously defective was extremely unlikely to imbue a population with the spirit of work sacrifice, deferred gratification, etc., even if that spirit had a resonance with the general behaviour of the host society. And in the relevant parts of Ghana—notably Ashanti and the coast—this was certainly not the case. Security seems to be a major social value and in an underdeveloped society security is extremely hard to obtain and this was the case even in 'Socialist' Ghana. For example, poverty was a major calamity which brought in its train a host of problems: 'A poor man's suit is summarily disposed of'; 'Poverty has no friends', 'Money is sharper than the sword'; 'The rich man is the man of authority.'[60] To meet this possibility a number of strategies are possible. Religious consolation and explanation of social or economic travail can be sought. Thus 'between 1910 and 1925, during which time the country's annual cocoa output rose from about 2,000 tons to 200,000 tons, the earliest of the modern protection-shrines were established'.[61] Another possibility, that adopted by cautious gamblers and peasants, is to spread one's risks over a wide number of possibilities so that if one fails the result is not disaster. Thus traders in Ghana typically do *not* aim at a maximum expansion of their business but rather at diversification into cocoa farming, house ownership and, less usually, into lorry ownership. All of these are relatively low risk, high return projects and are essentially a cautious response to socially structured uncertainty.[62]

Amongst the poorer people the appropriate technique is to attach oneself if at all possible to a more successful kinsman from whom one derives some sort of a living whilst the richer man gains status and acclaim. Thus both the incentive to save and re-invest in the one case and to find employment in the other is systematically undermined. And under both the socialist and the capitalist systems in Ghana the pressure was always on the established and wealthy to provide for relations and, equally significant, to constantly demonstrate and affirm the status of 'Big Man' by lavish expenditure. Hence, Ghana's very high propensity to consume imports and especially big cars, big houses and expensive drinks:

Question: 'Yes, but why does Busia need a big car?'
Answer: 'Every big man must ride in a big car. . . . Do you wan Busia to drive in a small car like a Volkswagon?'
Question: 'But what's wrong if Busia uses a small car?'
Answer: 'Me, I no respectam if he use a small car.'[63]

There is no evidence at all that the CPP top ranks behaved any differently to many other Ghanaians in this respect although in terms of *scale* they were able, at public expense, to be greatly more lavish.

Thus, the picture is of a very weakly committed elite attempting to change popular behaviour by means of propaganda. And a vast body of psychological research into mass persuasion indicates that success in such conditions is almost impossible—at best one obtains verbal acquiescence.[64]

A final factor meriting brief consideration in a discussion of the failure to change popular attitudes so that they became consonant with delayed consumption and immediate sacrifice is the social structure of Ghana. The immediate point is that the modern economy of Ghana whilst in many respects 'fragile' is, nevertheless, an extremely well established one dating in all early years of the twentieth century: 'Ghana of 1960 could still belong to the same category of structures as the 1911 Gold Coast, albeit at a generally higher (double) level of G.D.P. *per capita*.'[65] And the 'modern' economy is actually quite well integrated into the traditional structure.[66] It is also quite well integrated into the 'modern' political structure in two senses. Many people who are successful in, for example, politics, trade unions and the bureaucracy retain close connections and buy land in their natal town or village. Again, it is almost certain that a majority of politically relevant people in Ghana—including military officers—come from trade and cocoa farming backgrounds. From the very beginning the CPP was 'colonised' by smaller traders and, as we have seen, the bigger men were in process of accommodation.[67] The CPP was, quite simply, unwilling or unable to move this massive and entrenched interest.

At a local level the same process of accommodation or integration can also be observed. Writing of Larteh, a town in southern Ghana, Brokensha observes that it displayed a 'remarkable syncretic capacity to absorb new institutions so that even the powerful CPP . . . emerges as a Larteh rather than a national institution'.[68] In another survey of a southern town the author concludes that the CPP in Swedru 'was both a local and a national institution. The CPP was a compromise organization par excellence.'[69] Age-old political struggles which involved issues almost lost in antiquity were both seized upon by the CPP and also seized by the party: '. . . two facts—the existence of two paramount stools in Agona—for they are the pivots around which political conflict in Agona today revolve'.[70] And even when the party did impose its will and install CPP chiefs the result was 'local reconciliation with the party in previously hostile areas; this in turn tended to diffuse the local CPP'.[71] Similarly in Parliament the CPP back-benchers, if they were conscientious, seem to have regarded themselves primarily as spokesmen for constituency or regional interests.[72]

Unfortunately we have no detailed day-to-day studies of CPP activists—both the professional full-timers and amateurs—in the numerous small towns and larger villages of Ghana so in fact very little at all is known of the success or otherwise of the party in ideologizing at this level. One's suspicion is that locally the CPP activist resembled Bailey's Indian village 'brokers' who mediate between the villagers and the authorities doing 'privately and discreetly all those jobs which rulers of modern institutions forbid'. Such jobs include getting licences, placing bribes, filling forms, obtaining rights and so on. In a dominantly illiterate community such services *are* enormously important *but* in terms of attitudinal re-orientations the snag is that the services do not necessitate a meeting of minds but rather they 'provide pragmatic contracts (and therefore) render unnecessary normative communion'.[73] Since there was little ideology anyway it is almost certain that at the grass roots the party cadre . . . initially sought votes and latterly simply passivity in return for minor services. In its turn the local cadre could bargain with higher echelons of the party 'promising to deliver the votes of his followers in return for favours for himself, his followers, or his village in general'.[74]

Hence, at all levels of Ghanaian society the ideology of the CPP failed to change the behaviour of either party member or of the population at large. Despite constant hectoring to get party members to take ideology seriously it is obvious that socialism as a work and savings ethic had little appeal in Ghana which is relatively short on Puritanism.

CONCLUSIONS

It is a fact that the relationship between rapid economic development and the priority of attitudinal re-jigging is a highly debatable one with at the very least the possibility that structural change is greatly more important than attitudinal change in determining economic growth. Assuming that attitudinal changes consonant with development are necessary we have seen that Weber's Protestant ethic can be compared with socialism in the sense that both, hopefully, may underpin a need or a sense of achievement in work. Socialism is widely thought of as *the* ideology of development. In Ghana, despite great public efforts, socialism failed to obtain any real purchase on popular patterns of behaviour and, on the contrary, socialism almost certainly served mainly as a rather transparent smokescreen. As a matter of fact most of the 'big men' in the party did not even attempt to look like abstemious Puritans, but rather behaved like 'big men' always behaved in Ghana. Such behaviour may well be normatively sanctioned but it is possible to interpret it simply as a form of insurance taken out in good times against possible later bad times.

The evidence from the economic behaviour of Ghanaian traders and farmers suggests that their major interest is in security rather than in potentially profitable, but necessarily risky, innovation. Hence, the willingness to build houses, expand cocoa farms, buy lorries and support a network of half-employed hangers-on. Concerning the behaviour of most rural Ghanaians under the Nkrumah regime, there is little doubt that it remained exactly as it always had, and equally little doubt that beyond a plethora of words the CPP did little to change that behaviour. Some of the causes of this failure have been mentioned, but it would be perfectly possible to produce further reasons. For example, the urban worker in Ghana is relatively easily able to withdraw and place himself in a rural situation if factory discipline becomes too onerous. There is not the land shortage that would act to cut off this retreat and hence make adjustment to urban discipline a necessity. Again, the population of Ghana was always exposed to competing and more alluring messages—from magazines, returned travellers, from neighbouring countries, the cinema— than those of Nkrumah's belt-tightening and delayed consumption. In short the evidence is that as an ideology socialism failed to attract Ghanaians. On the other hand a good deal of evidence does suggest that a considerable measure of state *dirigisme* is necessary to move the economy from its present structure. The irony is that its present structure began and became solidly established with a cash economy and the 'economic miracle' must have required people willing to take tremendous entrepreneurial risks. But once established the production of cocoa became a relatively risk-free enterprise which probably absorbs much of the pool of Ghanaian entrepreneurial talent.

NOTES AND REFERENCES

1. See K. Marx, *The German Ideology* (London, Lawrence & Wishart, 1965); A. Gerschenkron, *Economic Backwardness in Historical Perspective* (London, Praeger, 1962), pp. 22-6; E. Shils, 'The Intellectuals in Political Development', *World Politics*, Vol. 12, 1960, pp. 329-68.

2. H. Lasswell, 'Power and Personality' in H. Eulau (ed.), *Political Behaviour* (Glencoe, Free Press, 1956), pp. 90-103.

3. D. Apter, *The Politics of Modernization* (London, University of Chicago Press, 1965); P. Sigmund, *The Ideologies of the Developing Areas* (London, Praeger, 1967), p. 3 describes the seventeenth and eighteenth centuries in Europe as the age of ideology and as a time of change when 'men became conscious of the variety of alternative paths open to them in their own personal lives, in their religious, philosophical, and political creeds, and in the ordering of society'.

4. D. Bell, *The End of Ideology* (New York, Collier Books, 1961), pp. 393-4.

5. E. Hoffer, *The True Believer* (New York, Mentor, 1951), p. 119.

6. C. Geertz, 'Ideology as a Cultural System' in D. Apter (ed.), *Ideology and Discontent* (New York, Free Press, 1963), p. 64.

7. As a matter of fact, even in the *Protestant Ethic and the Spirit of Capitalism* (London, Allen & Unwin, 1965), p. 21 Weber mentions the importance of 'a regular market' and he also lays emphasis on the need that capitalism has 'of a calculable legal system and of administration in terms of formal rules', p. 25. See also S. Eisenstadt (ed.), *The Protestant Ethic and Modernization* (New York, Basic Books, 1968), p. 75 who cites Weber as claiming that 'He sought no "psychological determination of economic events", but rather emphasized the "fundamental importance of the economic factors" '.

8. Ibid., p. 24.

9. Ibid., p. 2.

10. Ibid., p. 112. Weber mentions in passing that this 'psychological sanction . . . could doubtless in itself have been furnished by various different religious motives', p. 128. D. C. McClelland, *The Achieving Society* (Princeton, Van Nostrand,

1961) takes up this hint and suggests that the psychological sanction was 'need to achieve' which may well have been produced unintentionally by parents encouraging self-reliance in their children.

11. Ibid., p. 2, Weber, ibid., p. 65 found the spirit of capitalism most often in the 'rising strata of the lower industrial middle class'. See E. Hagen, *On the Theory of Social Change* (Homewood, Ill., Dorsey, 1962) who attempts to trace the psychological origins of these pushing *parvenu* to patterns of encouragement/discouragement of initiative in the home.

12. Ibid., p. 71. F. Helleiner, 'The Moral Conditions of Economic Growth', *Journal of Economic History*, Vol. 11 (1951), pp. 97-116 adds that the Christian ethic also devalues leisure and he suggests that 'It is only when religious inspiration furnishes incentives for both forms of self-denial—restriction of consumption *and* of leisure—that asceticism results in accumulation.' Commenting on Britain, S. Pollard, 'Investment, Consumption and Industrial Revolution', *Economic History Review*, Vol. XI (1958), pp. 215-26 argues that 'The absence, during industrial revolutions, of wide social approval for such conspicuous consumption . . . is too marked to be altogether ignored.'

13. A. Gouldner, *The Coming Crisis of Western Sociology* (London, Heinemann, 1971), p. 63. See Ch. 3 'Utilitarian Culture and Sociology' for a splendid account of the development of utility as a standard of moral political and economic worth.

14. See R. H. Tawney, Introduction to Weber, ibid., pp. 1-11; McLelland, op. cit., pp. 367-70; T. Roper, 'The Reformation and Economic Change' in M. Kitch (ed.), *Capitalism and the Reformation* (London, Longman, 1967), pp. 24-36; B. Supple, 'The Great Capitalist Man Hunt' in Kitch (ed.), pp. 191-201.

15. C. Hill, 'Protestantism and the Rise of Capitalism' in Kitch (ed.), *Capitalism and the Reformation* (London, Longman, 1967), pp. 1-8. B. Ward, *Nationalism and Ideology* (New York, Norton, 1966), p. 50 makes perhaps the largest claim for the Weber thesis: 'It is even possible that without this attitude, Europe would never have acquired enough capital to launch the capitalist system.' Although more concerned with structural change, H. Habakkuk, 'The Historical Experience on the Basic Conditions of Economic Progress' in S. Eisenstadt, *Comparative Perspectives on Social Change* (Boston, Little, Brown, 1968), pp. 30-45 also stresses that the 'sector of English society characterized by a high preference for leisure was probably smaller than elsewhere'.

16. Weber, op. cit., p. 57.

17. E. Thompson, *The Making of the English Working Class* (London, Pelican, 1968), p. 377. See also M. Flinn, 'Social Theory and the Industrial Revolution' in T. Burns and S. Saul, '*Social Theory and Economic Change*' (London, Tavistock, 1967), pp. 9-34.

18. See Kerr *et al.*, *Industrialism and Industrial Man* (London, Heinemann, 1962), pp. 170-4. Gerschenkron, op. cit., p. 9 argues that cutting the umbilical cord between worker and the land is difficult and that the 'creation of an industrial labour force that really deserves its name is a most difficult and protracted process'.

19. Pollard, op. cit.; Flinn, op. cit., p. 14. C. Black, *The Dynamics of Modernization* (New York, Harper & Row, 1957), p. 79, 'It appears that in some countries for as much as a generation there may have been an absolute decline in the standard of living for significant sections of the population.'

20. Flinn, op. cit. See also Thompson, op. cit., Ch. 11 'The Transforming Power of the Cron'.

21. Weber, op. cit., p. 62.

22. Ibid., p. 54.

23. F. Parkin, *Class Inequality and Political Order* (London, MacGibbon & Key, 1971), especially Ch. 3.

24. Weber, op. cit., p. 281.

25. Weber, op. cit., p. 226, was aware that it was a lengthy process.

26. E. Rogers, *Modernization Among Peasants* (New York, Holt, Rinehart, Winston, 1969), Ch. 2.

27. R. Brabianti and J. Spengler (eds.), *Tradition, Values, and Socio-Economic Development* (Durham, N.C., Duke University Press, 1961), p. 4.

28. For example, see A. Frank, *Capitalism and Underdevelopment in Latin America* (Harmondsworth, Penguin, 1971) and his important essay 'The Sociology of Development and the Underdevelopment of Sociology', *Catalyst* No. 3 (summer 1967).

29. See, for example, S. Kunkel, 'Values and Behaviour in Economic Development', *Economic Development and Cultural Change*, Vol. 13 (1964-5), pp. 257-77 for a discussion of a project in Latin America, R. Szerszewski, *Structural Changes in the Ghana Economy* (London, Weidenfeld & Nicholson, 1965) for a detailed African example, and R. Krishna, 'Agricultural Price Policy and Economic Development' in H. Southworth and B. Johnston (New Jersey, Cornell University Press, 1967), pp. 497-540 who, in a study of Indian peasants' reactions to changes in the economic structure, concludes 'that, wherever a minimal development of transport and monetization has occurred the behaviour of traditional and commercial farmers becomes similar'. For a general discussion see F. Bailey, 'The Peasant View of the Bad Life', in T. Shanin (ed.), *Peasants and Peasant Society* (Harmondsworth, Penguin, 1971), pp. 299-321.

30. K. Nkrumah, *Ghana* (Edinburgh, Nelson, 1959) p. x, and K. Grundy, 'Nkrumah's Theory of Underdevelopment', *World Politics*, Vol. 15 (1962-3), pp. 438-54.

31. See A. Diamant, 'Political Development: Approaches to Theory and Strategy' in J. Montgomery and W. Siffin (eds.), *Approaches to Development* (New York, McGraw-Hill, 1966), pp. 15-47, and J. Spengler, 'Economic Development: Political Pre-conditions and Political Consequences', *Journal of Politics*, Vol. XXII (1960), pp. 384-416.

32. See M. Owusu, *Uses and Abuses of Political Power* (University of Chicago Press, 1970), pp. 3-5.

33. Barrington Moore, *Social Origins of Dictatorship and Democracy* (Harmondsworth, Penguin, 1967), p. 506.

34. Spengler, op. cit. See also B. Folson, 'The Development of Socialist Ideology in Ghana, 1949-59', *Ghana Social Science Journal*, Vol. 1 (1971), pp. 1-20.

35. K. Nkrumah, *I Speak of Freedom* (London, Heinemann, 1961), p. 169 and again in *Africa Must Unite* (London, Heinemann, 1963), p. 55 when he refers to the CPP as 'representative of the broad mass of the people'. Even during his later 'Scientific Socialist' period in 1965-6 Nkrumah did not deny that the fundamental reality of Ghana was communal. See Nkrumah, 'African Socialism Revisited', *African Forum*, Vol. 1 (1966), pp. 3-9.

36. Cocoa producers, who were paid 57 per cent of the world price, were, naturally enough, not overly happy with the CPP. Although Nkrumah invited foreign capital into Ghana, during 1954-60 there was only a minute influx.

37. W. Birmingham, J. Neustadt, E. Omaboe (eds.), *A Study of Contemporary Ghana*, Vol. 1 (London, Allen & Unwin, 1966), pp. 55 and 27.

38. R. Genoud, *Nationalism and Economic Development in Ghana* (London, Praeger, 1969), p. 197.

39. D. Rimmer, 'The Crisis in the Ghana Economy', *Journal of Modern African Studies*, Vol. 4 (1966), pp. 17-32 notes that these measures from 1961 meant 'the assertion on behalf of the economy of its nationalism, of its sovereign independence'.

40. K. Nkrumah, *Africa Must Unite*, p. 105. C. Andrain, 'Patterns of African Socialist Thought', *African Forum*, Vol. 1 (1966), pp. 41-60, writes that 'in many

respects, African socialist ideology sounds very much like the language of Puritanism, with its focus on achievement, hard work and saving'.

41. 'Our Civic Duty' (Publicity Secretariat of CPP, n.d. Accra). In a radio broadcast to the nation, April 1962, Nkrumah appealed to workers for a 'total effort' arguing that 'we must all in our present stage of development discard completely our old ideas about work', 'Appeal to National Workers' (Accra, 1962).

42. Nkrumah, ibid., p. 123.

43. C. Kerr, Dunlop, Harbison and Myers, *Industrialism and Industrial Man* (London, Heinemann, 1962), p. 200. 'The detailed rules on discipline and pace may be reinforced by the protestant ethic, the communist ideal or dedication to a nationalist mission, but some moral sanctions underlies the rules of the work place on discipline and pace in each industrialising society.'

D. Apter, *The Politics of Modernization*, p. 329, 'The common element of the various forms of socialism . . . is the emphasis on development of goals for which individuals must make sacrifices.'

44. M. Matossian, 'Ideologies of Delayed Industrialization' in K. Kautsky (ed.), *Political Change in Underdeveloped Countries* (New York, Wiley, 1962), pp. 252-264.

45. Actually Nkrumah was profoundly ambiguous about the part to be played by businessmen since he both excoriated them as capitalists and encouraged them as producers, see, for example, Chapter 3 of the *Seven Year Development Plan* (Accra, n.d. 1963) together with 'Call to Businessmen' (Accra, Ministry of Information, 1963).

46. P. Garlick, *African Traders and Economic Development in Ghana* (London, Oxford University Press, 1971), p. 146.

47. For example, see P. Hill, *The Gold Coast Cocoa Farmer* (London, Oxford University Press, 1956), p. 102. 'The wealthier a farmer becomes the greater the demands made on him by an ever-widening family circle.'

48. W. Friedland and C. Rosberg (eds.), *African Socialism* (London, Oxford University Press, 1964), p. 30. 'The tendency towards this new society is not a product of planned choice as much as it is a consequence of many decisions taken by the political leaders as they come to grips with the difficult economic, political and social problems of independence.'

49. J. Mohan, 'Nkrumah and Nkrumahism' in R. Miliband and J. Saville (eds), *Socialist Register* (London, Stevens, 1967), pp. 191-228.

50. C. Anderson, F. van der Mehden and C. Young, *Issues of Political Development* (New Jersey, Prentice Hall, 1967), p. 205.

51. See K. Grundy, 'The "Class Struggle" in Africa', *Journal of Modern African Studies*, Vol. 2 (1964), pp. 378-93.

52. Evidence for this is presented in R. Dowse, *Modernisation in Ghana and the USSR* (London, Routledge & Kegan Paul, 1969), pp. 76-80.

53. See R. Dowse, 'Ghana: One Party or Totalitarian?', *British Journal of Sociology*, Vol, 18 (1967), pp. 251-68 for an account.

54. P. Canverse, 'The nature of Belief Systems in Mass Politics', in D. Apter (ed.), *Ideology and Discontent* (Glencoe, Free Press, 1964), pp. 206-61.

55. Thus Nkrumah simultaneously praised the African personality and advocated industrialization that would destroy it; he excoriated neo-colonialism and sought foreign investment.

56. C. Wright Mills, *Power, Politics and People* (New York, Ballantine, 1963), p. 467, writes that 'the central methodological problem of the social sciences springs from a recognition that often there is a disparity between lingual and social-motor types of behaviour'. Writing of Japan, R. Dore explains that 'It is easy enough to document the dominance of this ideology'—of work and sacrifice for the nation—'But how far is this ideology a clue to the really operative motives?' 'The Legacy

of Togugawa Education' in M. Jansen (ed.), *Changing Japanese Attitudes Toward Modernization* (Princeton University Press, New Jersey, 1965), pp. 93-131.

57. J. Kraus, 'Nationalism and Social Change in Ghana', *Journal of Modern African Studies*, Vol. 7 (1969), pp. 107-30. This is a judgement with which *all* commentators on Ghana agree.

58. That this is the case was perfectly evident before the spate of inquiries initiated by the military government following the coup, for example, Nkrumah, Dawn Broadcast in 1961 and the Abraham Commission of January 1966.

59. See H. Johnson, 'A Theoretical Model of Economic Nationalism in New and Developing States', *Political Science Quarterly*, Vol. LXXX (1965), pp. 169-85.

60. Akan proverbs cited in W. Abraham, *The Mind of Africa* (London, Weidenfeld, 1967), pp. 73-4.

61. M. Field, *Search for Security* (London, Faber 1960), p. 29. Thus, the Weber relationship in Ghana seems to be reversed: 'new shrines, all designed to give supernatural protection and help to people increasingly pre-occupied with a sense of insecurity,' p. 13. But see C. Baeta, *Prophetism in Ghana* (London, SCM Press, 1962), p. 6, who denies that Ghanaian *Christian* sects are patronized by 'persons suffering any psychological malaise, or extraordinary emotional strains and stresses'.

62. Garlick, op cit., *passim.*

63. Fragment of conversation between a sociology student and a tro-tro driver recorded in *Transition*, No. 39 (1971). Owusu, op. cit., indicates that the materialist or utilitarian attitudes just mentioned go quite deep into Ghanaian social, historical and religious experience.

64. A good general discussion of media impact will be found in D. McQuail, *Towards a Sociology of Mass Communications* (London, Collier-Macmillan, 1969), A more politically orientated discussion can be found in R. Dowse and J. Hughes, *Political Sociology* (London, Wiley, 1972), Ch. 8.

65. Szereszewski, op cit., p. 97.

66. Owusu, op. cit., *passim.*

67. The ideological peregrinations of the Asantehene are instructive in this respect: anti-CPP; co-sponsor of NLM; supports CPP; opposes CPP; supports NLC.

68. D. Brokensha, *Social Change at Larteh; Ghana* (London, Oxford University Press, 1966), p. xix. Similarly cocoa farming 'has been regulated to a great extent by traditional Larteh culture', p. 43.

69. Owusu, op. cit., p. 284.

70. Ibid., p. 29. See also D. Austin, *Politics in Ghana* (London, Oxford University Press, 1964), pp. 293-7 on the Brong-Ahafo dispute.

71. J. Kraus, 'Political Change, Conflict and Development in Ghana', in P. Foster and A. Zolberg (eds.) *Ghana and the Ivory Coast: Perspectives on Modernization* (University of Chicago Press, 1971), pp. 33-72.

72. See J. H. S. Frimpong, *The Ghana Parliament, 1957-1966*, Ph.D Thesis, University of Exeter, 1970, pp. 315-55. Frimpong also shows that opposition MPs behaved in a similar manner.

73. Bailey, op. cit.

74. C. Lande, *Leaders, Factions, and Parties* (Yale University, South East Asia Studies, Monograph No. 6., 1966), p. 11. Lande is writing about the Philippines, but the process seems very familiar: 'What tied the follower to the political leader was, therefore, not charisma but economic necessity, a reciprocal connection that at times assumed the form of a patron-client relationship. . . . The relationship held so long as the patron honoured his material and economic obligation, and the client his duty to vote at elections and perform various other services for the patron,' Owusu, op. cit., p. 251.

Ideology, Policy and Capitalism in South Africa[1]

HAROLD WOLPE

There is undoubtedly a high degree of continuity in the racist ideological foundations of Apartheid[2] and of the policy of Segregation which prevailed in the Union of South Africa prior to the election of the Nationalist Party to power in 1948. It is, perhaps, this continuity which accounts for the widely held view that, fundamentally, Apartheid is little more than Segregation under a new name. (See, for example, Legassick 1972; Walshe 1963, 360; Bunting 1964, 305.) As Legassick expresses it: 'After the Second World War segregation was continued, its premises unchanged, as *apartheid* or "separate development"' (Legassick 1972, 31).

According to this view, such differences as emerged between Segregation and Apartheid are largely differences of degree. More specifically, the argument continues, in the political sphere Apartheid entails a considerable increase in White domination through the extension of the repressive powers of the State; the Bantustan policy involves the development of limited local government which, while falling far short of political independence and *leaving unchanged the economic and political functions* of the Reserves, nevertheless, in some ways, goes beyond the previous system in practice as well as in theory; and, in the economic sphere Apartheid 'modernizes' the system of cheap *migrant* labour and perfects the instruments of labour coercion: '*Apartheid*, or separate development, has meant merely tightening the loopholes, ironing out the informalities, eliminating the evasions, modernizing and rationalizing the inter-war structures of "segregationist" labour control' (Legassick 1972, 47).

While it will be necessary, at a later stage, to question this characterization of the differences between Segregation and Apartheid, it is relevant to consider at this point how the variance between the two 'systems' summarized above has been explained.

Generally,[3] the explanations advanced account for the increased racial oppression manifested by Apartheid on the basis of the contention that the governing Nationalist Party's ideology is more racist than that of their predecessors, and for the intensified political repression by reference to the Party's totalitarian ideology. According to this view, the Government, in pursuance of its racist ideology, and even at the cost of economic rationality, introduced a series of measures which extended racial discrimination to its limits. The effect of this was to produce widespread opposition which the Government met, acting in pursuance of its totalitarian ideology, with a drastic curtailment of political rights and an elaborate system of State security. This set in train a vicious cycle of resistance and repression which also led, in due course, to international condemnation of, and pressure on, South Africa. The Bantustan policy of separate development was the response to these combined internal and external political pressures and was (and is) designed both to divert opposition and to transfer conflict out of the 'White' urban areas to the African rural 'homelands' (Szeftel 1971).

Although such explanations are open to a number of objections I want here to focus on only one. As I have argued elsewhere in relation to South Africa (Wolpe 1970), since a racist ideology may be actualized in a number of alternative ways, it is not sufficient merely to spell out the ideology in order to explain specific political policies which are being pursued. This is all the more obvious when different policies (Apartheid and Segregation) are said, as in the present case, to flow from the same basic ideology. Nevertheless, a few exceptions apart (e.g. Legassick 1971, 1972; Wolpe 1970, 1971; Trapido 1971; Johnstone 1970), the literature—radical, liberal and racist alike (e.g. Simons and Simons 1969; Asherson 1969; Van der

Horst 1965; Van den Berghe 1967; Rhoodie 1969)—analyses and describes the society in terms of racial concepts and explains its functioning in terms of the racist ideologies held. Even where the relationship between classes is incorporated into the discussion, race is nevertheless treated as the dominant and dynamic force (e.g. Simons and Simons 1969, 614-15). Racial segregation, separate development, racial discrimination, racial groups (African, White, Coloured and Asiatic), colour-bar, White ruling-class, race-relations, etc.—these are the concepts of the analysis of South Africa. The predominance of these concepts can, no doubt, be attributed to the opaqueness of racial ideology which is reflected, *inter alia*, in the formulation of laws in racial terms, in the content of the mass media, in the policies and ideological statements of all the political parties and organizations and in almost the entire intellectual product of the society.

The overwhelming importance accorded to race in these approaches is apparent, above all, in their treatment of the relationship between racially oriented action and 'the economy' Thus, on the one hand, the content of 'Native' or 'Bantu' policy (to use the official terms) which can be found in the legislative programmes, government policies and commission reports both before and after 1948,[4] is analysed in its own terms and treated as being concerned solely with the regulation of 'race relations'. On the other hand, whether the economy is conceived of in terms of liberal economics (Van der Horst 1965; Van den Berghe 1967; Hutt 1964; Horwitz 1967) or in Marxist terms as a capitalist mode of production (Simons and Simons 1969; Asherson 1969), racial beliefs are treated as a force external to, but productive of, distortions in the otherwise rational economic system.[5] In its most advanced form this leads to the 'theory' of the plural society which both reflects the dominant ideology and provides an apparently scientific corroboration of it. This approach (see for example, Kuper and Smith 1970; Van den Berghe 1967) accepts, precisely by reference to the racial or ethnic content of the laws, policies and ideologies current in the society, the critical salience of race to the exclusion of the mode of production. The basic structure of the society is seen, in this and the other analyses referred to, in the relationship between a dominant White group and a dominated Black group.

It is of fundamental importance to stress that in this perspective the State in South Africa comes to be treated as the instrument of oppression of Whites over Blacks but (precisely because class relationships are not normally included in the analysis) as neutral in the relationship between classes. It in no way detracts from the conception of the State as an instrument of White domination, however, to insist that the South African State is also an instrument of class rule in a specific form of capitalist society. Indeed, while there have been, of course, variations in emphasis and detailed policy (variations which stem, in part, from the specific class composition of and alliances in the parties that have ruled from time to time, from the conflicts between classes and segments of classes and from changing socio-economic conditions), nevertheless, since the establishment of the Union of South Africa in 1910 (to go back no further), the State has been utilized at all times to secure and develop the capitalist mode of production.

It is not possible in this paper to discuss in detail the historical evidence which demonstrates this;[6] it is sufficient here merely to note that the State apparatus has been utilized throughout to foster and aid capitalist development, to coerce workers (both Black and White) on behalf of or in support of employers as the occasion arose and to enforce the laws which guarantee the perpetuation of capitalism.

It is precisely the racial terms used in these laws that gives rise to the dense ideological screen which overlays the capitalist relations they sustain. The enactment of laws, the express purpose of which is the regulation of relationships between racial groups and the ordering of the conduct of the members of legally defined racial categories, is both an expression of racist ideology and a means of reinforcing that ideology. This is so because not only do racial laws, in common with many other laws, appear as neutral to the capitalist structure of the society by taking that structure as given, but more importantly, they actively operate both to mask the capitalist nature of the society altogether and the consequence they have for the functioning of that system.

However, viewed from the standpoint of this paper, racist ideology and policy and the State appear now not only as the means for the reproduction of segregation and racial discrimination generally, but also as what they really are, the means for the reproduction of a particular mode of production.[7]

It follows from what has been argued above that what is necessary for an adequate explanation of South Africa is a specification of the historical conjuncture between ideology, political practice and the mode of production. Concretely the relevant historical conjunctures may be stated as follows: whereas Segregation provided the political structure appropriate to the earlier period of capitalist development in which the relationship between the capitalist sector and the African pre-capitalist economies was dominant, Apartheid, including separate development, can best be understoed as the *mechanism specific to South Africa* in the period of secondary industrialization, of maintaining a high rate of capitalist exploitation through a system which guarantees a cheap and controlled labour force, under circumstances in which the conditions of reproduction (the redistributive African economy in the Reserves) of that labour force is rapidly disintegrating.[8] It is these critical points of articulation between ideology, racial politics and the mode of production or, more precisely, the modes of production which I want now to examine more fully.

Laclau (1971, 33) has drawn a distinction, of particular importance in the present context, between the concept of 'mode of production' and that of 'economic system'. He states:

We understand by 'mode of production' an integrated complex of social productive forces and relations linked to a determinate type of the means of production. . . . An 'economic system', on the other hand, designates the mutual relations between the different sectors of the economy, or between different productive units, whether on a regional, national or world scale. . . . An economic system can include, as constitutive elements, different modes of production—provided always that we define it as a whole . . . (Laclau 1971, 33).

The economic system in South Africa has always included different modes of production and, before proceeding further, the 'constitutive elements' of the system in the period with which we are concerned need to be stated.

This history of South Africa[9] shows the emerging *dominance*, first through British imperialism, and then also through internal capitalist development, of the capitalist mode of production, that is, of a mode of production in which the fundamental economic relationship through which the surplus product is extracted is that of the sale by the direct labourers, who do not own the means of production, of their labour-power to the owners of the means of production who are non-labourers.

In the areas of African concentration (particularly those areas which later became known as the Reserves), there existed the pre-capitalist modes of production and familial communities of the African societies characterized by kinship obligations and redistributive economies. This is *not* to argue either that other forms of production were not developing in the interstices of these societies[10] or that they were not continuously undergoing profound changes in their relations of production. On the contrary, as will be elaborated later, the central argument of the present paper is based on the occurrence of such transformations. What must be stressed, however, is that in the period of capitalist development (from, say, 1870) African redistributive economies constituted the predominant mode of rural existence for a substantial (for much of the period, a majority), but continuously decreasing, number of people.

The simultaneous existence of two modes of production within the boundaries of a single state has given rise to the notion of the 'dual economy' (see Hobart Houghton 1964). As Frank (1967, 1969) and others have shown for Latin America, however, the assumption that different modes of production can be treated as independent of one another is untenable. In South Africa the development of capitalism has been bound up with, first, the deterioration of the productive capacity and then, with increasing rapidity, the destruction of the pre-capitalist modes of production.

In the earlier period of capitalist development in South Africa the relationship between the capitalist and pre-capitalist sectors was soon reduced to the provision by the backward sector of a supply of cheap labour-power to the capitalist sector. The peculiar feature of this labour-force is that it is migrant and temporary, returning to the Reserves in between periods of work, and that it retains means of production in the African economy or has a claim on such means. The exploitation of migrant labour-power of this kind enables the capitalist sector to secure an increased rate of surplus value. How is this effected?

In the first place, in determining the level of wages necessary for the subsistence of the migrant worker and his family, account is taken of the fact that the family is supported, to some extent, from the product of agricultural production in the Reserves and consequently it becomes possible to fix wages at the level of subsistence of the individual worker. Arrighi (1970) has shown this to be the basis of cheap labour in Rhodesia. (See also Schapera 1947.)

In the second place, as Meillassoux (1972, 102) has pointed out: 'The agricultural self-sustaining communities, because of their comprehensiveness and their *raison d'être* are able to fulfill functions that capitalism prefers not to assume . . . the functions of social security.' That is to say, the social security functions of the African communities relieves the State of the necessity of expending resources on Africans.

By these means, a portion of the product of the Reserves is indirectly appropriated by the capitalist sector with the result that an increased proportion of the working day is devoted to the production of surplus value. This effect is represented diagrammatically on the opposite page.

The interest of the capitalist sector in preserving the relations of the African familial communities is clear—if the network of reciprocal obligations between migrant and family were broken, neither the agricultural product nor the social security 'services' of the African society would be available to the worker. It is no accident that the South African State has consistently taken measures, including the recognition of much of African law and custom, the recognition of and grant of powers to chiefs, the reservation of areas of land, etc., aimed at preserving the 'tribal' communities. In the period of Segregation, whatever political functions of social control may have been served by the African social structures, the economic function of these societies in providing means of subsistence for migrant labourers, when not directly engaged in production in the capitalist sector or before or after they enter that sector, was the primary one for the capitalist sector.

The production and reproduction of the migrant labour-force depended upon the existence of a rough equilibrium between production, distribution and social obligation in the Reserves—the level of production in the Reserves together with wages being *more or less* sufficient to meet the (historically determined) subsistence requirements of migrants and their families, while land tenure and familial community relation-ships ensured the appropriate distribution of the Reserve product. This equilibrium was, however, inherently fragile and subject to irresistible pressures.

The relative proportion of surplus to necessary labour in the Capitalist sector where:

(a)	(b)
The working-class is wholly dependent upon wages for its reproduction	The working-class derives a portion of its means of repro-duction from the Reserve Economy

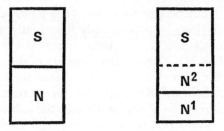

Where: S = surplus labour time/product

N = labour time/product necessary for reproduction of labour-power.

N^1 = the decreased proportion of labour time/product devoted to the reproduction of labour-power by the capitalist sector where a portion of the necessary means of subsistence is provided by the Reserve Economy (N^2)

Given the developed incapacity (due to the competitive dominance of the capitalist sector) of the Reserves to generate a surplus product, the limited area of land available (fixed by the Native Land Act 1913), the increasing pressure of popu-lation and, therefore, congestion on the land, the loss, at any given time, of a large proportion of the economically active

287

adults to temporary employment in the capitalist sector, the relatively backward and inefficient farming methods, and the tendency (related to the traditional culture and economy) of Africans to accumulate cattle and thereby overstock the land available, the only possibility of ensuring appropriate levels of agricultural production is through investment by the capitalist sector. Large-scale investment, however, (unless it could be met from the resulting surplus, a situation which would itself create other intractable problems since it implies the development of an economically powerful class of African agricultural producers or a retardation of the flow of migrants) would negate the very purpose served by a migrant labour force. That is to say, the effect of large-scale investment in the Reserves would be to make cheap labour-power costly in the sense that the accumulation advantages to capitalism deriving from such labour-power would be lost or reduced if the surplus was utilized in the African rural areas. In fact, the State's expenditure on agricultural development in the Reserves has always been extremely low, increasing only marginally as conditions of production worsened. The immediate consequence of the resulting decline in the productive capacity of the pre-capitalist economies was a decrease in the agricultural product available for consumption in the Reserves and, therefore, a decrease in the contribution of the Reserves towards the subsistence necessary for the reproduction of the labour force.[11] This threatened to reduce the rate of surplus value through pressure on wages in the urban areas and posed, for capital, the problem of preventing a fall in the level of profit.

The solution for capital to this problem must take account of the complementary effect of the erosion of the economic foundations of cheap migrant labour-power, upon both the African rural societies and the urbanized African industrial proletariat. Increasing rural impoverishment, since it removes that portion of the African industrial workers' subsistence which is produced and consumed in the Reserves, also intensifies urban poverty if wages are not increased. This twofold effect of capitalist development tends to generate conflict, firstly about wages, but also about all aspects of urban and rural life and brings into question the structure of the whole society. This broadening and intensification of conflict is met by political measures which in turn lead to an increasingly political re-action. Clearly, the nature, form and extent of the conflicts generated by the structural conditions will depend not only upon the measures of State control but on the complex con-juncture of political ideologies and organization, trade unions, the cohesion of the dominant sector, and so on. Although these may vary, what is continuously present, it must be stressed, is the tendency for the structural conditions to generate conflicts, in one form or another, which centre on the system of cheap labour.

This struggle began long before 1948 when the conditions discussed above began to emerge (and control measures to be taken), but the particularly rapid urbanization and industriali-zation fostered by the Second World War sharpened and in-tensified the trends we have been discussing and the resultant conflicts. The 1940s were characterized by the variety and extent of the industrial and political conflicts, especially in the urban, but also in the rural, areas. In the period 1940-9 1,684,915 (including the massive strike of African mineworkers in 1946) African man-hours were lost as compared with 171,088 in the period 1930-9. Thousands of African workers partici-pated in squatters' movements and bus boycotts. In 1946 the first steps were taken towards an alliance of African, Coloured and Indian political movements and this was followed by mass political demonstrations. Towards the end of the 1940s a new force—militant African intellectuals—appeared on the scene. There were militant rural struggles at Witzieshoek and in the Transkei. These were some of the signs of the growing assault on the whole society and the structure of cheap labour that underpinned it, which confronted the capitalist State in 1948.

The policy of Apartheid developed as a response to this urban and rural challenge to the system which emerged inexorably from the changed basis of cheap labour-power. What was at stake was nothing less than the reproduction of the labour force, not in general, but in a specific form, in the form of cheap labour-power.[12] Within its framework Apartheid combined both institutionalizing and legitimating mechanisms and, overwhelmingly, coercive measures.

It is not possible, for reasons of space, to set out in any detail the structure of Apartheid erected by the Nationalist Govern-ment. In a fuller account it would be necessary to do this and to

K

show how Apartheid, as a response to the principal contradiction between capital and cheap African labour, ramifies out
and penetrates into the secondary contradictions which in turn
have, to some extent, a reciprocal effect on the system. Here it
will be possible only to touch upon two of the superficially
similar, but in reality substantially different, aspects of Segregation and Apartheid.

It is true, as was pointed out earlier, that Apartheid differs
from Segregation in the degree to which it perfects the mechanisms for ordering the Non-White population. However, while
the important measures introduced by the Nationalist Government relating to African job and geographical mobility have
the same purpose of maintaining the cheapness of African
labour-power, they do so under conditions that are radically
altered and in a new way. The nature and meaning of these
measures has been obscured by the terms of the relevant laws and
the Government's policy statements to the effect that Africans
were to be regarded only as temporary migrants in the urban
areas, there only as long as they ministered to White needs.

The Pass Laws and the Native Urban Areas Act 1925 which
regulated the right of residence in urban areas were, of course,
available in 1948. The 'modernization' of the Pass Laws—
under the Native (Abolition of Passes and Co-ordination of
Documents) Act—and the establishment of labour bureaux,
which serve to direct African workers to where White employers
require it, has been effected through a battery of amendments
to old laws and the introduction of new laws which give the
State exceptionally wide powers to order Africans out of one
area and into another. There are practically no legal limitations
on these powers which can be used to remove 'excess' Africans
from areas where their labour is not required or 'troublesome'
Africans to outlying, isolated areas where they will be politically
harmless. All Africans are, legally, only temporary residents in
the urban areas.

These facts have been interpreted as meaning that the
Government has elaborated and perfected the migrant labour
system. Control over residence and movement is clearly one
essential element of a system based on a migrant labour force,
but it is not the only one. Therefore, to treat the increase in the
State's legal power to declare Africans temporary sojourners in

the urban area and to move them as exigencies demand as constituting the 'modernization' of the system, without taking account of changes in its economic basis, is insufficient. In the present case it results in the failure to grasp the essential changes in the nature of capitalist exploitation in South Africa. For in South Africa the migrant labour force, *properly speaking*, did not mean *merely* a mobile labour force, or a labour force that could be made mobile, that is, that could be directed and redirected to where it was required. Above all, a *migrant* labour force is a labour force which is both mobile *and* which has a particular economic basis in the pre-capitalist Reserve economy. With the disappearance of that economic basis the problems of curtailing industrial action and of political control over Africans in the urban areas became extremely acute. That control is exercised, in part, by repressive measures including, importantly, the elaboration of the State's power over the residence and movement of labour. The extension of the State's power over the residence and movement of the labour force which adds importantly to the State's repressive control over it (precisely, one feature of Apartheid) is a function of the economic changes in the Reserves which generate a threat to the cheapness of labour-power.

In its application to the urban areas, Apartheid appears predominantly and with ever-increasing thoroughness in its coercive form. In its application to the Reserves it has undergone a number of changes in content—culminating in the programme of separate development—in which the attempt both to establish forms of control that Africans would regard as legitimate and to institutionalize conflict has been an increasingly important ingredient although coercion is never absent. This policy towards the Reserves has been, whatever other purpose it may have had in addition, centrally concerned, as in the past, with the control and supply of a cheap labour force, *but in a new form.*

Separate development is the mode of reproducing cheap labour-power in the Reserves (complementing that in the urban areas) which takes as given the changes in the African 'tribal' economies and erects, under the overarching power of the capitalist State, an institutionalized system of partial political control by Africans. That is to say, the practice and policy of separate development must be seen as the attempt to retain, in a modified form, the structure of the 'traditional' societies, not, as in the past, for the purposes of ensuring an economic supplement to the wages of the migrant labour-force, but for the purposes of reproducing and exercising control over a cheap African industrial labour force, in or near the 'homelands', not by means of preserving the pre-capitalist mode of production but by the political, social, economic and ideological enforcement of low levels of subsistence.

The Transkei Constitution Act was passed in 1963[13] and although it need hardly be stressed that the arrangements consequent upon it in no way approach political independence, at the same time it must not be overlooked that within limits, set both by the Constitution and the available resources, the Transkeian Government exercises real administrative power. By this means the South African State is able to secure the execution of certain essential social control and administrative functions at low cost, particularly as a considerable portion of Government expenditure can be obtained through increased general taxes. Thus in 1971 the Transkeian Government's budget was £18 million of which £$3\frac{1}{2}$ million was obtained through taxation of Transkeian citizens.

It is, however, in the sphere of economic development and in particular in the State's policy of industrial decentralization that the emerging role of the Reserves can be seen most clearly. This policy which has been the subject of Government commissions and legislation is also the concern of a Permanent Committee for the Location of Industry. At all times the policy of decentralization has been tied to the Bantustan policy and this meant, at first, the establishment of 'White' industries on the borders of the Black 'homelands'. Between 1960 and 1968 some £160 million was invested in industrial plant in the border and approximately 100,000 Africans were employed in these industries which were absorbing 30 per cent of Africans entering jobs each year by 1969. By 1971 there were plans for a rapid expansion (including car factories and chemical plants) of industrial development in the border regions. The point has correctly been made that, to date, most border industries have been established in areas close to the main industrial regions of South Africa, including Johannesburg, Pretoria and Durban.

This is due to the fact that in remoter border regions the State, in the main, has not provided the necessary infrastructure of transport, communications and so on. But, why decentralize to the borders in any event? One answer has been to suggest that the purpose of border development is to stem the drift of Africans into 'White' South Africa. The question is why? I would suggest that the policy of border industrial development can only be understood it if is seen as an alternative mechanism of ensuring cheap labour-power. There are three aspects of the situation which need to be stressed.

Firstly, neither the provisions of the Industrial Conciliation Act nor Wages Act determinations made for other regions apply to the border industries. This is extremely important in two respects. Since the Industrial Conciliation Act is inapplicable, Section 77, which empowers the Minister of Labour to reserve certain jobs for particular racial groups, also does not apply and neither do the provisions of industrial agreements which reserve the higher-paid skilled jobs for White workers. This being so it becomes possible to employ Africans in jobs which, in the 'White' areas, are the exclusive preserve of White workers. The effect of this, in conjunction with the inapplicability of wage determinations for other areas, is that a totally different and much lower wage structure becomes possible and has arisen.

Secondly, as elsewhere, African trade unions are not recognized and the provisions of the Natives (Settlement of Disputes) Act apply.

The third, and in some ways perhaps the most important aspect, relates to the conditions of life of the African workers in the border industries. Not only, as has already been indicated, is the level of subsistence extremely low in the 'homelands' but in addition there are virtually no urban areas which might tend to increase this level. The assessment by the State, employers organizations and so on, of African subsistence requirements in the Reserves is much lower than in the main industrial centres. This fact is not altered (or, at least, will not be altered for a considerable period) by the necessity of establishing townships of some kind for the housing of workers employed in industry. It is an interesting index of the State's policy that a major item of expenditure for the so-called development of the

Reserves has been for town-planning. A United Nations Report (No, 26. 1970, 15) stated: 'Town planning has throughout been a major portion of expenditure. Thus in 1961 a five-year development plan for the reserves was inaugurated which projected an expenditure of £57 million, but *two-thirds* of this amount was allocated for town-planning, while the next largest item—£7·3 million—was for soil conservation.'

The towns planned will be, no doubt, simple in the extreme, supplying little in the way of the complex services and infrastructure of the 'White' urban areas. All the indications are that what will be established will be rural village slums,[13] alleviated marginally, if the Transkei is typical, by the allocation of garden allotments for the purpose of the production of vegetables, etc. which, incidentally, will no doubt provide the rationale for lower wages.[14]

Recently, the Government reversed its previous rejection of the Tomlinson Commission's recommendation that Whites be allowed under certain conditions to invest capital in the Reserves. As in the case of the border industries various incentives are held out to induce investment. These include 'tax-holidays', tariff reductions, development loans and so on. All the considerations discussed above in relation to the border industries apply with equal force to industrial development within the Reserves. It is still too soon to say anything about the likely level of investment inside the Reserves although some investment has already occurred. Nevertheless, the change in policy must be seen as a further significant step towards the establishment of an extensive structure of cheap labour-power in the Reserves.

CONCLUSION

The argument in this paper shows that Apartheid cannot be seen merely as a reflection of racial ideologies and nor can it be reduced to a simple extension of Segregation.

Racial ideology in South Africa must be seen as an ideology which sustains and reproduces capitalist relations of production. This ideology and the political practice in which it is reflected is in a complex, reciprocal (although asymmetrical) relationship with changing social and economic conditions. The response of the dominant classes to the changing conditions, mediated by these ideologies, produces the two faces of domination—Segregation and Apartheid.

The relationship between two modes of production, by virtue of its own contradictory necessity, increasingly produces the conditions that make impossible the continuation of the pre-capitalist relations of production in the Reserves. The consequence of this is the accelerating dissolution of these relations and the development towards a single, capitalist, mode of production. This results in important changes in the nature of exploitation and transfers the major contradiction from the relationship *between* different modes of production to the relations of production *within* capitalism. The consequence of this is to integrate race relations with capitalist relations of production to such a degree that the challenge to the one becomes of necessity a challenge to the other. Whether capitalism still has space (or time) for reform in South Africa is an issue which must be left to another occasion.

NOTES AND REFERENCES

1. This paper is a revised and shortened version of a paper entitled 'Capitalism and Cheap Labour-Power in South Africa: From Segregation to Apartheid' in *Economy and Society*, Vol. 1, No. 4. In preparing this version I have benefited from criticisms and comments made by R. Hallam and W. Clenaghen of the Department of Sociology and Law, Polytechnic of North London.

2. Although the term 'Apartheid' has more or less given way to 'separate development' in the language of the Nationalist Party, it remains the term most widely used to characterize the present system in South Africa. In this paper I intend to use 'Apartheid' as the generic term to refer to the period (its policies, practices and ideology) since the Nationalist Party took office in 1948—in this sense it subsumes the policy of 'separate development'. 'Racial Segregation' or 'Segregation' is employed throughout, unless the context indicates a contrary intention, to refer to the ideology, policies and practices prior to 1948. It need hardly be added that although 1948 is obviously a year of great importance it is not intended to suggest that in that year Apartheid replaced Segregation.

3. This is not Legassick's approach; he has a more complex analysis which cannot be dealt with here.

4. See for example:

Transvaal Local Government Commission of 1922 (Stallard Commission) T. P. 1-122.

Native Land Commission (Beaumont Commission) 26-1916.

Native Economic Commission 1930-1932 (U.G. 22, 1932).

Social and Economic Planning Council—Report No. 9:
The Native Reserves and Their Place in the Economy of the Union of South Africa (U.G. 32/1946).

Report of the Commission for the Socio-Economic Development of the Bantu Areas within the Union of South Africa (Summary) (U.G. 61/1955) (Tomlinson Commission).

Native Lands Act 1913.

Native Trust and Lands Act 1936.

Native (Urban Areas) Consolidation Act 1945 and subsequent amendments.

Bantu Authorities Act 1951.

5. For a critique of this approach see Wolpe (1970).

6. Considerable historical material on this point can be found in Simons and Simons (1969).

7. Althusser's (1971) essay 'Ideology and Ideological State Apparatuses' is relevant on this point. Althusser (p. 124) suggests that: ' . . . in order to exist, every social formation must reproduce the conditions of its production at the same time as it produces, and in order to be able to produce. It must therefore reproduce:

1. the productive forces,
2. the existing relations of production.'

The reproduction of both the forces (that is, labour power) and the relations of production are secured for the most part ' . . . by the exercise of State power in the State Apparatus, on the one hand the (Repressive) State Apparatus, on the other the Ideological State Apparatus' (Althusser 1971, 141). See also, Poulantzos, N., 'The Problem of the Capitalist State', *New Left Review*, November-December 1969, No. 58, p. 67.

8. While the present paper is restricted to a consideration of African rural economy in the Reserves, to some extent African agriculturists outside the Reserves on 'White' land had a similar relationship to migrant labour. Both this aspect and, as pointed out to me in a personal communication by M. Legassick, the relationship of Reserve migrants to White capitalist agriculture, would need to be incorporated in a full study.

9. For a good outline of this history see Legassick (1972).

10. There is a serious lack of adequate material or analysis of African societies. It is clear that no adequate account of the dynamics of South African society can be arrived at without a proper history of these societies.

11. For evidence regarding the decline of the Reserves see the various Commission Reports cited in note 4.

12. A number of different analyses have been made of the position of different classes in the development of Apartheid. See, for example, Legassick (1972) and Clenaghen (1972). It is not necessary in the present paper, given its concern with the central relationship between White capital and cheap African labour, to pursue this point here.

13. Other Bantustans are in various stages of formation.

14. In a new appendix to the new (1971) edition of his book Mayer (1962) provides an account of a 'dormitory town' which shows that this is exactly what is happening.

BIBLIOGRAPHY

ALTHUSSER, L. (1971) *Lenin and Philosophy* (London, New Left Books).

ASHERSON, R. (1969). 'South Africa: Race and Politics', *New Left Review* 53, January-February 1955.

BUNDY, C. (1971), 'The Response of African Peasants in the Cape to Economic Changes, 1870-1910: A Study in Growth and Decay', unpublished Seminar Paper, Institute of Commonwealth Studies, London.

BUNTING, B. P. (1964), *The Rise of the South African Reich* (Harmondsworth, Penguin Books).

CLENAGHEN, W. (1972), 'The State in South Africa,' unpublished Seminar Paper.

FRANK, G. A. (1967), *Capitalism and Underdevelopment in Latin America* (London, Monthly Review Press).

FRANK, G. A. (1969), *Latin America: Underdevelopment or Revolution* (London, Monthly Review Press).

GERVASSI, S. (1970), *Industrialization, Foreign Capital and Forced Labour in South Africa*, United Nations, ST/PSCA/Set.A./10.

HOUGHTON, D. Hobart (1964), *The South African Economy* (London, Oxford University Press).

HORWITZ, R. (1967), *The Political Economy of South Africa* (London, Weidenfeld & Nicholson).

JOHNSTONE, R. (1970), 'White Prosperity and White Supremacy in South Africa Today', *African Affairs*.

KUPER, L. and SMITH, M. G. (1969), *Pluralism in Africa* (University of California Press).

LACLAU, E. (1971), 'Feudalism and Capitalism in Latin America', *New Left Review*, No. 67, May-June, p. 19.

LEGASSICK, M. (1971), 'Development and Underdevelopment in South Africa', unpublished Seminar Paper for the Southern Africa Group, The Royal Institute of International Affairs, Chatham House, London.

LEGASSICK, M. (1972), 'South Africa: Forced Labour, Industrialization, and Racial Differentiation,' to be published in a forthcoming volume in a series on the political economy of the Third World edited by Richard Harris.

MAYER, P. (1962), *Townsmen or Tribesmen* (London, Oxford University Press).

MEILLASSOUX, C. (1972), 'From Reproduction to Production', *Ecomony and Society*, Vol. I, No. 1, p. 93.

RHOODIE, N. J. (1969), *Apartheid and Racial Partnership in South Africa* (Pretoria, Academica).

SCHAPERA, I. (1947), *Migrant Labour and Tribal Life* (London, Oxford University Press).

SZEFTEL, M. (1971), 'The Transkei: Conflict Externalization and Black Exclusivism', unpublished Seminar Paper, Institute of Commonwealth Studies, London.

SIMONS, H. J. and R. E. (1969), *Class and Colour in South Africa, 1850-1950* (Harmondsworth, Penguin African Library).

TRAPIDO, S. (1971), 'South Africa in a Comparative Study of Industrialization', *Journal of Development Studies*, Vol. 7, No. 3, 309.

VAN DER HORST, S. (1971), *Native Labour in South Africa* (London, Frank Cass).

VAN DER HORST, S. (1965), 'The Effects of Industrialization on Race Relations in South Africa' in HUNTER, G. (ed.), *Industrialization and Race Relations* (London, Oxford University Press).

VAN DEN BERGHE, P. (1967), *South Africa: A Study in Conflict* (University of California Press).

WALSHE, A. P. (1963), 'The Changing Content of Apartheid,' *Review of Politics* Vol. 25, 343-61.

WILSON, M. (1971), 'The Growth of Peasant Communities' in WILSON, M. and THOMPSON, L. (eds.), *The Oxford History of South Africa*, (London, Oxford University Press), Vol. II, Ch. II.

297

WILSON, F. (1971), 'Farming', in WILSON, M. and THOMPSON, L. (eds.), *The Oxford History of South Africa* (London, Oxford University Press), Vol. II, Ch. III.

WOLPE, H. (1970), 'Industrialization and Race in South Africa', in ZUBAIDA, S. (ed), *Race and Racialism* (London, Tavistock Publications).

WOLPE, H. (1971), 'Class, Race and the Occupational Structure in South Africa', Paper delivered to the World Sociology Congress, September 1970.

Black Nationalism and
Anti-colonialism

MALCOLM CROSS

The assertion that colonialism induced a reactive demand by subject people for self-determination is neither novel nor surprising. But this response produced ideological positions that vary in relation to a particular phase of decolonization and, at any one point in time, to exigencies of social stratification. This paper will draw on examples from the West Indies to illustrate this process.

Colonialism was not a simple force and neither was its reaction. It tended to have within it a number of crucial strands. Of these I wish to isolate three: economic domination, political domination, and racial domination. I do not wish to suggest that the content of anti-colonial movements was entirely reactive for this is far from being true (especially outside the West Indies) but the understanding of ideological movements aiming at some form of self-determination is facilitated by conceiving of responses to the challenge of colonialism along these same three dimensions.

The approach to nationalism, defined as a group's claim for self-determination, that focuses on its essentially reactive properties is hardly original. Lord Acton certainly perceived it in this manner. He was careful to point out, however, that if it is to serve a truly political role or if it is to act as a vehicle for social change, then, however oppressive the situation may be, the reaction has to be conjoined with some positive notion of a new unity or greater freedom. Thus '... though oppression may give rise to violent and repeated outbreaks, like the convulsions of a man in pain, it cannot mature a settled purpose and plan of regeneration, unless a new notion of happiness is joined to the sense of present evil'.[1] In terms of the threefold division used in the present discussion the problem becomes one of understanding the situations where this 'notion of happiness' is defined in racial or cultural terms, in political terms and finally in economic terms, although there is no attempt to suggest that these three are necessarily distinct in all concrete examples.

In the West Indian case there is some sense in viewing this division in a temporal sequence although it is clear that even in modern objections to economic domination there is ofter a racial or cultural element. The sequence is important, however, for even if it cannot always be shown to have occurred there is little doubt that the path to economic demands, especially of a far-reaching kind, has lain through the gradual removal of racial barriers, then political ones, until the economic reality was apparent to more than the prescient few.

There seems to be little reason for limiting the discussion to the quest for state nationalism through political independence since an important part of the ideological reaction to colonialism has been concerned with freedom or unity at either a sub-state or pan-state level. This is not to deny the importance of the state nationalist idea but it misses the main point of the colonial experience merely to suggest that nationalism is an example of cultural influence from Europe. Astonishingly, there are even those today who view it as a part of Europe's civilizing mission: 'African societies contributed no Kants, no Beethovens, no Michelangelos. Intellectually and politically this was virgin soil. Suddenly the whole area was opened up to the civilizing process—to European laws, customs, traditions, and business. Along with European ideas and ideologies came the flags of nationalism'.[2] It is certainly the case that European ideas were influential but merely to see the quest for state nationalism as the natural result of cultural borrowing avoids crucial questions concerning the constraints colonialism engendered on the types of leaders and policies that were possible. In addition such a view precludes consideration of communal feelings of such national minorities as, say, Indians in Trinidad or Guyana (where they form a numerical majority) or international sentiments expressed in Garveyism or *négritude*. While there are considerable difficulties in this approach, Peter Worsley is right to insist that 'the analysis of modern nationalism outside Euro-America . . . must begin by distilling the experience of modern imperialism'.[3] This experience may best be understood in terms of the *colonial situation*.[4] That is, black nationalism is conceived as a manifestation of conflict inherent in a colonial crisis situation.

I

RACIAL AND CULTURAL REJECTION

In discussing the difference between the nineteenth-century English and French views on nationality, Acton pointed out that in the former case the claim was inspired by a commitment to 'the theory of freedom' while in the latter the principle of unity was of major significance. Both claims have validity in the colonial context for in operation colonialism was a denial of unity and freedom. It is also true in the West Indies that examples of racial and cultural responses took different forms in the English and French colonies. *Négritude* did indeed seek what could almost be described as a spiritual unity of black races, exemplified by an identifiable culture, while Garveyism sought freedom from colonialism for all blacks.

GARVEY AND GARVEYISM

There have been no other movements more significant for promoting black racial consciousness than Marcus Garvey's Universal Negro Improvement Association (UNIA) which he founded in Jamaica in 1914. The movement propounded racial solidarity and the migration of New World Negroes back to the African Homeland. One of Garvey's many projects, the Black Star line shipping company, was intended to bring about this latter objective.

Garvey spent the ten most crucial years of his life (1916-26) in the United States and it was among the American blacks that his movement had the greatest following—sometimes estimated at 3 million by 1920.[5] It is also usually accepted that Garvey's influence was crucial in the rise of African nationalism and UNIA branches were set up in Lagos and in Liberia.[6]

Garveyism is more important for its effects than for its substance, since the man himself propounded a mixture of racism and utopian politics that has been described as 'pitiable rubbish' by the black Marxist writer C. L. R. James, who went on to draw similarities between Garvey and Hitler.[7] The important point was that he rejected the colonial system and the oppression of blacks in the United States. He did not, however, reject capitalism, but saw Africa developing a European or American-styled economic system. Thus an editorial in his *Blackman* newspaper commented:

With the help of capital from the West Indian and American Negro the development (of Africa) will be enhanced. In the not very distant future, Africa will bloom forth and startle the world, not as the dark continent, not only as the richest cupboard in the world but rather as the homeland of a Black Commonwealth and as the greatest single continent on the globe.[8]

The crucial point for Garvey was the ejection of the European from Africa so that her riches could accrue to all Africans, whether in the 'Homeland' or in the New World. His views were really Pan-African in the racial rather than the geographical sense. All 'persons of Negro blood and African descent' were regarded as ordinary members of the UNIA and the constitution of 1918 declared the aims of the organization to be:

To establish a Universal Confraternity among the race; to promote the spirit of pride and love; to reclaim the fallen; to administer to and assist the needy; to assist in civilizing the backward tribes of Africa; to assist in the development of Independent Negro Nations and Communities; to establish Commissionaries or Agencies in the principal countries and cities of the world for the representation and protection of all Negroes, irrespective of nationality; to promote a conscientious Spiritual worship among the native tribes of Africa; to establish Universities, Colleges, Academies and Schools for the racial education and culture of the people;

to conduct a worldwide Commercial and Industrial Intercourse for the good of the people; to work for better conditions
in all Negro communities.[9]

Whatever else may be said of Marcus Garvey, he could not
be said to have lacked vision and ambition!

Garvey returned to Jamaica in 1927 after federal charges
for fraudulently using the mail had been preferred against him
and, apparently undaunted, launched the Sixth Annual
International Convention of the Negro Peoples of the World
in Kingston, Jamaica, during August 1929.[10] This resulted in
the launching of the *Blackman* newspaper, which survived
until 1931.

Garvey's influence in the West Indies derives less from precept and example than it does from racial identification. But
there were times when such identification overruled political
ideology. For example, Garveyism received a fillip with the
Italian invasion of Abyssinia in 1935. In Trinidad the efforts
of the British Government to disavow any support for Mussolini
were not strong enough to prevent an outspoken racial condemnation of all white men for complicity in this attack on
the heart of Africa. The radical newspaper, the *People*, attacked
the Pope, the League of Nations, South Africa and the United
States in a sudden burst of racial awareness which is typified
in this unsigned article of 1935: 'It is evident from the behaviour
of a certain section of the white race (that) their civilization
will ultimately be destroyed because it is barbarous, it is
savage, it is ungodly, it is nearly everything that is bad. . . .'[11]
This particular newspaper, which was highly influential in
the 1930s, pronounced West Indians to be Ethiopian and
demanded the unity of Indians and Negroes against the continued white domination of their society.

However, in a vein that recurs in 1970, there were many who
realized that while anti-white sentiment could be a powerful
weapon in destroying colonialism, pro-Negro feeling could
destroy any possibility of united Indian-African opposition
in the racially divided societies of Trinidad and British Guiana.
When Garvey visited Trinidad in 1937, at the time of intense
unrest and rioting, the *People* warned that the '. . . aim of
Africans should not be the substitution of an African imperial-

ism for European imperialism but the rejection of imperialism itself in any form'.[12]

The Garveyite movement in the West Indies was most powerful in Garvey's native Jamaica where it has contributed, together with the Ras Tafari sect, to the wave of political and economic demands that have followed the emergence of radical black movements after political independence in 1962. Even though the arguments are now far more sophisticated and profound, the content of Garveyism can still be found easily, although it tends to be expressed in the framework of black socialism rather than black capitalism. A report on Garvey's son, Marcus Garvey jnr., in 1970 quotes him as saying:

> The major black power movements in Jamaica are true to the principles of Marcus Garvey because they advocate preparing for a return to Africa. We are racially exclusive national socialists favoring the African socialist concept of Ujamaa and we don't believe Indians, Chinese, or Arabs should be with us.[13]

Despite their comparative lack of organization, current black-power movements are not, as we shall see, 'true to the principles of Marcus Garvey'; they are far more revolutionary. It is perhaps because of this that they have never been allowed to organize in the way that Garvey was able to do.

NÉGRITUDE

Négritude does indeed seek unity and, at least in the eyes of some, is intrinsically cultural rather than political in its tenets. The word was coined by the Martiniquan poet and politician, Aimé Césaire, in his justly famous political poem, *Cahier d'un retour au pays natal*.[14] The ideas that the ideology contains are, however, essentially Haitian in origin and, through the writing of Leopold Senghor, Jean-Paul Sartre and Franz Fanon, almost worldwide in significance.[15]

The basic principle of *négritude* is simply the affirmation of the cultural value of blackness and the intrinsic worth of the black man.[16] Like Garveyism its importance lies in stimulating a consciousness of black identity rather than in setting forth principles of political or economic action. Not that writers like Césaire were apolitical; on the contrary *négritude* provided the shared understanding without which *black* politics would have been impossible. One could not make purposive statements or act to break the colonial ties without a belief in one's intrinsic worth. Colonialism itself sought to deny this by promoting a culture with nothing but a European reference and it was out of this conflict, between the denial of legitimacy and the necessity for action, that both *négritude* and Garveyism were born.

To some, *négritude* could be more a political movement than for others. Thus '. . . whereas for Senghor *négritude* postulates an intrinsic moral worth in the negro for its own sake, for Césaire *négritude* is a set of values whose purpose it is to set in motion forces that can bring about a political revolution.'[17] Senghor recently restated his position in the Paris-based journal of *négritude*, *Présence Africaine*: '*Négritude* is a cultural fact. It is a collection of values—economic and political, intellectual and moral, artistic and social—not only of African people but also among the black minorities of America, Asia and Australasia.'[18] He does go on to recognize its future political importance but it was really Fanon who transcended *négritude's* almost reactionary elements to forge the most powerful statement of decolonization yet to appear.[19]

Négritude was not itself revolutionary. It marks a response to the racism inherent in colonialism; sensed first by the intelligentsia and adopted by those who sought the unattainable—integration into white society on the basis of equality. As La Guerre put it:

> (*Négritude*) was originally conceived as an ideology of protest and an assertion of equality, if not superiority in certain respects. Many saw it as a powerful weapon in the struggle for national liberation. But it was soon to become the ideology of the middle class. Its limitations were soon to become apparent, and in an age of independent African states it was doomed to irrelevance.[20]

The importance of *négritude* lies not in its direct relevance or irrelevance but in the way that it made possible the political challenge to colonial domination. Like Garveyism it provided self-respect and confidence to the new leaders; unlike Garvey-ism, *négritude* never really affected the masses. *Négritude* demanded an extension of French culture to include the black man, Garveyism denied the possibility of this and sought independence. The policy of assimilation for the French Antilles as opposed to political independence is not unrelated to this fact.

II

POLITICAL SELF-DETERMINATION

Nationalist demands in the English-speaking West Indies, in so far as they have been political in intent, have largely operated within a constitutional framework. Typically the path to political power was seen to lie in a direction firmly indicated by the Colonial Office.

It is a fact, explicable only in terms of colonialism's unique contradictions, that the founder of black nationalism in the West Indies was a white man, Captain Arthur Cipriani. Cipriani, the descendant of a white Creole planter and former officer in the West India Regiment, revived the Trinidad Workingman's Association after the Great War and used it as a vehicle for ardent and effective campaigns of opposition to the colonial administration.

By 1939 Trinidad was still an archetypal crown colony with a minority of representatives, elected on a highly restricted franchise, facing an official and nominated majority in the local legislature. Effective power here, as elsewhere in the West Indies, lay in the Governor's hands although influenced to some degree by an Executive Council which was itself dominated by business and government interests. The TWA had by this time formed itself into a political party (the Trinidad Labour Party) modelled on the British Labour Party and it sought a revised national constitution. But, above all, it demanded a federation with dominion status. The important point is that the TLP, one of the earliest and best organized political parties in the region, saw the solution to the problems of Trinidad and the West Indies in essentially British terms, that is, a politically independent union but with British-style institutions.

A good example of this is contained in the evidence submitted by the TLP to the West India Royal Commission of 1938/9 which had been sent to provide a general investigation after a whole series of riots and disturbances in the previous few years.[21] Cipriani wrote in the Party's memorandum to the Commission:

> Our aim is ultimately to have a Federation—a Federated West Indian Commonwealth, recognised as a Dominion, with insular Constitutions and a federal constitution with, if necessary, reserved powers given to the Governor, the Federal Constitution, and to the Colonial Office; with proper planning for the encouragement of West Indian development in industries, political advancement, cultural progress, and political emancipation; with a local negro of coloured or mixed electorate devoted to the service of the British Crown and working in accordance with British traditions, British methods, and educating itself on British lines.[22]

Although it would never be made so explicitly again, the TLP's statement represents the pattern which the major nationalist parties of the post-war phase, such as the People's National Party of Jamaica, the Jamaica Labour Party and the People's National Movement in Trinidad, were to follow. It is striking the way that these movements, that were later to become the inheritors of political power, were anti-colonialist but not anti-imperialist. As such they, with the imperial power herself, were the true carriers of what has effectively been called 'neo-colonialism'.

It must be said that not all nationalists fell into this category. In Jamaica, Richard Hart and the small group of PNP radicals with which he was associated were exceptions, as were Dr Tito P. Achong and Adrian Cola Rienzi in Trinidad. Achong, for example, who was later to become Mayor of Port of Spain, would have none of what he called 'the stark British cant of political gradualism'. In a sentence which could have been found in the statements of the 1970 insurgents, Achong declared: 'We, the people, have had enough of glorified injustice, unconscionable exploitation of coloured labour by white capital, lying imperialist propaganda and economic dogmas expedient to monopoly enterprises.'[23] In the Jamaican case, Richard Hart, who was a founder member of the PNP parted company with it in 1952 over the attitude of the party to economic as opposed to political self-determination.[24]

This conservative, pro-British nationalism has to be viewed in the light of the constitutional model that Britain insisted upon. In fact it was more than a model for it embraced an ideology. The phrase 'Westminster model' is often used but is not particularly apposite since no West Indies government has had the *de facto* autonomy of Westminster and, in the early days, prior to independence, they could not possibly be said to be even democratic on any reasonable meaning of that over-used word. However, it is a fact that crucial constraints operated to perpetuate middle-class governmental organizations.

The whole experience of British colonialism, of course, made the acceptance of the British demands inevitable. As a recent writer on Jamaican society put it: '. . . the completeness of colonialism placed a premium on the assimilation of white culture and devalued either surviving Africanisms or "creole" syntheses which emerged'.[25] Ideas of nationalism and governmental structures were no exceptions to this, although it could be argued that working-class opinion was often well aware of the contradiction between their class position and the acceptance of a middle-class nationalism. The important point is that the period leading to independence marked the rise to power of the West Indian middle class as a result of which the years following independence were relatively calm and peaceful. The 'transition' was easily accomplished but only because it was a very superficial transition.[26]

The British thus bequeathed a class system of politics and political institutions to the West Indies—a system designed for the middle class and one that could be operated in their interests simply by continuing previous policy. It did not take account of regional problems, the most striking of which concerned societies where loyalties of race and religion (notably Trinidad and Guyana—formerly British Guiana) outweighed those of class. Trinidad has, as over one-third of its population, the descendants of indentured Indian labourers, while in Guyana this proportion rises to over one-half. It may well be that the trappings of the Westminster model exist but one should not imagine that they necessarily operate in the same way. Thus:

> That there are two major parties in Trinidad and Tobago is not because the electoral system tends to exaggerate the strength of two large parties at the expense of smaller parties. Rather, it is because political development under colonial rule left the two large racial groups as the prime inheritors of, as well as competitors for, political power.[27]

The same could perhaps be said of Guyana, although in this case the actions of the British and American governments dictated not merely the structure of government but the type of political ideology that was permitted, even against the express wish (in so far as voting figures indicate this) of the populus.

The facts of the suspension of the constitution, in what was then British Guiana, 133 days after the return of the People's Progressive Party at the first elections under adult suffrage in 1953 are well known.[28] Unexpectedly the election resulted in an overwhelming victory for the PPP which at that time represented a multi-racial party committed to radical socialist reform. Although the party was structured along rather similar lines to the British Labour Party, it soon became clear that any other similarity was more apparent than real since neither the party leader, East Indian dentist Dr Cheddi Jagan, nor its chairman, African lawyer, Forbes Burnham, were going to be satisfied with Fabian gradualism or Gaitskellite reform. British colonialism in the West Indies, even at its most radical, has tended to view the decolonization process as an attempt to persuade the vested economic interests to tolerate the 'burden' of welfare and social service provision. Any more radical proposal, such as any participatory democracy would entail, was beyond the limits of debate. It is perhaps too easy now to accept the extraordinary decision to suspend the constitution and return to full Crown Colony control as born of pre-Suez high Toryism and the prevailing anti-communist hysteria of McCarthyism. As Colin Henfrey has recently pointed out, the problem is much deeper and more pervasive.[29] Even after the return of the Labour Party in 1964 the policy of Anglo-American collusion to remove the 'extremist'

Jagan from power (the PPP had been returned again in 1957 and 1961) continued.

The result of such intervention is beyond the scope of this paper but to put it very briefly the earlier period from 1953-61 produced a racial polarization between Indian and African together with a period of economic stagnation, the middle period, 1962-4 resulted in racial riots and complete dislocation of the country's economy, while from 1964 the more 'acceptable' People's National Congress has held power and consolidated its position through every expedient possible. There are a number of indicators that suggest that the PNC government, particularly after 1968, does not feel itself to be encumbered by the normal constraints of the democratic process.

The Guyana example is a good limiting case on too glib a use of the phrase 'Westminster model' for it is not normally taken to mean government by fiat and force and elections that almost no one accepts as valid. Conversely the post-independence government in Guyana is as emulative as any (notwithstanding the use of romantic concepts like 'Co-operative Republic' implying participation, or even 'socialist' policies of nationalization) for the tradition of political corruption does not start with the PPP or PNC, or any other political party, but with British colonial practice and United States policies on international affairs.[30]

In terms of purely political nationalism the example of the West Indies reveals the culmination of colonial culture. In an area where the British influence has been more pervasive and telling than anywhere else in the world, colonialism was so complete that hardly anyone challenged the smooth transfer of power from white middle-class Britons to black middle-class, crypto-British West Indians. Where any challenge did exist, as in Guyana, the troops could always persuade where historical precept and conditioning had failed. Indeed, so complete was the colonial socialization that, as in Jamaica, the colonial governor was often genuinely more interested in political decolonization than the leaders of the indigenous political parties.[31] But such events institutionalized the traditional gulf and lack of feeling between middle class and working class. The conspicuous consumption patterns of the former, together with their equally conspicuous lack of concern for the masses, was one factor in creating the conditions for the strengthening of the second wave of mass nationalism that is only now growing in the area. The other major set of conditions concerns the position of the masses themselves. The result was the most recent phase of black nationalism which, because of its concern for economic transformation, I have termed 'economic nationalism'.

III

ECONOMIC NATIONALISM

It was once true, and to some degree still is in some parts of the West Indies, that nationalist tendencies were mediated through racial and cultural associations. Later political groupings emerged with their own *elitist* nationalism but it was seldom the case that the objective conditions of poverty and privation were related to the demand for self-determination or decolonization. To some this is a general phenomenon, characteristic of underdevelopment:

> In under-developed countries, where, paradoxically enough, widespread poverty and hunger should make economic demands irresistible, in fact one sees nationalist or subnationalist divisive tendencies being strongly rooted in discontent which is located more nearly at the heart of the socio-religious superstructure than in the bureaucratic political infrastructure.[32]

The last five years in the West Indies have seen the crumbling of this tradition and the emergence of a series of radical mass movements that aim at economic transformation and 'real' decolonization.

They articulate the same kind of resentment expressed in the movements of racial and cultural rejection that we examined earlier but for two reasons they have focused almost exclusively on problems of economic organization. In the first place, political independence has been achieved but it clearly brought little amelioration of the conditions of poverty and unemployment. Indeed, for many the situation is far worse than it was before. Second, the movements are led by men of far greater understanding and sophistication than was ever the case in the past. The group of young radicals, now mostly affiliated to the University of the West Indies but making their initial impression through the pages of *New World Quarterly*, are particularly important. Their explanations of the nature of colonialism, of multi-national corporations, and the structure and consequences of 'plantation society' give these movements a profundity and purpose which their fore-bears lacked in the past. Men like 'Buzz' Butler, Marcus Garvey and the Rastafarians had to rely on anti-white senti-ment and fundamentalist Christianity as the vehicles for change. Even radicals like Rienzi, Hart and Jagan, who were all well versed in Marx and Engels, lacked the precise knowledge of local conditions that is now available. Today economists like George Beckford, Lloyd Best, Norman Girvan, Owen Jefferson and Clive Thomas are able to point to the way their societies have been 'underdeveloped' by the continuation of colonial economic associations.[33]

The work of these writers, among others, provides a firm base for political arguments advocating economic transfor-mation. But the frustrations are inevitably the same as before and, although the demands are different, such elements as the reference to race remain simply as the most visible badge of inequality—sometimes spontaneously referred to, other times invoked for purposes of political mobilization. Such movements inevitably attract the label 'Black Power' but did not originally seek it.

The banning of the Guyanese lecturer in history at the University of the West Indies, Walter Rodney, by the Jamaican Government in October 1968 marks something of a turning-point. It resulted in marches, riots and a period of considerable tension in Jamaica. Rodney was not putting forward radical proposals for change but he was making similar claims to Garvey, although he was much more informed about African history. He was certainly interested in *mass* mobilization although he never founded a political movement. There is always an element of Garveyite racialism in black-power movements and this receives a clear articulation in Rodney. For example, he writes: 'Black Power is about black people, for black people, preached by black people. I'm putting it to my black brothers and sisters that the colour of our skins is the most fundamental thing about us.'[34] Although one may find the same kind of sentiment expressed in *ABENG*, the paper that followed in the wake of the Rodney crisis, and elsewhere, the movements that have actually started are far more interested in radical economic change than racial rhetoric.

In Trinidad, for example, the National Joint Action Committee (NJAC), which instigated the marches in February, March and April 1970 that resulted in a state of emergency (that has been intermittently imposed since), certainly expressed 'anti-white' feelings but only directed at neo-colonialism in the form of continued ownership and control of major industries (oil, asphalt and sugar in particular) from outside the independent island. A pamphlet of theirs argued: 'It is quite clear that the whole pattern of economic activity was designed to keep the Black man down to ensure the continuation of white rule.'[35] Again, a spokesman for the NJAC responds to the specific charge of 'racism in reverse' from a white radical in the following words: '. . . it is not white individuals who are the real targets of Black anger but the racist capitalist system that was developed among them and which has been imposed on us.'[36] The same orientation, though with less rhetoric and more science, may be found in the TAPIA organization and particularly in the writings of its founder, Lloyd Best. To Best, 'Black Power expresses itself in large part as a demand for economic power'.[37] And this represents the nub of current protest movements in the West Indies; at once more powerful a call and more revolutionary an ideology than anything that has come before.

West Indian economists (and many play an important role in political movements) point to the social, psychological and economic effects of the plantation. Economic nationalism does not just demand the nationalization of the plantations but their dissolution since their continuance in any form militates against a peasantry. As Clive Thomas put it: 'the birth of an independent peasantry is the destruction of the plantations'.[38]

Similarly, the current wave of economic nationalism, in line with radical thought on neo-colonialism, condemns the extraction of basic resources by multi-national corporations.

On the industrial front the policy of 'industrialization by invitation', an almost universal middle-class solution to balance of trade problems and diversification, is rejected. Such manufacturing has not solved unemployment problems and despite rapid growth rates contributes little more to overall production than it did fifteen years ago. In addition industrialization has contributed to urban growth and thus urban squalor but, even so, has remained capital intensive. Often monopoly status and generous fiscal incentives are offered with little or no attempt to control prices, profits or standards; the result being a capital outflow that perpetuates and indeed strengthens economic dependence and hence political subordination.

Ideas such as these are clearly not new and yet the economic nationalist movements of the West Indies represent the theoretical articulation of a new form of black nationalism in the Afro-American world.[39] The fact is, of course, that despite repression and external intervention the societies of the West Indies are small and potentially self-contained entities with the economic resources and educational skills to form black socialist experiments that are impossible in Brazil or the USA.[40] And that, after all is what these latest movements are about.

CONCLUSION

In this paper I have argued that black nationalism, in an area where whites are a tiny minority, has three faces; a demand for racial equality and freedom, political self-determination and an end to neo-colonialism. The second of these, and the series of movements most commonly associated with 'nationalism' (i.e. state nationalism), made its impression on the middle classes. The first represents both the initial rejection of colonialism and also a continuing theme in later movements. The importance of racial sentiment in movements of self-determination lies either in its ability to provide crude articulation of class-based protests or as a weapon to be used by middle-class politicians for establishing or retaining loyalty.

This latter function parallels the use made of 'tribalism' and indeed the similarity extends to the phenomenon itself. So-called 'tribalism' may have significance in dictating kinship loyalties but as a modern political force it owes much to middle-class competition and the imputation that cultural differences possess political importance. They might under certain conditions but in a rural area of Nigeria where everyone is Ibo inter-tribal conflicts do not exist. The propinquity and uncertainty of the city demands a primordial attachment and where the salaried *élite* is concerned this is not likely to be on class lines. Ethnicity in the form of 'tribalism' fills that gap.[41]

Unfortunately it has a mystifying influence just as reference to race has in the West Indies. Archie Mafeje could have been referring to 'racial nationalism' in the West Indies when he charged that the ideology of 'tribalism' '. . . oversimplifies, mystifies, and obscures the real nature of economic and power relations between Africans themselves, and between Africa and the capitalist world . . .'[42] Despite this, racial awareness is a direct product of colonialism and, as Lowenthal shows so well, the West Indies are steeped in this tradition.[43]

There is an important sense in which the three categories of protest movements are related. Race and ethnic differences may not in themselves be very significant in objective terms but as subjectively interpreted symbols their significance is enormous.[44] The consequence of nationalism founded upon the perceived differences between colonizers and colonized results in a change of personnel but not of policy. In other words, given the tradition of colonial culture, the type of leader and policy at the time when the movement for political emancipation was in progress was not in question—only his race and cultural identity. That this suited the British is another reason why it succeeded.

The colonial *élite* thus brought into being a mass response that would ensure its own departure but would not ensure any structural alteration. The inheritors of power, as middle class as the colonizers before them, have themselves created an opposition which cannot be sidetracked by the mystifications of race and culture (notwithstanding the influence of American blacks). In the West Indies it is this which provides the direct parallel between the riots of the 1930s and those after 1968. Patterns of self-determination are thus intimately associated with local class systems and the nature of colonialism itself.

In the light of this one might expect that Marxist analyses of colonies and former colonies would be fruitful. In fact they are conspicuous by their absence. A major reason for this is the almost obsessive current concern to show that Third World countries are no more or no less than appendages of the West.[45] One has sympathy with Anthony Smith when he recently complained: 'The more rigorous the Marxist analysis employed, the less important appears the role of the colonial system of rule and the colonial situation. The less important too becomes the territorial unit of rule, the colony itself.'[46] No one would wish to deny that the incorporation of dependent economies into a metropolitan system was not of crucial importance but the understanding of colonial or post-colonial ideologies requires a more detailed analysis of the individual societies themselves.

It is too early to judge the effects of 'economic nationalist' movements in the West Indies but aside from the racial rhetoric used by the less perspicacious leaders there is little doubt that they are clear portents for the future. As *The Financial Times* was quick to recognize in a report on Jamaica: 'Any Black Power movement in Jamaica must be considered as based on purely economic grounds.'[47] There is a sense in which the new movements represent a return of 'black-power' thought to the West Indies after West Indians like Marcus Garvey, George Padmore, C. L. R. James, Franz Fanon and Stokely Carmichael have spread its message to Africa and North America. Of much greater importance is the fact that the recent black nationalist movements often show a concern for the masses untrammelled by racial rhetoric and, as yet, by political opportunism. Perhaps they represent the product of the first non-colonial generation—and that at least makes their slogan of 'Power to the People' a possibility.

NOTES AND REFERENCES

1. Lord Acton, *Essays on Freedom and Power* (Glencoe, Free Press, 1949), p. 166.
2. Louis Snyder, *The New Nationalism* (Ithaca, Cornell University Press, 1968), p. 110. Cf. William R. Bascom, 'Tribalism, Nationalism and Pan Africanism', *Annals of the American Academy of Political and Social Science*, 342, July 1962, pp. 21-9.
3. Peter Worsley, *The Third World* (London, Weidenfeld & Nicholson, 1967), p. 84.

4. George Balandier, 'The Colonial Situation: A Theoretical Approach' in Immanuel Wallerstein (ed.), *Social Change: The Colonial Situation* (New York, John Wiley, 1966), pp. 34-61.

5. See A. J. Garvey, *Garvey and Garveyism* (London, Collier-Macmillan, 1970); *Philosophy and Opinions of Marcus Garvey* (London, Frank Cass, 1967). Also E. D. Cronin, *Black Moses* (Wisconsin, University of Wisconsin Press, 1955).

6. J. A. Langley, 'Garveyism and African Nationalism', *Race*, 11 (2) (1969), pp. 157-72.

7. C. L. R. James, 'Marcus Garvey', *Black Lines*, 1 (3) (1971), p. 11. Reprinted from *A History of Pan-African Revolts* (New York, Drum & Spear Press), 1969.

8. 'Editorials from Marcus Garvey's *Blackman* Newspaper' in Trevor Munroe and Rupert Lewis (eds.), Readings in *Government and Politics of the West Indies* (Mona, Jamaica, U.W.I., 1971), p. 205.

9. 'Constitution of the UNIA' in A. C. Hill and M. Kilson (comp.), *Apropos of Africa: Sentiments of the Negro American Leaders on Africa from the 1800s to the 1950s* (London, Frank Cass, 1969), p. 185.

10. It is likely that the charge against Garvey was used as an excuse to deport a particularly troublesome Negro. For example, W. F. Elkins examines the evidence of J. Edgar Hoover's involvement in the case and concludes: '(Garvey's) conviction for fraud must be considered as the outcome of the intention of government officials to effect his deportation.' See W. F. Elkins, 'Marcus Garvey, The *Negro World*, and the British West Indies', *Science and Society*, 36 (1) (1972), p. 76. Cf. Robert G. Weisbord, 'Marcus Garvey: The View From Whitehall', *Race*, 11 (4) (1970), pp. 419-29.

11. *People* (23 November 1935).

12. *People* (13 November 1937).

13. *New York Times* (25 April 1970).

14. Aimé Césaire, '*Cahier d'un retour au pays natal*' (Paris, *Présence Africaine*, 1956).

15. On the origins see G. R. Coulthard, *Race and Colour in Caribbean Literature* (London, Oxford University Press for the IRR, 1962). Espec. Ch. IV. Cf. David Caute, *Fanon* (London, Fontana, 1970).

16. On the tradition of biological differences see David Nicholls, 'Biology and Politics in Haiti', *Race*, 13 (2) (1971), pp. 204-14.

17. John La Guerre, 'Colonial Intellectuals in Politics: The British and French Experience', unpublished Ph.D. thesis, University of Manchester, 1971, p. 160.

18. L. S. Senghor, 'Problématique de la Négritude', *Présence Africaine*, 78 (2) (1971), p. 6.

19. Franz Fanon, *The Wretched of the Earth* (Harmondsworth: Penguin, 1967).

20. La Guerre, op. cit., 501.

21. *Report of the West India Royal Commission*, Cmd. 6607 (London, HMSO, 1945).

22. Memorandum of the TLP to the West India Royal Commission, dated 15 February 1939, p. 6. PRO, CO 950/776.

23. Memorandum from Tito P. Achong to the West India Royal Commission. PRO, CO 950/853. Despite the fact that Achong was a prominent citizen he was not called upon to give verbal evidence before the Commission.

24. See Hart's review of nationalism in Jamaica in 'Jamaica and Self-Determination, 1660-1970, in *Race*, 13 (3) (1972), pp. 271-97.

25. Trevor Munroe, *The Politics of Constitutional Decolonization: Jamaica, 1944-62* (Jamaica, I.S.E.R., 1972), p. 176.

26. Ibid., Ch. 6, pp. 179-92.

27. Lewis Bobb, 'The "Westminster Model" and its Relevance to Constitutional Change in Trinidad and Tobago', *Seminars on Contemporary Issues III: Constitutional Change in Trinidad and Tobago* (Trinidad, U.W.I., 1972), pp. 16-17.

28. The most important sources of information on this event are *British Guiana: Suspension of the Constitution*, Cmd. 8980 (London, Colonial Office, 1953); *Report of the British Guiana Constitutional Commission*, Cmd, 9274 (London, HMSO, 1954); Cheddi Jagan, *The West on Trial: My Fight for Guyana's Freedom* (London, Michael Joseph, 1966); Philip Reno, *The Ordeal of British Guiana* (New York, Monthly Review Press, 1964); Gordon K. Lewis, *The Growth of the Modern West Indies* (London, MacGibbon & Kee, 1968), Ch. X. For a recent review of events see Malcolm Cross, *The East Indians of Guyana and Trinidad* (London, Minority Rights Group, 1972).

29. Colin V. F. Henfrey, 'Foreign Influence in Guyana: The Struggle for Independence' in Emanuel de Kadt (ed.) *Patterns of Foreign Influence in the Caribbean* (London: Oxford University Press for the RIIA, 1972), p. 73.

30. Henfrey, op. cit. and Raymond T. Smith, 'Race, Class and Politics in Post-Colonial Society', in Malcolm Cross (ed.), *Race, Pluralism and Power: Essays on Race and Social Stratification* (London, Oxford University Press for the IRR (forthcoming)).

31. Munroe, op cit., pp. 64-74.

32. T. V. Sathyamuxthy, 'Sociology of Contemporary Nationalism: Tribe, Religion, Technology', *Civilizations*, 20 (3) (1970), p. 351.

33. See G. L. Beckford, *Persistent Poverty: Underdevelopment in Plantation Economies of the Third World* (London, Oxford University Press, 1972); Lloyd Best, 'Outlines of a Model of Pure Plantation Economy', *Social and Economic Studies*, 17 (3) (1968); Norman Girvan, *Foreign Capital and Economic Underdevelopment in Jamaica* (Jamaica, I.S.E.R., 1972); Owen Jefferson, *The Economic Development of Jamaica in the Post-War Period* (Jamaica, I.S.E.R., 1972); Havelock Brewster and Clive Y. Thomas, *The Dynamics of West Indian Economic Integration* (Jamaica, I.S.E.R., 1967).

34. Walter Rodney, *The Groundings With My Brothers* (London, Bogle-L'Ouverture Publications, 1969), p. 16.

35. NJAC, 'Slavery to Slavery: NJAC on the Economic System', reprinted in part in Munroe and Lewis (eds.), op. cit., p. 235.

36. Aiyegoro, 'Positive Achievements of the NJAC,' *Tapia* 27 (18 May 1972), p. 10.

37. Lloyd Best, 'Black Power and the Afro-American in Trinidad and Tobago', *New World*, 5 (4) (1971), p. 5.

38. C. Y. Thomas, 'Conceptualization and Policy: An Essay on Two Aspects of the West Indian Economy', *New World*, 5 (4) (1971), p. 31.

39. Studies like Nkrumah's have, of course, been particularly influential. See Kwame Nkrumah, *Neo-Colonialism: The Last Stage of Imperialism* (London, Heinemann), 1968.

40. On the problem of continuing U.S. involvement see the following report which appeared following the uprisings in Trinidad during April 1970: 'The United States flew a planeload of weapons, including mortars and machine guns, to Trinidad today at the urgent request of the black government there, which is seeking to put down a mutiny inspired by black-power elements.' *New York Times* (23 April 1970). A leading article of the same date reported that ships, ostensibly sent to evacuate U.S. citizens, were in fact '. . . carrying marines'.

41. See Pierre van den Berghe, 'Pluralism at a Nigerian University: A Case Study,' *Race*, 12 (4) (1971), pp. 429-42. Reprinted in Cross (ed.), op. cit., Also 'Ethnicity: the African Experience.' *International Social Science Journal*, 23 (4) (1971), pp. 507-17.

42. Archie Mafeje, 'The Ideology of Tribalism', *Journal of Modern African Studies*, 9 (2) (1971), p. 261.

43. David Lowenthal, *West Indian Societies* (London, Oxford University Press for the IRR, 1972). Despite the veracity of this claim, Lowenthal's massive work

fails to relate such expressions to colonialism or the political and economic structure of individual territories.

44. See Malcolm Cross, 'On Conflict, Race Relations and the Theory of the Plural Society', *Race*, 12 (4) (1971), pp. 486-88.

45. See Andre Gunder Frank, *Latin America: Underdevelopment or Revolution* (New York, Monthly Review Press, 1969).

46. Anthony D. Smith, *Theories of Nationalism* (London, Duckworth, 1971), p. 79.

47. *The Financial Times* (6 January 1970).

Index

L

South Africa—*contd.*
  Apartheid 280-1, 284, 289-91, 294-5, 296*n*
  Bantustan policy 280, 281
  border industries 292
  economic system 284-9
  Industrial Conciliation Act 293
  migrant labour force 290-1
  Nationalist Party 280, 281
  Native (Abolition of Passes and Co-ordination of Documents) Act 290
  Native Land Act (1913) 287
  Native Urban Areas Act (1925) 290
  Natives (Settlement of Disputes) Act 293
  Reserves, 284 *ff.*, 292 *ff.*, 296*n*
  Segregation policy 280, 281, 284, 286, 290, 294-5
  Transkei Constitution Act (1963) 292
Southcott, Joanna 20
Spark 270
Spectator 197
Spencer, Herbert 161, 181, 183-4, 184-5, 189, 197, 198, 199, 200, 204, 248
  Man versus the State 156
Spengler, J. 264
Spinoza, Benedict de 58
Spiro, Melford E. 39
Stalin, Joseph
  Concerning Marxism in Linguistics 112*n*
Stalinists and Stalinism 108, 109
Stanley, Oliver 193
Stewart, J. D. 139, 140, 142
Stirner, Max 107
Storing, Herbert, J. 149*n*
Strachey, John St Loe 197, 203
Structural functionalism 248, 251, 256*n*
Studdert-Kennedy, Gerald 140, 141
Sutton, F. X. 247
Suarez, Francisco (*Tractatus de legibus*) 156
Suyin, Han 24
Swanson, Guy 39
Switzerland (federation) 154, 164, 169
Syndicalism 40, 160
Sydney (Sydney, Algernon) 155

Tawney, R. H. 79, 137, 184, 225, 260
  Commonplace Book 208
Taylor, Charles 80
Theology 38-40

Theology, German 40-41
Thomas, Clive 312, 313
Thompson, E. P. 18, 19-33, 222
  The Making of the English Working Class 18, 19-33
Tocqueville, Alexis de 117, 132-3, 148*n* 152
Tönnies, Ferdinand 247
Tracy, Destutt de 43, 55*n*
Trade unions and trade unionism 14, 216-17, 263
Trades Union Congress (TUC) 139, 146
Trinidad 303, 306, 308-9
  Indians 300-1
  National Joint Action Committee 313
  People's National Movement 307
  Trinidad Labour Party 306-7
  Trinidad Workingman's Association 306
Trotsky, Leon 127
Truman, David 133, 148, 149*n*
Tucker, Robert W. 238-40

USSR
  Constitution 175*n*
  Federation 166, 175*n*
  Foreign policy 230
United States
  Bill of Rights 163
  Confederation 164, 175*n*
  Constitution 162-3, 164-5
  Federalist Party 176*n*
  Federation 154, 163-5, 166-7, 168-9, 170, 175*n*
  Foreign Policy 227-44
Universal Negro Improvement Association 301, 302-3
University of the West Indies 312

Vauvenargues 59
Vietnam war 123, 227, 231, 233, 234, 235, 236
Violence 77
Voltaire, François-Marie Arouet 59, 117

Walkland, S. A. 141
Walzer, Michael 39
Webb, Sidney and Beatrice 27, 28, 184
  Beatrice Webb's diary 192
Weber, Max 16, 32, 39, 61, 78-80, 82, 247, 259-63, 274, 276*n*